The Scandal of Standardized Tests

The Scandal of Standardized Tests

Why We Need to Drop the SAT and ACT

EDITED BY
Joseph A. Soares

TEACHERS COLLEGE PRESS
TEACHERS COLLEGE | COLUMBIA UNIVERSITY
NEW YORK AND LONDON

Published by Teachers College Press,® 1234 Amsterdam Avenue, New York, NY 10027

Cover design by Holly Grundon / BHG Graphics. Cover composite: Hand holding paper by flas100, Scannable test by Wittayayut, Flames and smoke by vaitekune, all via iStock by Getty Images.

Library of Congress Cataloging-in-Publication Data is available at loc.gov

ISBN 978-0-8077-6331-5 (paper)
ISBN 978-0-8077-6332-2 (hardcover)
ISBN 978-0-8077-7821-0 (ebook)

Printed on acid-free paper
Manufactured in the United States of America

This work is dedicated to
the memory of
Professor David Riesman

Contents

Preface

The SAT and ACT are peculiarly American institutions. Admissions tests were supposed to be the standardized gatekeeper keeping watch like the proverbial Saint Peter at the intersection between locally controlled K–12 schools and autonomous institutions in higher education. They were to pass objective judgment on candidates, stamped by unequal childhood schoolings, to enter a world of higher education populated by thousands of colleges each fiercely proud of its distinct brand. Yet colleges, made short-sighted by rivalries, signed on to a standardized test in the relentless race for prestige. The inadequacy of a multiple-choice standardized test to measure the variety of qualities thousands of separate colleges would want got overlooked. Its inability to tap into personal creativity, grit, collaborative skills, and real-world problem-solving abilities got ignored. Over time, the gatekeeper became the beneficiary of a multibillion-dollar industry and test scores became for America's youths a stigmatizing ordeal. Yet test scores were then, as now, more a reflection of one's social origin than of one's merited academic destination. Rather than providing for an objective and fair means of social mobility, the tests were a tracking mechanism limiting the odds of improving on one's family's economic and social position in America.

The history of college admissions testing is anything but saintly. The SAT aptitude test in particular was designed from the beginning to facilitate social Darwinism, selecting for White Anglo-Saxon males; Jim Crow segregation, eugenics, and protecting the Ivy League's racial stock provided the legal and cultural context in which the SAT was born. Those IQ-type tests always correlated academic criteria with social attributes. Current research shows, despite claims to the contrary, that the social biases of these tests have not been removed. They do not work as IQ tests or achievement tests; they do not predict one's academic promise better than high school grades. They are a detour from real education and an impediment to equal opportunity.

Sadly, the admissions test industry is a product of decisions made by thousands of colleges obsessed with building their prestige on the backs of how many student applicants each could reject; fortuitously, high-stake tests can be undone by colleges looking to advance their mission to uplift and transform young people's lives by going test-optional. The problem was created by colleges; it can be resolved by them too. Test-optional is a reality at 43% of America's 4-year degree-granting institutions. The tipping point is close.

This book is for me a third book on the misrecognition of privilege disguised as academic merit, the first two being *The Power of Privilege: Yale and America's Elite Colleges* (Stanford University Press, 2009) and *SAT Wars: The Case for Test-Optional College Admissions* (Teachers College Press, 2012).

I want to thank my editor at Teachers College Press, Brian Ellerbeck, for seeing the point of providing an updated companion work to our *SAT Wars* book; Lori Tate and Kathy Caveney of TCP for herculean copy editing; the authors of the chapters in this book for their scholarly dedication to fair college admissions; the youths and families who have gone for test-optional colleges; the more than one thousand test-optional colleges in America; and FairTest.org for its tireless role in this movement. Also, I thank Anthony Carnevale, Research Professor and Director of the Georgetown University Center on Education and the Workforce, for comments on my chapter on the "adversity index." Finally, and always, I thank my spouse, Felicitas Opwis, and my son, Axel and daughter, Isabella, for their loving support.

—Joseph A. Soares

Introduction

"Toss That Test"

Joseph A. Soares

Back in the 1980s, Bates College and Bowdoin College stood alone as the only liberal arts colleges not to require applicants to submit SAT or ACT test scores. By June 2019, 1,030 institutions, 43% of America's 4-year nonprofit colleges (National Center for Education Statistics [NCES], 2019), had rejected the idea that a standardized test score should determine a student's future. The ranks of test-optional institutions include hundreds of prestigious private institutions, such as the University of Chicago, George Washington University, Wesleyan University, and Wake Forest University. The list also includes hundreds of public universities, such as George Mason University, Evergreen State College, and Old Dominion University (Soares, 2018).

The tide turned definitively against the SAT/ACT at a Berkeley conference on November 22, 2019. California's adoption of the SAT back in 1968 gave that test a national standing, and in the second decade of the 21st century, California threatens to take that national authority away. At the conference, "UC Berkeley Chancellor Carol T. Christ and UC Provost Michael Brown said . . . that research had convinced them that performance on the SAT and ACT was so strongly influenced by family income, parents' education and race that using them for high-stakes admissions decisions was simply wrong" (Watanabes, 2019). Saul Geiser, author of Chapter 1 of this book, and I both spoke at that event. The Berkeley forum contributed to the discussion of a faculty task force for the University of California examining the role of standardized tests in admissions and came on the heels of a lawsuit announced against the California Regents over the discriminatory impact of the SAT/ACT tests. The lawsuit moves the debate from the field of empirical research into the legal arena of unequal access to higher education in California. The tests exclude black and Latinx and low-income youths from attending university when by all other measures those youths are fully qualified (Nadworny, 2019). Whether by an act of the Regents, faculty, or the courts, the future for college admissions without the SAT or ACT in California and the nation is bright.

As noted in a book I edited, *SAT Wars: The Case for Test-Optional College Admissions* (Soares, 2012), critics had claimed that test-optional colleges wouldn't be able to select students of merit, standards would collapse, and underachieving youths would run amok. The critics were wrong.

At Wake Forest, where I work, we've never had academically stronger students with as much racial, ethnic, and economic diversity from across America than since 2009, when we went test-optional. As reported in the *New York Times Magazine* (Balf, 2014), the average high school GPA of our incoming students went up after we stopped requiring standardized test scores. Prior to going test-optional, the percentage of first-year students who were in the top 10% of their high school class was in the low 60s. Afterward, the newspaper reported, that figure rose to 79%. Our students are better because we look at the whole person, not a high-stakes test score.

It is a myth that standardized scores predict college performance better than high school grades. Though many parents and academics are surprised by this, it remains true that high school grades have always done a better job in predicting college grades than test scores. As the emeritus president of the University of California, Richard Atkinson, and Berkeley sociologist Saul Geiser remind us, "irrespective of the quality or type of school attended, cumulative grade point average (GPA) in academic subjects in high school has proved to be the best overall predictor of student performance in college. This finding has been confirmed in the great majority of 'predictive-validity' studies conducted over the years, including studies conducted by the testing agencies themselves" (Atkinson & Geiser, 2012, p. 24). In technical articles, for statistical cognoscenti, the College Board concedes that high school grades matter most, but for hoi polloi of the press, they go "truth optional" and unabashedly claim that the test predicts best (Ruiz, 2011).

If the SAT and ACT tests are less predictive than the high school record, the real question is, how much value do they add? Youths and their families should not have to suffer through the time, expense, and effort to take a test that stands outside the high school curriculum, unless it raises to a higher level our ability to identify college-ready talent. When statisticians attempt to model outcomes, in this case college grades, they use linear multiple regressions to measure the contribution that each variable makes to the explanatory power, or R-square, of the model. The test industry claims to find an 8-point boost, raising one's R-square from 13% with high school GPA alone, to 21% with the SAT (Kobrin, Patterson, Shaw, Mattern, & Barbuti, 2008; Morgan, 1989; Zwick, 2017, p. 82). Independent researchers, however, most often find an increase of merely 2 points (Soares, 2012). As one can see from examples in my book, *SAT Wars*, institutional validity studies show that the SAT increased Johns Hopkins' R-square by two percentage points, raising their models' explanatory punch from an R-square of 18 to 20; at the University of Georgia it added one percent, raising their R-square from 30 to 31; and at DePaul the ACT was found to contribute one percent, raising their R-square from 19 to 20. Independent scholars found that neither the SAT nor the ACT adds more than a few percentage points to what is already known from high school GPAs. For a billion-dollar industry, this is pretty pathetic value added for the money.

If the SAT/ACT improves one's predictive model by just one or two percentage points, how could that be worth the costs? Those tests do not lift college admissions out of the realm of practical wisdom into the realm of applied science. With approximately 80% of the variance in college grades left unexplained by our statistical models, it is time to acknowledge that admissions professionals do not have a reliable diagnostic tool; they are making decisions that remain more art than science. A false sense of scientific precision is one type of collateral damage done by the test industry. When test scores are used to set floors below which admissions staff will not go, we are doing an injustice to thousands of students; and when we decide between students based on a test score difference, we are relying on a tool that delivers many false negatives. Fairness and merit are better served in a holistic review than in a numeric cutoff.

Many opponents of standardized, factory-production-line, timed tests build on the work of Howard Gardner (1983) and Robert Sternberg (2003) on multiple intelligences. The SAT/ACT are limited by a narrow psychometric concept of cognitive skill that rewards speed over depth. Contrary to the lesson taught by the children's tale, with these tests the hare always beats the tortoise (Gladwell, 2019). Wisdom, practical abilities, creativity, and perseverance are not qualities captured by multiple-choice timed tests.

Narrow standardized tests with weak predictive powers should not be a barrier, deterring many, including high achievers from low-income families, from even applying to college (Soares, 2013). These predictively weak tests are also saddled by the weight of social biases. Why should we require a test that is biased against low-income youths, against women, Latinx, and Blacks? As noted in Chapter 6 of *SAT Wars,* written by Jay Rosner (2012) of the Princeton Review Foundation, math questions in the experimental parts of the SAT where women outperform men and verbal questions where Black youths outperform White youths are eliminated from future versions of the test that count. Apparently, a question is invalid if women and Blacks do better on it than White men.

Rosner documents this test question selection bias by working with data on 2 years of SAT questions, 276 in total. Rosner provides multiple examples of experimental questions on the SAT that Black youths did relatively better on than White youths and questions on which White youths did relatively better than Black youths. Then he asks, how many of the questions that counted were White-advantage questions or Black-advantage questions? "Each and every one of the 276 questions were white [advantage] questions in this white/black comparison," Rosner wrote (2012, p.

114). Life is unfair enough without the added inequalities imposed by a racist and sexist test.

High school transcripts are where you will find hints about a student's grit, creativity, and accomplishments. SAT or ACT standardized test scores tell us nothing about community engagement or which students are striving to achieve meaningful lives. Look at how well admission based on rank in one's local high school works in California and Texas. Both the University of Texas and the University of California admit all who graduate near the top 10% of their individual high school. They do so without harm to academic standards, and doing so opens doors to a better life for thousands of young people from low- and middle-income households.

Some researchers have expressed the concern that high school grade point average (HSGPA) might be more correlated with family socioeconomic status (SES) than is the case for SAT scores (Sternberg, Bonney, Gabora, & Merrifield, 2012). An argument used to defend the SAT/ACT is that these tests level the playing field, providing for a nationally normed test that reduces disparities among high schools due to the property values of the neighborhood and the SES composition of the student body. But University of California researchers found the opposite. Geiser and Santelices (2007) "reported that the SAT-V correlated at the .32 level with family income, and at the .39 level with parents' education; similarly, SAT-M scores correlated respectively at .24 and .32, but HSGPA correlated with family income at the .04 level, and with parents' education at the .06 level" (p. 2). If Geiser and Santelices are right, HSGPA is far from being a proxy for social class. Since HSGPA retains its punch, without conveying social disparities, then why not save money, energy, and incalculable family anxiety by dropping the SAT/ACT?

Tests and college admissions have a century-long troubled history. Public universities, roughly between the 1890s and the late 1950s, used to admit everyone with a high school degree from a certified public high school. Then, in the 1950s, midwestern public universities developed the ACT as an alternative to the SAT. Once the University of California, under Kerr's presidency, wanted to compete with Harvard, it signed up for the SAT in 1968, against the recommendations of every study produced by the university, making standardized testing rather than high school grades the passkey to higher education (Soares, 2007, pp. 146–152). The direct link between public universities and public high schools was cut mid-20th century.

Private institutions launched the College Board in 1900 to set common exams on academic subjects that would give bragging rights to the private sector. Private colleges did not accept just any high school graduate, but only those who could do college level work in a particular subject as signified by their College Board exam scores. Then the Jewish community in New York blew by that academic hurdle, creating at Columbia University a foothold on the college/social mobility ladder. Fearing a Jewish invasion,

Yale and Princeton wanted an IQ test that would show, according to the Princeton psychologist who oversaw the design of the test, the superiority of their Nordic youths over inferior racial stock: the Alpine, Mediterranean (including Jews), and Negro (Soares, 2007, pp. 22–23). In the 1920s, IQ eugenics was not just an intellectual subculture, but rather the reverse—it was the law of the land with "separate but equal," forced "three generations of imbeciles are enough" sterilization, and strict immigration quotas. When the SAT was introduced in 1926, it was supposed to be an IQ test that would measure intrinsic intellectual aptitude, not academic subject mastery; it was supposed to help sort between the gems in the Nordic race from the subject-test grinds in the "Jewish race." It did not work to exclude Jews, but other tactics introduced in the 1930s of requiring mother's maiden name and place of birth, were more effective toward that goal. It also did not work to predict grades; Yale and Princeton knew that as early as 1930 (Soares, 2007, p. 30). But the private sector clung to the test, first for the invidious distinction over public universities of requiring a national normed measuring stick, and later because of the convenient way it disguised SES selection as academic selection, paying the bills along the way.

What those college entrance exam scores do reliably signal is the ability of a student's family to pay tuition fees and living costs. The SAT works better as a proxy for family income than it does as a predictor of college performance. As the *New York Times* points out, "For the math geeks out there, the R2 [r-square] for each test average/income range chart is about 0.95" (Rampell, 2009); remember that the SAT's r-square for predicting college grades is just 0.13. Or, as I argue in a different book, *The Power of Privilege* (Soares, 2007), test score selection is selection for bank accounts disguised as selection for brains.

The test industry is about profits, not pedagogy. Standardized testing and test prep in America are worth in excess of $13 billion (Strauss, 2015) per year. The way I see it, testing is a gold mine for the industry and a sweat shop for America's youths. The energy, anxiety, effort, time, and money spent on SAT or ACT tests for college admissions is wasted. The test industry takes time away from real learning, from literature, foreign languages, arts, and sciences. It is time to toss those admissions tests.

This book contributes to the case for test-optional admissions with scholarship that sheds significant light on key problems. In Chapter 1 Saul Geiser, one of Berkeley's top sociologists on college admissions, provides 25 years' worth of data in "Norm-Referenced Tests and Race-Blind Admissions: The Case for Eliminating the SAT and ACT at the University of California." Geiser finds that over time the predictive power of the test has declined while its correlation with race and family income has grown. The test serves as such a strong proxy for race that "race blind" admissions, as mandated by California law, cannot be done so long as one relies on test scores to sort youths.

The effects on educational attainments of the correlation between test scores and family income are vividly highlighted by Paul Fain in Chapter 2, "Wealth's Influence on College Enrollment and Completion." He uses the best and most recent data available to show how the odds of attending a 4-year college, let alone a very selective one, are overwhelmingly stacked against low-income, working-class youths; the linear relationship between family income and test scores makes a mockery of meritocratic equal opportunity.

In Chapter 3 William Kidder, a legal scholar, and Jay Rosner, former executive director of the Princeton Review Foundation, explore the legal case against standardized college admissions tests. Due to the racial and ethnic biases contained in the test, they offer a "disparate impact" legal case against the constitutionality of using SAT/ACT scores for college admission.

In Chapter 4, "The 'Landscape' or 'Dashboard Adversity Index' Distraction: A Clumsy Attempt at Damage Control," I address how the College Board has been forced to acknowledge the roles played by family, community, and schools in the production of test scores, even as it attempts to ignore the role played by race. The "landscape" is intended by the Board to provide background context with which to interpret SAT scores. The index, as it currently stands, is either an artful distraction or the beginning of the end for the academic legitimacy of the test. I show how the "adversity index" noise could be turned into a scientific index signaling strivers or slackers, following in the footsteps of Anthony Carnevale, a former ETS vice president, currently in charge of Georgetown University's Center on Education and the Workforce.

In Chapter 5 Robert Schaeffer, the public education director for FairTest.org, provides a national balance sheet and practical guide for going test-optional in "The SAT/ACT Optional Admissions Growth Surge: More Colleges Conclude 'Test Scores Do Not Equal Merit.'"

Next there are two chapters giving solid findings on the experiences of test-optional colleges. Chapter 6, "Wake Forest's Ten Years of Test-Optional Admissions: A Review of Students Who Did Not Submit Versus Those Who Did," is a case study by Michael DeWitt and Philip Handwerk of Wake Forest's Office of Institutional Research. Chapter 7, "Defining Access: How Test-Optional Works," by Steven Syverson, Valerie W. Franks, and William C. Hiss, is the best, most extensive national study of test-optional colleges. This study poses the right questions and provides answers: Does test-optional increase social class and racial diversity? Are Pell grant recipients and first-generation students disproportionately among the non-submitters? Are there any differences between submitters and non-submitters in GPA or college graduation rates?

Reflections on the nation's biggest admissions scandal, which involved parents paying as much as $200,000 and $6.5 million (Chappell & Kennedy, 2019) for falsified test scores and fake athletic credentials, are offered in "Final Thoughts: The FBI Sting and Moments that Define a Profession," by

Jon Boeckenstedt. He was formerly the associate vice president for Enrollment Management at De Paul University, and is currently the vice provost of Enrollment Management for Oregon State University. Boeckenstedt sees the "deception and fraud" charges for "fake test scores, fake credentials" (Chappell & Kennedy, 2019) involving at least 50 individuals, including entertainment celebrities, as a turning point in the nation's troubled relation to standardized admission tests.

REFERENCES

Atkinson, R. C., & Geiser, S. (2012). Reflections on a century of college admissions tests. In J. A. Soares (Ed.), *SAT wars: The case for test-optional college admissions* (pp. 23–49). New York, NY: Teachers College Press.

Balf, T. (2014, March 6). The story behind the SAT overhaul. *New York Times Magazine*. Retrieved from www.nytimes.com/2014/03/09/magazine/the-story-behind-the-sat-overhaul.html

Chappell, B., & Kennedy, M. (2019, March 12). U.S. charges dozens of parents, coaches in massive college admissions scandal. Retrieved from www.npr.org/2019/03/12/702539140/u-s-accuses-actresses-others-of-fraud-in-wide-college-admissions-scandal

Gardner, H. (1983). *Frames of mind: The theory of multiple intelligences.* New York, NY: Basic Books.

Geiser, S., & Santelices, M. V. (2007, June). *Validity of high-school grades in predicting student success beyond the freshman year: High-school record vs. standardized tests as indicator of four-year college outcomes* (Research & Occasional Paper Series: CSHE.6.07). Berkeley, CA: Center for Studies in Higher Education. Retrieved from cshe.berkeley.edu/publications/validity-high-school-grades-predicting-student-success-beyond-freshman-yearhigh-school

Gladwell, M. (2019). *Puzzle rush* [Audio podcast]. In *Revisionist History* (Season 4, Episode 1). Retrieved from revisionisthistory.com/episodes/31-puzzle-rush

Kobrin, J. L., Patterson, B. F., Shaw, E. J., Mattern, K. D., & Barbuti, S. M. (2008). *Validity of the SAT for predicting first-year college grade point average* (College Board Research Report No. 2008-5). New York, NY: The College Board. Retrieved from eric.ed.gov/?id=ED563202

Morgan, R. (1989). *Analyses of the predictive validity of the SAT and high school grades from 1976 to 1985* (College Board Report No. 89-7; ETS RR No. 89-37). New York, NY: College Entrance Examination Board. Retrieved from eric.ed.gov/?id=ED562586

Nadworny, E. (2019) Lawsuit Claims SAT and ACT are Illegal in California Admissions. www.npr.org/2019/12/10/786257347/lawsuit-claims-sat-and-act-are-illegal-in-california-admissions

National Center for Education Statistics (NCES). (2019, May). Figure 3. Number of degree-granting institutions, by level and control of institution and enrollment size: Fall 2017. In *Characteristics of degree-granting postsecondary institutions.* Retrieved from nces.ed.gov/programs/coe/indicator_csa.asp

Rampell, C. (2009, August 27). SAT scores and family income [Blog post]. In *Economix, The New York Times.* Retrieved from economix.blogs.nytimes.com/2009/08/27/sat-scores-and-family-income/

Rosner, Jay (2012). The SAT: Quantifying the unfairness behind the bubbles. In J. A. Soares (Ed.), *SAT wars: The case for test-optional college admissions* (pp. 104–117). New York, NY: Teachers College Press.

Ruiz, R. (2011). A New Book Argues Against the SAT. Retrieved from http://thechoice.blogs.nytimes.com/2011/11/09/sat/

Soares, J. A. (2007). *The power of privilege.* Stanford, CA: Stanford University Press.

Soares, J. A. (Ed.). (2012). *SAT wars: The case for test-optional college admissions.* New York, NY: Teachers College Press.

Soares, J. A. (2013). Private paradigm constrains public response to challenges of 21st century. *Wake Forest Law Review, 48*(2), 427–443.

Soares, J. A. (2018, January 10). More colleges than ever have test-optional admissions policies—and that's a good thing. In *The Conversation.* [Website]. Retrieved from theconversation.com/more-colleges-than-ever-have-test-optional-admissions-policies-and-thats-a-good-thing-89852

Sternberg, R. J. (2003). *Wisdom, intelligence, and creativity synthesized.* New York, NY: Cambridge University Press.

Sternberg, R. J., Bonney, C., Gabora, L., & Merrifield, M. (2012). WICS: A model for college and university admissions. *Educational Psychologist, 47*(1), 30–41.

Strauss, V. (2015, March 11). Five reasons standardized testing isn't likely to let up. *The Washington Post.* Retrieved from www.washingtonpost.com/news/answer-sheet/wp/2015/03/11/five-reasons-standardized-testing-isnt-likely-to-let-up/

Watanabes, T. (2019, November 23) Drop the SAT and ACT as a requirement for admission, top UC officals say. *Los Angeles Times.* www.latimes.com/california/story/2019-11-23/uc-officials-recommend-dropping-sat-admission-requirement

Zwick, R. (2017). *Who gets in? Strategies for fair and effective college admissions.* Cambridge, MA: Harvard University Press.

Part I

THE CASE AGAINST THE SAT/ACT

CHAPTER 1

Norm-Referenced Tests and Race-Blind Admissions

The Case for Eliminating the SAT and ACT at the University of California

Saul Geiser

THE GROWING SOCIAL COSTS OF ADMISSIONS TESTS

Admissions tests like the SAT and ACT have both costs and benefits for colleges and universities that employ them. Their chief benefit is predictive validity, that is, their purported ability to predict student performance in college and thereby provide a standardized, numerical measure to aid admissions officers in sorting large numbers of applicants. Their chief cost is that test scores are strongly influenced by socioeconomic factors, as shown in Table 1.1. The findings shown here are based on an initial sample of 1,144,047 California high school graduates who applied for freshman admission at UC between 1994 and 2011. The sample was provided to the author by UC Office of the President (UCOP). Subsequently, UCOP institutional research staff replicated and extended the author's findings for the years 2012 through 2016, expanding the total sample to over 1.6 million applicants. Findings for 2012-2016 reported in later figures and tables below were kindly provided by UCOP research staff.

Compared to other admissions criteria like high school grades or class rank, scores on nationally norm-referenced tests like the SAT and ACT are more highly correlated with student background characteristics like family income, parents' education, and race or ethnicity. To the extent that test scores are emphasized as a selection criterion, they are a deterrent to admission of low-income, first-generation college, and underrepresented minority applicants.

At institutions that continue to employ the SAT and ACT, this cost/benefit trade-off is, of course, well-known. While many smaller colleges have

Table 1.1. Correlation of Socioeconomic Factors with SAT/ACT Scores and High School GPA

	Family Income	Parents' Education	Underrepresented Minority
SAT/ACT scores	.36	.45	-.38
High school GPA	.11	.14	-.17

Note. UC Corporate Student System is source of data on all California residents who applied for freshman admission between 1994 and 2011 for whom complete data were available on all covariates.

gone "test-optional," most highly selective universities have not. At those institutions, a détente has emerged that accepts SAT/ACT scores as an indicator of individual differences in readiness for college, yet acknowledges that test scores are affected by disparities in students' opportunity to learn. Rather than eliminate tests, colleges and universities make accommodations in how tests are used. Almost all selective institutions now consider SAT/ACT scores as only one of several factors in their "holistic" admissions process, and not necessarily the most important factor. Many institutions also give admissions preferences to applicants from socioeconomic categories most adversely affected when test scores are emphasized as a selection criterion. These and other accommodations serve to offset the adverse statistical effect of SAT/ACT scores on admission of low-income, first-generation college, and underrepresented minority applicants.

Yet the balance of costs and benefits has changed over time, and the uneasy détente over testing has become more difficult to sustain. This is evident at the University of California. Over the past 2 decades, the correlation between test scores and socioeconomic factors has increased sharply among UC applicants, as shown in Figure 1.1.

In 1995, family income, parental education, and race/ethnicity together accounted for 23% of the variance in test scores among UC applicants, compared to 5% of the variance in high school grades. By 2016, those same factors accounted for 40% of the variance in SAT/ACT scores, compared to 9% for high school GPA. What this means is that 40% of the variation in students' SAT/ACT scores is attributable to differences in socioeconomic circumstance. It also means that test scores have become a deterrent to admission of poor, first-generation college, and Latinx and African American applicants at UC.[1]

UC AS A TEST CASE FOR "RACE-BLIND" ADMISSIONS

To be sure, UC has taken extraordinary steps to offset the adverse impacts of test scores and to expand admission of students from disadvantaged

Figure 1.1. Variance in SAT/ACT Scores and High School GPA Explained by Family Income, Parents' Education, and Race/Ethnicity, 1994 to 2016

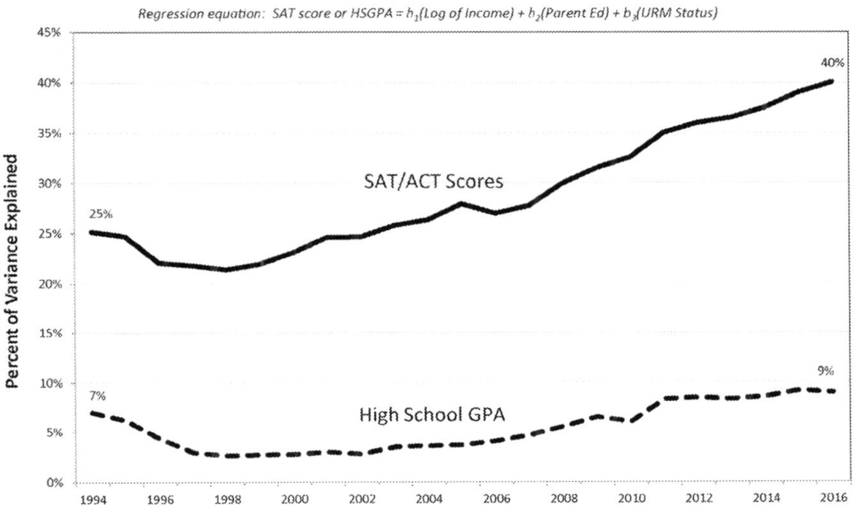

Note. UC Corporate Student System is source of data on all California residents who applied for freshman admission from 1994 through 2016 for whom complete data were available on all covariates.

backgrounds. In addition to holistic review, UC introduced the Eligibility in the Local Context (ELC) program in 2001, extending eligibility for admission to the top 4% of students in each California high school based on their grades in UC-required coursework, irrespective of test scores. ELC was expanded to include the top 9% of students in each school in 2012. UC also gives admissions preferences for low-income and first-generation college students, other qualifications being equal. A common denominator in these reforms is their deemphasis on test scores as a selection factor in favor of students' high school record and socioeconomic circumstances.

UC's reforms have been closely watched for their national implications. California is one of eight states to bar consideration of race as a factor in university admissions, either through state referenda, legislative action, or gubernatorial edict. The other 42 states allow public colleges and universities to take applicants' race into account as one among several admissions factors under U.S. Supreme Court guidelines reiterated most recently in *Fisher v. University of Texas* (2016).

California is viewed as a test case for "race blind" admissions. Some argue that race-neutral or "class-based" affirmative action— admissions preferences for low-income and first-generation college applicants—can be as effective as race-conscious affirmative action in boosting underrepresented minority enrollments indirectly and without the political controversy those programs have attracted. Some advocates have characterized UC's reforms as a promising step in that direction (e.g., see Kahlenberg, 2014b).

Admissions reforms undertaken at UC in the aftermath of Proposition 209 have substantially improved the number and proportion of low-income and first-generation college students. By 2014, 42% of UC undergraduates were eligible for Pell grants (federal financial aid for low-income students) and 44% were first-generation college students. Both figures are far higher than other comparable universities, public or private. Four UC campuses now individually enroll more Pell-eligible students than the entire Ivy League combined. If class-based affirmative action can be an effective proxy for race-conscious affirmative action, the effect should be evident in California.

But the racial impact has been limited. Underrepresented minority enrollments—Black, Latinx, and American Indian students—plummeted after Proposition 209 took effect at UC in 1998 and did not return to pre-209 levels until 2005. Today, underrepresented groups account for about 28% of all new UC freshmen, up from about 20% before affirmative action was ended.

Almost all that growth, however, is the result of underlying demographic changes in California. The racial/ethnic composition of the state has changed dramatically in the past quarter-century, especially among younger Californians and particularly Latinx. White enrollments in the state's public schools declined in both absolute and relative terms between 1993 and 2012, Asian enrollments held steady as a proportion of California's school population, and Black enrollments increased numerically but decreased proportionately. The number of Chicanx and Latinx students increased by 68%, becoming a majority of K–12 public school enrollments (Orfield & Ee, 2014). That demographic shift accounts for most of the growth in underrepresented minority enrollments at UC since Proposition 209 took effect. In fact, as measured by the gap between their share of new UC freshmen and their share of all college-age Californians, underrepresentation of these groups has worsened at UC since then.[2]

RACE VERSUS CLASS AS CORRELATES OF TEST SCORES

Closer analysis of UC test score data challenges an underlying assumption of class-based affirmative action: that racial and ethnic differences in test scores are mainly a byproduct of the fact that Latinx and Black applicants come disproportionately from poorer and less educated families. UC data show, to the contrary, that race has a large, independent, and growing statistical effect on students' SAT/ACT scores after controlling for other

Figure 1.2. Relative Weight of Family Income, Parents' Education, and Race/Ethnicity in Predicting SAT/ACT Scores, 1994 to 2016

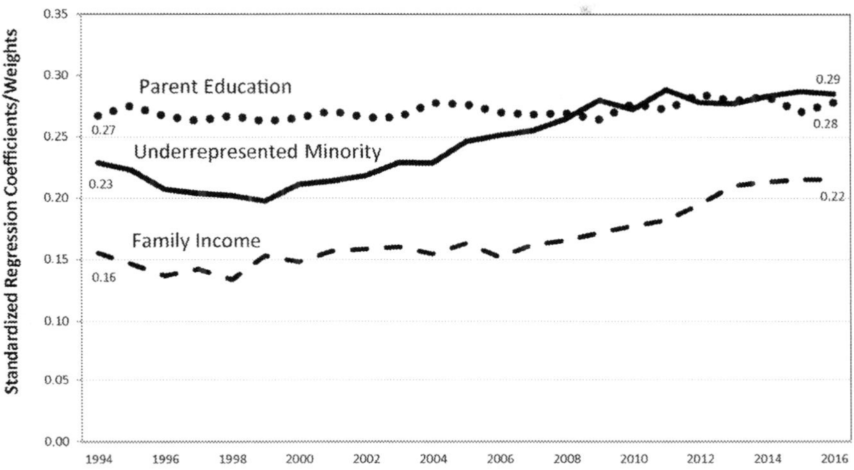

Note. UC Corporate Student System is source of data on all California resident freshman applicants from 1994 through 2016 for whom complete data were available on all covariates. All coefficients are statistically significant at .001 confidence level.

factors. Race matters as much as, if not more than, family income and parents' education in accounting for test score differences.

This is not to suggest that family income, parents' education, or race/ethnicity "cause" test score differences in any simple or direct fashion. Socioeconomic factors are mediated by other, more proximate experiences that affect test performance, such as access to test prep services or the quality of schools that students attend. Nevertheless, without being able to observe those intermediating experiences directly, regression analysis enables one to measure the relative importance of different socioeconomic factors in accounting for test score differences. Figure 1.2 shows standardized regression coefficients for family income, parental education, and race/ethnicity in predicting test score variation among UC applicants. The coefficients represent the predictive weight of each factor after controlling for the effects of the other two, thus allowing comparison of the relative importance of each.

Parents' education—the education level of the student's highest-educated parent—has long been the strongest predictor of test scores among UC applicants. In 1995, at the beginning of the period covered by this analysis, the predictive weight for parental education was 0.28. This means that for each one standard-deviation increase in parents' education, SAT/ACT scores rose by .28 of a standard deviation, or about 50 points, controlling for other factors. The predictive weight for parental education has remained about the same since then.

Family income, perhaps surprisingly, has the least effect on test scores after controlling for other factors, although it has shown a small but steady increase. The coefficient for income grew from 0.16 in 1995 to 0.22 in 2016. The latter represents a test score differential of about 40 points.

But the most important trend has been the growing statistical effect of race and ethnicity. The standardized coefficient for race increased from 0.22 in 1995 to 0.29 in 2016 (about a 55-point test score differential), the last year for which the author has obtained data. Underrepresented minority status—self-identification as Latinx or African American—became the strongest predictor of test scores for the first time in 2009.[3]

A key implication of these findings is that racial and ethnic group differences in SAT/ACT scores are not simply reducible to differences in family income and parental education. Statistically, being born to Black or Latinx parents is as much of a disadvantage on the SAT or ACT as being born to poor or less-educated parents.

RACIAL SEGREGATION AND THE "TEST SCORE GAP"

What accounts for the growing statistical correlation between race and test scores among UC applicants? It has occurred within a relatively short time span, less than a generation, so that any suggestion of a biogenic explanation is moot.

Over 20 years ago the publication of Jencks and Phillips' (1998) *The Black–White Test Score Gap* sparked an extraordinary burst of research on the relationship between race and test scores. Most of that research focused on Black–White differences and is not as directly relevant to the California experience as one might wish. The explosion of California's Chicanx and Latinx population together with continued growth among different Asian ethnic groups have overtaken the traditional, Black–White dichotomy. Yet the earlier research has much to tell us.

Studies of the Black–White test score gap can be divided into two strands: Those that seek to explain the gap primarily by reference to general socioeconomic factors, such as differences in family income and wealth, and those that emphasize factors specifically associated with race, such as discrimination and segregation.

A great deal of research on the Black–White test score gap has favored the first type of explanation. Those studies have emphasized, among other influences, differences in family income (Magnuson & Duncan, 2006; Magnuson, Rosenbaum, & Waldfogel, 2008), parental education (Cook & Evans, 2000; Haveman & Wolfe, 1995), and quality of schools (Corcoran

& Evans, 2008) as factors underlying Black–White test score differences. As a group, Black students are disproportionately affected by all these factors. For example, Black students have, on average, fewer resources in and out of the home, poorer health care, and less effective teachers, all of which can have an impact on test scores (Magnuson et al., 2008; Phillips, Crouse, & Ralph, 1998).

The main problem with this body of research is that it leaves much of the Black–White gap unexplained. Though class differences account for a portion of the test score gap, they by no means eliminate it entirely. Conventional measures of socioeconomic status leave a large portion, even a majority of the gap, unexplained (Haveman, Sandefur, Wolfe, & Voyer, 2004; Meyers, Rosenbaum, Ruhm, & Waldfogel, 2004; Phillips & Chin, 2004).[4]

Others who have studied the Black–White test score gap have long noted the coincidence between trends in racial segregation and changes in the size of the gap. Following the U.S. Supreme Court's decision in *Brown v. Board of Education* (1954), racial segregation in U.S. schools decreased dramatically during the 1960s and 1970s. The Black–White test score gap narrowed significantly during the same period. School desegregation stalled in the 1990s as the result of court decisions restricting busing and other integration measures. Progress in narrowing the test score gap stalled at the same time.

The coincidence of these trends has prompted a great deal of research to determine whether they are causally linked. Berkeley economists David Card and Jesse Rothstein's (2006) study of SAT score gaps in metropolitan areas across the United States is generally regarded as dispositive: "We find robust evidence that the Black–White test score gap is higher in more segregated cities" (p. ii).

RESURGENCE OF RACIAL SEGREGATION IN CALIFORNIA SCHOOLS

Racial segregation has increased sharply in California over the past quarter-century, as documented by Gary Orfield and his colleagues at the UCLA Civil Rights Project (Orfield & Ee, 2014). In 1993 about half of California's public schools were still majority White schools, and only one-seventh were "intensely segregated," meaning 90% or more Latinx and Black. By 2012, 71% of the state's schools had a majority of Latinx and Black students and 31% were intensely segregated.

California's schools now rank among the most segregated of all the states, including those in the deep South, on some measures. Measured by Black students' exposure to White students, California ranks next to last. For Latinx students, it ranks last. Today the typical Latinx student attends schools where less than 6% of the other students are White.

A clear pattern of co-segregation of Latinx and African American students has emerged. Slightly more than half of all Latinx students now attend intensely segregated schools, and the comparable figure for Black students in California is 39%. At the same time, "double segregation" by race and poverty has become increasingly common as the result of rising poverty levels within segregated school districts. Black students in California, on average, attend schools whose populations are two-thirds poor children, and Latinx attend schools that are more than 70% poor. Double segregation by race and poverty is overlaid with "triple segregation" by language, as these same schools enroll high proportions of English language learners. On top of all, intensely segregated schools are typically underresourced and staffed by teachers with weaker educational credentials.

Racial segregation is associated, in short, with multiple forms of disadvantage that combine to magnify test score disparities among Latinx and Black students.

> There are two aspects to this conclusion: First, social and economic disadvantage—not poverty itself, but a host of associated conditions—depresses student performance, and second, concentrating students with these disadvantages in racially and economically homogenous schools depresses it further. (Rothstein, 2014, p. 1)

If segregation does have an independent effect on test scores, as much research on the Black–White gap suggests, that explanation is consistent with observed trends in the California data: why the correlation between race and test scores has grown for Latinx as well as Black students, and why the correlation remains after controlling for conventional measures of socioeconomic status.

HOLISTIC REVIEW AND PROPOSITION 209

In 1998 the Educational Testing Service (ETS) proposed a new test score measure, known as the "Strivers" proposal (Carnevale & Haghighat, 1998). ETS researchers compared students' actual SAT scores with their predicted scores based on socioeconomic and other factors, including race. Students whose actual score significantly exceeded their predicted score were deemed "strivers." As an ETS official explained, "A combined score of 1000 on the SATs is not always a 1000. When you look at a Striver who gets a 1000, you're looking at someone who really performs at a 1200. This is a way of measuring not just where students are, but how far they've come" (quoted in Marcus, 1999). The proposal was later withdrawn after it sparked controversy and was rejected by the College Board.

Yet the underlying idea of the Strivers proposal remains very much alive at selective universities, like UC, that practice holistic admissions. "Holistic" or comprehensive review considers the totality of information in applicants' files. Admissions staff who read files are "normed" and trained to evaluate indicators of academic achievement, such as test scores, in light of applicants' educational and socioeconomic circumstances. Though far less algorithmic than the Strivers proposal, holistic admissions shares the same impulse to assess "achievement in context," as emphasized in UC admissions policy:

> Standardized tests and academic indices as part of the review process must be considered in the context of other factors that impact performance, including personal and academic circumstances (e.g., low-income status, access to honors courses, and college-going culture of the school). (UC Academic Senate, 2014, p. 3)

UC's holistic review process differs, however, from that at most other selective universities in one key respect: UC admissions readers cannot consider race as a contextual factor when evaluating applicants' SAT or ACT scores. Proposition 209 amended the California state constitution to prohibit "preference" in public education on the basis of race, sex, or ethnicity. While it made no mention of affirmative action, Proposition 209 was widely viewed as a referendum on that policy. Until then, UC had considered underrepresented minority status a "plus factor" in selection decisions. Supporters of the ballot measure saw it as a vehicle to end "reverse discrimination" in university admissions.

Race was removed from applicant files after Proposition 209 took effect in 1998. UC continues to collect data on applicants' race and ethnicity, but that information is not given to admissions readers. Proposition 209 has thus had the effect of eliminating any attention to race, whether as a "plus factor" or a socioeconomic disadvantage, in UC's admissions process. In barring consideration of race as an admissions criterion, it has also effectively barred consideration of how other admissions criteria—like SAT and ACT scores—are themselves conditioned by race.

A BRIEF HISTORY OF VALIDITY STUDIES AT UC

Of course, tests may have adverse statistical effects without necessarily being biased. If tests are valid measures of student readiness for college, test score gaps between different groups may simply reflect real, if unfortunate, differences in opportunity to learn. The validity of admissions tests like the SAT and ACT is measured by their ability to predict student performance in college. How well do test scores predict student success at UC?

Early Validity Studies by BOARS

The relatively weak predictive validity of the SAT and ACT is a longstanding issue that prevented their adoption at UC until later than most other selective U.S. universities. UC experimented with the SAT as early as 1960, when it required the test on a trial basis to evaluate its effectiveness. In 1962 Charles Jones, chair of the Board of Admissions and Relations with Schools (BOARS), [5] came to the following conclusion: "Extensive analysis of the data, leave the Board wholly convinced that the Scholastic Aptitude Test scores add little or nothing to the precision with which the existing admissions requirements are predictive of success in the University." BOARS voted unanimously to reject the test (quoted in Douglass, 2007, p. 90).

Lobbied by the Educational Testing Service, in 1964 UC conducted another major study of the predictive value of achievement exams such as the SAT II Subject Tests, which assess student knowledge of specific college-preparatory subjects, like chemistry or U.S. history. The study again showed that test scores were of limited value in predicting academic success at UC, although achievement exams were slightly superior to the SAT. High school GPA remained the best indicator, explaining 22% of the variance in university grades, while subject tests explained 8%. Combining high school GPA and test scores did yield a marginal improvement, but the study concluded that the gain was too small to warrant adoption of the tests at UC. Again, BOARS's decision was to reject the tests (Douglass, 2007, pp. 91–92).[6]

Growing Use of Test Scores in UC Eligibility and Admission

If UC was slow to embrace the national exams, the "tidal wave" of California high school graduates that Clark Kerr and the Master Plan architects had foreseen would soon tip the scales in favor of the SAT, if for reasons other than predictive validity. The growing volume of UC applications made test scores more useful as an administrative tool to cull UC's eligibility pool and limit it to the top 12.5% of California high school graduates prescribed by the Master Plan. In 1968 UC for the first time required all applicants to take the SAT or ACT but restricted use of test scores to specific purposes such as evaluating out-of-state applicants and assessing the eligibility of in-state students with very low GPAs (between 3.00 and 3.09), who represented less than 2% of all admits. Test scores were still not widely used at this time.

UC began using the SAT and ACT more extensively as part of its systemwide eligibility requirements in 1979, following a 1976 study by the California Postsecondary Education Commission (CPEC). The CPEC study showed that UC eligibility criteria then in place were drawing almost 15% of the state's high school graduates, well in excess of the Master Plan's 12.5% target. Rather than tightening high school GPA requirements,

BOARS chair Allan Parducci proposed an "eligibility index," combining grades and test scores, to address the problem. The index was an offsetting scale that required students with lower GPAs to earn higher test scores, and the converse. The effect was to extend a minimum test score requirement to most UC applicants. The proposal was controversial because of its anticipated adverse effect on low-income and underrepresented minority applicants, and it was narrowly approved by the regents in a close vote (Douglass, 2007, pp. 116–117).

The SAT would soon feature more prominently in UC admissions as well, and for the same reason: its utility as an administrative tool to sort the ballooning volume of applications after the UC system introduced multiple filing in 1986. Multiple filing enabled students to submit one application to all UC campuses via a central application processing system. The volume of applications increased sharply the first year, and Berkeley and UCLA for the first time received vastly more applications from UC-eligible students than they were able to admit.

The UC system responded in 1988 with a new policy on "admissions selection" at heavily impacted campuses. The policy established a two-tier structure for campus admissions. The top 40% to 60% of the freshman class were admitted based solely on high school grades and SAT/ACT scores. The remainder were admitted based on a combination of academic and "supplemental" criteria. Race and ethnicity were explicitly included among the supplemental criteria. The guidelines were, in effect, a compromise between the competing goals of selectivity and diversity. The compromise would hold for only a few years, however, before being shattered in 1995 by UC regents' resolution SP-1, eliminating race as a supplemental admissions criterion.

2001 UC Validity Study

It might be assumed that UC's increasing reliance on the SAT and ACT during this period was accompanied by concurrent improvements in the validity of the tests, but that assumption would be mistaken. In the aftermath of SP-1 (and a year later, passage of Proposition 209), UC undertook a sweeping review of all admissions criteria, with a special focus on standardized tests, in an effort to reverse plummeting minority enrollments. The findings of that review were strikingly similar to what BOARS had found 40 years earlier.

A 2001 study commissioned by BOARS showed once again that test scores yielded only a small incremental improvement over high school GPA in predicting freshman grades at UC. High school GPA accounted for 15.4% of the variance in first-year grades (see Table 1.2 for study results).

Adding students' scores from the SAT into the prediction model improved the explained variance to 20.8%. SAT scores provided an

Table 1.2. Percent of Variance in UC First-Year Grades Predicted by High School GPA and Test Scores

Predictor Variables/Equations	Explained Variance
(1) HSGPA	15.4%
(2) HSGPA + SAT	20.8%
(3) HSGPA + Subject Tests	22.2%
(4) HSGPA + Subject Tests + SAT	22.3%
SAT increment (4–3)	0.1%

Note. Data were taken from "UC and the SAT: Predictive Validity and Differential Impact of the SAT I and SAT II at the University of California," by S. Geiser(with R. Studley, 2002, *Educational Assessment, 8*(1), p. 6 (Table 2). Results were based on a sample of 77,893 first-time freshmen entering UC from 1996 through 1999.

incremental gain, in other words, of about five percentage points, close to what BOARS had found in 1964.

The 2001 study replicated another result from BOARS's earlier studies: Achievement exams such as the SAT II Subject Tests were slightly superior to the SAT I "reasoning test" in predicting first-year performance at UC. The subject tests provided an incremental gain of about seven percentage points over high school GPA alone. After taking account of high school GPA and SAT II Subject Test scores, SAT I scores yielded little further incremental improvement and became almost entirely redundant. Based in part on this finding, then-UC-president Richard C. Atkinson (2001) proposed eliminating generic, norm-referenced tests like the SAT or ACT in favor of curriculum-based achievement exams like the SAT II Subject Tests.[7]

The College Board responded with a revised SAT in 2005. The new test eliminated two of its more controversial item types, verbal analogies and quantitative comparisons, and added a writing test, thus addressing many of Atkinson's and BOARS's criticisms and moving the exam more in the direction of a curriculum-based assessment. But the changes did not alter the test's basic design and, like the ACT, it has remained a norm-referenced assessment. Nor have the changes improved the test's predictive validity. According to the College Board: "The results show that the changes made to the SAT did not substantially change how well the test predicts first-year college performance" (Kobrin et al,, 2008, p. 1).[8]

Later Validity Studies

The SAT and ACT are designed primarily to predict freshman grades, and most validity studies published by the national testing agencies have focused on that outcome criterion. Later studies by independent researchers have examined whether the tests are useful in predicting other measures of success in college, like graduation, that many would regard as more important. The most definitive study of U.S. college graduation rates to date is Bowen, Chingos, and McPherson's (2009) *Crossing the Finish Line*. Based on a massive sample of freshmen at 21 state flagship universities and 4 state higher education systems, the late William G. Bowen and his colleagues found that

> High school grades are a far better predictor of both four-year and six-year graduation rates than are SAT/ACT test scores— a central finding that holds within each of the six sets of public universities that we study, . . . Test scores, on the other hand, routinely fail to pass standard tests of statistical significance when included with high school GPA in regressions predicting graduation rates. (pp. 113–115)[9]

With respect to first-year outcomes, later research has shown that traditional validity studies overstate the predictive value of the tests. Validity studies conducted by the College Board and ACT typically consider only two predictors: high school grades and SAT/ACT scores. This simple, two-variable prediction model can be misleading, however, because it masks the effects of socioeconomic factors on prediction estimates. Socioeconomic status (SES) is correlated both with test scores and with outcomes like first-year grades, so that much of the apparent predictive value of test scores reflects the "proxy" effect of SES. When SES is included in the model, the predictive value of test scores falls. An independent analysis of UC test score data by Berkeley economist Jesse Rothstein (2004) has found that the proxy effect is substantial:

> The results here indicate that the exclusion of student background characteristics from prediction models inflates the SAT's apparent validity, as the SAT score appears to be a more effective measure of the demographic characteristics that predict UC FGPA [freshman grade-point average] than it is of preparedness conditional on student background. . . . [A] conservative estimate is that traditional methods and sparse models [i.e., those that do not take socioeconomic factors into account] overstate the SAT's importance to predictive accuracy by 150 percent. (p. 297)

How Well Do Test Scores Predict Student Success at UC?

As this brief history teaches, the answer depends not only on the outcome measure chosen but on what other academic and socioeconomic information is included in the prediction model. The advent of holistic review in UC admissions has substantially added to the body of information considered in admissions decisions. After taking that information into account, how much do test scores *uniquely* add to the prediction of student success at UC?

An answer is provided in a 2007 study by institutional researchers Sam Agronow and Roger Studley of UC Office of the President. In a regression model predicting first-year grades, the researchers entered all available data from the UC application. In addition to high school GPA and test scores (including SAT II Subject Test scores as well as scores on the SAT), those variables included: number of UC-required "a-g" courses taken, number of AP or honors courses taken, class rank in high school, family income, parental education, race/ethnicity, language spoken in the home, participation in academic preparation programs, and the rank of the student's high school on the state's Academic Performance Index.

Entering all these factors into the prediction model, the researchers found that they explained 28.6% of the variance in UC freshman grades. When they eliminated test scores from the model, thus isolating their effect, the explained variance fell to 25.4%. Test scores, including SAT II Subject Tests as well as the SAT I, accounted for about 3% of the variance in students' first-year grades at UC.[10]

Test scores do add a statistically significant increment to the prediction of freshman grades at UC. But in the context of all the other applicant information now available, they are largely redundant, and their unique contribution is small.

THE PROBLEM OF PREDICTION ERROR

Some may argue that any improvement in prediction, however small, is useful if it adds information. More information is always better than less, on this view. Using SAT and ACT scores in tandem with other applicant data may improve the overall quality of admissions decision making and yield a stronger admit pool.

One problem with this argument is prediction error. In highly competitive applicant pools like UC's, where most applicants have relatively high scores, relying on small test score differences to compare and rank students yields almost as many wrong predictions as correct ones.

Consider two applicants who are evenly matched in all other respects—same high school grades, socioeconomic characteristics, and so forth—except that the first student scored 1300 on the SAT and the second 1400. The choice would seem clear. Test scores are sometimes used as a tiebreaker to choose between applicants who are otherwise equally qualified, and in this case the decision would go to the second student.

What this ignores, however, are two measurement issues. First, because SAT/ACT scores account for such a small fraction of the variance in college grades, their effect size is quite small. Controlling for other academic and supplemental factors in students' files, a 100-point increment in SAT or ACT-equivalent scores translated into a predicted improvement of just 0.13 of a grade point, or an increase in college GPA from 3.00 to 3.13 for the UC sample.

Second, the confidence intervals or error bands around predicted college grades are large and, indeed, substantially larger than the effect size itself. The confidence interval around predicted GPA for the UC sample was plus or minus 0.81 grade points at the 95% confidence level, the minimum level of statistical significance normally accepted in social science research. The error band around the predictions, in other words, was over six times larger than the predicted difference in the two applicants' test scores. For both students, the most that can be said is that actual performance at UC is likely to fall somewhere in a broad range between an A- and a C+ average.

Using SAT/ACT scores to rank applicants introduces a substantial amount of error in admissions decision making. Two types of error are involved. First are "false positives," that is, students admitted based on higher test scores who later underperform in college. Second are "false negatives," that is, individuals denied admission because of lower test scores who would have performed better than many of those admitted. Both types of error are inevitable when the predictive power of tests is low and score differences are small.

It might be countered that some predictive error is the price to pay for the utility of the SAT and ACT at large public institutions that receive huge numbers of applications. Even if their predictive power is small, test scores do have a statistically significant effect "on average," that is, over large numbers of students. Whatever random errors they produce in individual cases may be outweighed by their utility as an administrative tool.

The problem is that the effects of the SAT and ACT are nonrandom. When used as a tool to rank applicants, SAT/ACT scores create greater racial stratification than other admissions criteria. More information is not always better than less if the new information introduces systematic bias in admissions decisions.

NORM-REFERENCED TESTS AND RACIAL STRATIFICATION

Norm-referenced tests like the SAT and ACT magnify racial stratification among UC applicants, as Figure 1.3 will illustrate. All UC applicants were first ranked into 10 equal groups, or deciles, based on their high school grades. The same students were then ranked into deciles based on their SAT/ACT scores, and the proportion of Latinx and Black students in both distributions was compared.

The difference is dramatic. Although SAT/ACT scores and high school GPA both create racial stratification, the demographic footprint of the tests

Figure 1.3. Proportion of Black and Latinx Applicants by SAT/ACT vs. High School GPA Deciles

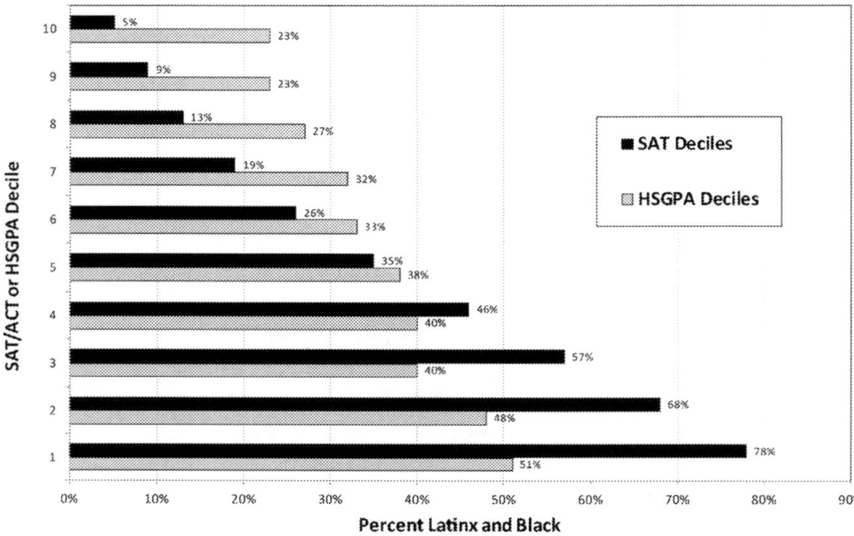

Note. UC Corporate Student System is source of data on all CA resident freshman applicants from 2016.

is far more pronounced. At the bottom of the pool, underrepresented minorities comprise 78% of the lowest SAT/ACT decile, compared to 51% of the lowest HSGPA decile. Conversely, at the top of the pool—those most likely to be admitted— Latinx and Blacks make up 23% of the top HSGPA decile but just 5% of the top SAT/ACT decile. Underrepresented minority applicants are far less likely to rise to the top of the pool when ranked by test scores in place of high school grades.

The tendency of test scores to magnify racial and ethnic differences stems in part from the way norm-referenced assessments like the SAT and ACT are designed. Before going further, it should be emphasized that test publishers such as the College Board and ACT take strenuous measures to eliminate test bias, so that any such effect is unintentional. Gone are the days when test items such as "runner is to marathon as oarsman is to regatta" would survive the rigorous, multistep review process that test publishers now follow.

Despite this, there are grounds for believing that exams like the SAT or ACT may unintentionally disadvantage Latinx and Black applicants because of the way those tests are developed. Before any item is included in the SAT, it is reviewed for reliability. Reliability is measured by the internal correlation between performance on that item and overall performance on the test in a reference population. If the correlation drops below 0.30, the item is typically flagged and dropped from the test. Some test experts argue that the test-development process tends systematically to exclude items on which minority students perform well, and vice versa, even though the items appear unbiased on their face:

> Such a bias tends to be obscured because Whites have historically scored higher on the SAT than African Americans and Chicanos. The entire score gap is usually attributed to differences in academic preparation, although a significant and unrecognized portion of the gap is an inevitable result of . . . the development process. (Kidder & Rosner, 2002, p. 159)

One measure of bias is known as *differential item functioning*, or DIF. DIF occurs "when equally able test takers differ in their probabilities of answering a test item correctly as a function of group membership" (AERA/APA/NCME, 2014, p. 51).[11] Although test developers go to great lengths to eliminate items that exhibit DIF, there is evidence that some residual DIF remains on the finished exams. One of the most rigorous studies to date is by psychometricians Veronica Santelices and Mark Wilson of Berkeley's Graduate School of Education. Based on analysis of several SAT test forms offered in different years, the researchers found that about 10% of all items exhibited large DIF for Black examinees and 3% to 10% for Latinx examinees, depending on the year and form. Moderate-to-low levels of DIF were found on a substantially larger percentage of items for both subgroups (Santelices & Wilson, 2012, p. 23).[12]

Yet item bias may be less important than the general design of norm-referenced tests in understanding why test scores tend to magnify racial differences. Before the SAT, the original "College Boards" were written exams designed to measure students' academic preparation. Multiple-choice exams like the SAT and ACT did not come into prominence until later, as admissions became more competitive and colleges needed to make finer distinctions within applicant pools where most students were high performers. The SAT and later the ACT were designed to meet that need.

Although they differ in some other ways, both the SAT and ACT are *norm-referenced* tests, designed to compare an examinee's performance with that of other examinees. They differ from *criterion-referenced* assessments that measure student performance against a fixed standard. A student's SAT or ACT score measures how he or she performs relative to other test takers. How others perform matters as much as one's own performance in determining one's score. Scores on norm-referenced exams tell admissions officers where an applicant falls within the national test score distribution.

Norm-referenced tests are designed to produce the familiar bell curve so beloved of statisticians, with most examinees scoring in the middle and

Figure 1.4. Frequency Distribution of Test Scores Among California SAT Takers

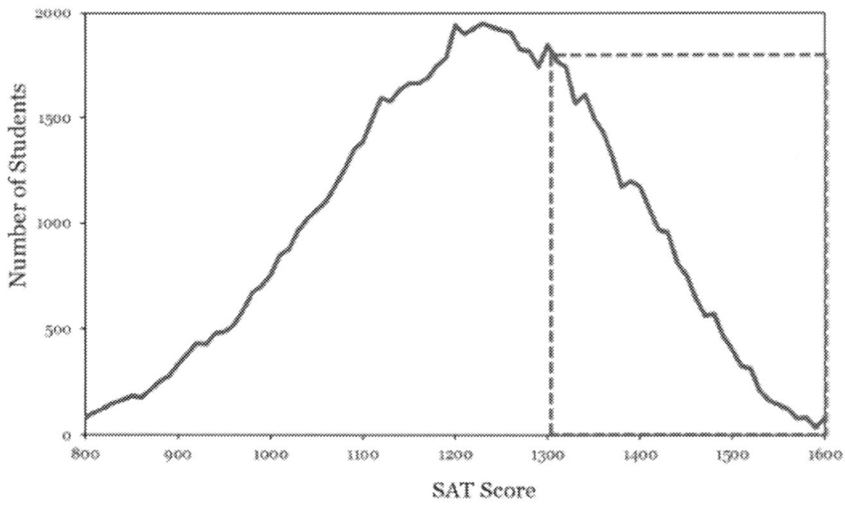

Source: College Board College-Bound Seniors Report for California (n.d.).

sharply descending numbers at the top and bottom. To create this distribution, test designers must make the test neither too easy nor too hard. Designers adjust test difficulty by using plausible-sounding incorrect answers, or *distractors,* to make multiple-choice items harder, and by the *speededness* of the test, or how many items the student must complete in a short space of time. Most important is the choice of items to be included. The ideal test item is one that splits the test-taking population evenly. Items that too many students can answer correctly are dropped from the test.

The resulting bell curve is especially useful for admissions officers at highly competitive institutions like UC (see Figure 1.4), where most applicants are concentrated in the higher-scoring, right-hand tail of the distribution. At those institutions, the problem is how to select from an applicant pool where most students are high performing. Norm-referenced tests assist by accentuating the importance of small score differences at the high end of the test score range. There the distribution is steepest, and a small difference in test scores makes a bigger difference in a student's percentile rank. This has led to the creation of an entire test-prep industry, as students and their parents seek any small advantage in an increasingly competitive admissions environment. It is not surprising that tests designed to magnify the importance of small score differences should magnify underlying racial, economic, and educational differences at the same time.

NATIONAL STANDARDS FOR FAIRNESS IN TESTING

In 2014 the American Educational Research Association (AERA), American Psychological Association (APA), and National Council on Measurement in Education (NCME) jointly issued the latest revision of their *Standards for Educational and Psychological Testing*. First issued in 1955, and previously revised in 1974, 1985, and 1999, the *Standards* address all aspects of test design, development, and use for educational purposes. While they do not carry the force of law, the *Standards* provide guidance on the responsibilities of test users to ensure "fairness in testing." What guidance can they offer UC regarding the difficult issues of race and testing?

The *Standards* obligate test users to be vigilant about the adverse effect of test scores on different social groups, such as racial and ethnic minorities. Adverse statistical effect is not enough by itself, however, to judge whether a test is unfair or biased. Where there are group differences in students' "opportunity to learn," a test may have adverse statistical impact but still be a valid indicator of what it is designed to measure. Adverse impact must be weighed against test validity.

When score gaps between groups are observed, the *Standards* advise test users to look for deeper psychometric warning signs, or "threats to fairness," that may indicate a problem with the validity of the test. "Group differences in testing outcomes should trigger heighted scrutiny for possible sources of test bias" (AERA/APA/NCME, 2014, p. 54). One warning sign is *test content*: Is there evidence that test items unfairly favor one group over another? Another is *text context*, that is, aspects of the testing environment that may favor or disfavor certain groups of examinees. Still another is *differential prediction*, as when a test predicts better for one group than another.

When tests exhibit such symptoms, the *Standards* offer this guidance to test users:

> Standard 3.16: When credible research indicates that test scores for some relevant subgroups are differentially affected by construct-irrelevant characteristics of the test or of the examinees, when legally permissible, test users should use the test only for those subgroups for which there is sufficient evidence of validity to support score interpretations for the intended uses. (AERA/APA/NCME, 2014, p. 70)

All of the warning signs the *Standards* describe are evident in the admissions tests that UC employs. Test content is a first issue. As noted above, UC psychometricians have found differential item functioning on the SAT. Despite efforts of test developers to remove it, some statistically significant DIF remains for both Black and Latinx examinees (Santelices & Wilson, 2012).

Test context is another issue for underrepresented minority students:

> Multiple aspects of the test and testing environment . . . may affect the performance of an examinee and consequently give rise to construct-irrelevant variance in the test scores. As research on contextual factors (e.g., stereotype threat) is ongoing, test developers and test users should pay attention to the emerging empirical literature on these topics so that they can use this information if and when the preponderance of evidence dictates that it is appropriate to do so. (AERA/APA/NCME, 2014, p. 54)

The *Standards*' reference to "stereotype threat" as a contextual factor in testing owes to the work of Stanford social psychologist Claude Steele. Steele and Aronson's (1995) study was the first to demonstrate that awareness of racial stereotypes has a measurable effect on SAT performance among Black examinees.

Finally, differential prediction, or prediction bias, is also evident in the UC test score data. This problem arises "when differences exist in the pattern of associations between test scores and other variables for different groups, bringing with it concerns about bias in the inferences drawn from the use of test scores" (AERA/APA/NCME, 2014, p. 51). For example, SAT/ACT scores are relatively weak predictors of graduation rates for all UC students, but they are even weaker predictors for Black and Latinx undergrads (Geiser, 2015, pp. 8–9). Tests predict least well for groups most disadvantaged by test scores.

When such warning signs are found, the *Standards* hold test users responsible for mitigating the adverse impact of their tests to ensure fairness for students from affected groups. In most states outside California, race and ethnicity can be taken into account in evaluating applicants' test scores, in the same way that family income and parental education are considered in identifying "strivers" who have overcome socioeconomic disadvantages. But how does Standard 3.16 apply in California and the seven other states where it is *not* "legally permissible" to consider race as a factor in admission to public colleges and universities?

In the end, the *Standards* are silent and punt the ball back to test users. As applied to UC admissions, a literal reading of Standard 3.16 would mean exempting Latinx, African American, and American Indian applicants from the test requirement if test validity was deemed insufficient for those groups. SAT/ACT scores would be used only in admitting other applicants. Such an outcome is highly unlikely in California. Exempting any racial or ethnic group from the test requirement would be construed as a violation of Proposition 209. If UC were to exempt underrepresented minority applicants from submitting SAT/ACT scores on grounds of insufficient test validity, it would need to exempt all applicants.

OPPORTUNITY TO LEARN AND ADMISSIONS TESTING

Yet the problem goes beyond race. The larger problem is that SAT/ACT scores systematically disadvantage applicants who have had less opportunity to learn in favor of those who have had more, even when individual ability is equal.

The current détente over use of SAT/ACT scores in U.S. college admissions rests crucially on the concept of opportunity to learn. The *Standards* define this as "the extent to which individuals have had exposure to instruction or knowledge that affords them the opportunity to learn the content and skills targeted by the test" (AERA/APA/NCME, 2014, p. 56). Differences in opportunity to learn are a threat to test validity and fairness. For example, if a school system establishes a test requirement for graduation, it is unfair to hold all students to the requirement if some have received inadequate instruction.

But the circumstances are different in college admissions, according to the *Standards*:

> It should be noted that concerns about opportunity to learn do not necessarily apply to situations where the same authority is not responsible for both the delivery of instruction and the testing and/or interpretation of results. For example, in college admissions decisions, opportunity to learn may be beyond the control of the test users and it may not influence the validity of tests interpretations for their intended use (e.g., selection and/or admissions decisions). (AERA/APA/NCME, 2014, p. 57).

Put differently, despite disparities in students' opportunity to learn and thus to perform well on the SAT and ACT, universities are justified in using them for admissions purposes if they are valid predictors of how students will perform in college.

The national détente over opportunity to learn in testing does not sit well in California. To start with, SAT/ACT scores don't predict student outcomes very well at UC. Test scores add little incremental validity in predicting UC student outcomes such as first-year grades or 4-year graduation rates. Another issue is the size of the effect of opportunity to learn on test scores. Student socioeconomic characteristics now account for about 40% of the variance in SAT/ACT scores among California high school graduates who apply to UC. Even granting that SES differences are beyond UC's control, the sheer size of the effect makes it difficult to justify using test scores to rank applicants.

SAT/ACT scores create "built-in head winds" (Kidder & Rosner, 2002). that reduce the chances of admission for socioeconomically disadvantaged students throughout the applicant pool. But the effect is most pronounced

Figure 1.5. Percent First-Generation College Applicants by SAT/ACT vs. HSGPA Quintiles

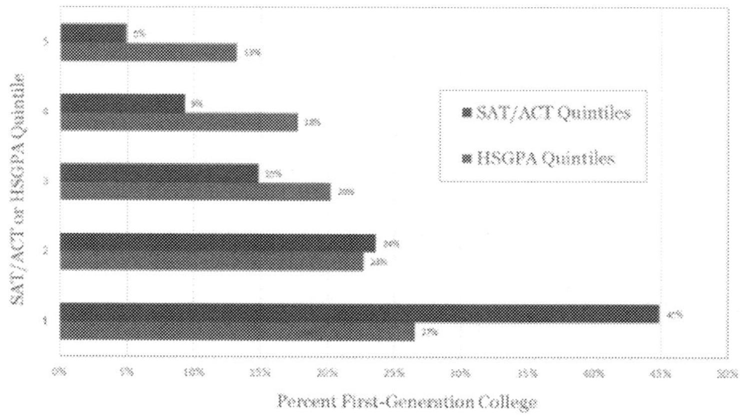

Note. UC Corporate Student System is source of data on all California residents who applied for freshman admissions between 1994 and 2011.

at the top of the pool, among the ablest students. Figure 1.5 shows the effect on first-generation college applicants at UC.

When applicants are ranked by test scores instead of grades, first-generation college applicants are much less likely to place within the upper strata of the pool, where the chances of admission are greatest. SAT/ACT scores systematically disfavor the ablest applicants—as measured by their achievement in school–who have had less opportunity to learn.

For this reason, norm-referenced admissions tests are ill-suited to the mission of public universities like UC. Public institutions have a special obligation to expand opportunity for able students from disadvantaged backgrounds. SAT/ACT scores create built-in deterrents to that mission. Only by making special accommodations to compensate for disparities in opportunity to learn, such as admissions preferences for low-income or first-generation college students, can their use be justified.

CONCLUSION: ELIMINATING THE SAT AND ACT IN UC ADMISSIONS

National standards for fairness in testing oblige test users to be vigilant about the differential impact of test scores on racial and ethnic minorities, beyond what may be warranted by test validity. Until 1998, UC met this obligation by means of a two-tiered admissions process. The top half of the pool was admitted based on grades and test scores only. The bottom half was admitted using a combination of academic and supplemental criteria, including race. Though far from ideal, two-tiered admissions did allow sensitivity to the differential validity of SAT/ACT scores for underrepresented minority applicants.[13]

All of this changed with SP-1 and Proposition 209, barring use of race as a supplemental admissions criterion. But that change has also effectively barred consideration of how other admissions criteria, like SAT/ACT scores, are themselves affected by race. The correlation between race and test scores has grown substantially among UC applicants over the past 25 years, mirroring the growing concentration of Latinx and Black students in California's poorest, most intensely segregated schools. Statistically, underrepresented minority status is now a stronger predictor of SAT/ACT scores than either family income or parents' education.

UC is thus faced with a choice of some consequence. One is to continue to employ a selection criterion with known collateral effects on underrepresented minorities, even while admissions officials are prevented by law from acting on that knowledge. Continuing to use the SAT and ACT under the constraints of Proposition 209 means accepting adverse impacts on Black and Latinx applicants beyond what is warranted by test validity.

The alternative is to eliminate use of SAT/ACT scores in UC admissions. If the university cannot legally consider race as a socioeconomic disadvantage in admissions, neither should it consider scores on nationally normed tests. Race-blind implies test-blind admissions.

The question remains: How would UC replace standardized test scores in its admissions process? Following are thoughts on four possible paths.

1. Test-Optional

One possibility is the "test-optional" approach taken by a number of U.S. colleges. In fact, the term is associated with a number of related, but distinct alternatives including "test-flexible" and "test-blind" admissions policies. Test-optional allows applicants to choose whether to submit SAT/ACT scores and have them considered in the admit decision. Test flexible allows students to pick from a larger smorgasbord of tests. Test-blind eliminates any consideration of test scores in admit decisions.

Test-optional admissions is the most widely employed approach at U.S. colleges and has been most studied (Soares, 2012). About half of national liberal arts colleges ranked in the "Top 100" by *U.S. News and World Report* no longer require ACT or SAT scores from all or most applicants. The list includes Bates, Bowdoin, Bryn Mawr, Holy Cross, Pitzer, Smith, and Wesleyan. As of this writing, the University of Chicago, ranked number 6 among national universities, is the first elite U.S. university to go test-optional.

Although disputed by the College Board and ACT Inc., most independent evaluations of test-optional admissions are generally positive (e.g., Bryn Mawr College, 2009; McDermott, 2008; see also Chapters 6 and 7 of this volume). Test-optional colleges report increases in application and enrollment rates for both low-income and underrepresented minority students, though the effect appears to be greater under a test-blind approach (Espenshade & Chung, 2012). At the same time, test-optional institutions report little if any change in college outcomes such as grades and graduation rates. An added attraction is that test-optional boosts SAT/ACT averages among applicants who do submit scores, a fact that has not gone unnoticed at colleges concerned to improve their institutional ranking.

Whether test-optional might work at UC is an open question. Test-optional does nothing to lessen the built-in advantage for those who do submit scores (and who have usually enjoyed the greatest opportunity to learn). For those who do not submit, it is unclear how UC would replace test scores as a tool for sorting the large volume of applications it receives. Also of concern is the potential for gaming the system that test-optional creates, both for institutions as well as students.

2. Strivers Approach

Another possible path is the Strivers approach, that is, controlling statistically for the effects of socioeconomic circumstance on SAT/ACT scores. The most thorough-going effort to assess how such an approach might work at UC is a UC Office of the President (UCOP) study by Roger Studley (2004). Based on a sample of California SAT takers who applied to UC, the study adjusted students' test scores to account for socioeconomic circumstance: neighborhood of residence (as defined by zip code), high school attended, and family characteristics including income, parents' education, and whether English was the students' first language. These factors were used to generate a predicted SAT score for each student. Students whose actual scores exceeded their predicted score were deemed high-ability applicants, as in the Strivers proposal.

The results showed that adjusting SAT/ACT scores for SES substantially reduced score deficits for Latinx and Black students relative to other applicants. To a lesser extent this was also true for Asian students, who tended to score higher than White students in similar circumstances (Studley, 2004). Of course, class-based adjustments cannot eliminate racial gaps entirely, as noted earlier. But a Strivers-type approach might reduce those gaps in significant measure.

3. Curriculum-Based Achievement Tests

Until 2012 UC was one of the few universities outside the Ivy League to require both curriculum-based achievement tests as well as nationally normed tests like the SAT and ACT. During the 1930s the College Board developed a series of multiple-choice tests to replace its older, written exams. These later became known as the SAT IIs and are now officially called the SAT Subject Tests. They are hourlong assessments that measure mastery of college-preparatory subjects and are offered in 20 subject areas, like chemistry or literature. Though used primarily to assess students' present level of achievement rather than predict future performance, UC validity studies have long shown that performance on a battery of three achievement tests predicts student outcomes at least as well as SAT/ACT scores.

In his 2001 speech to the American Council on Education, UC President Richard Atkinson argued that, as well as offering the same or better prediction, curriculum-based achievement tests were preferable to the SAT on educational grounds. Unbeknownst to Atkinson, BOARS had been moving independently to the same conclusion (Douglass, 2007, pp. 214–234; Pelfrey, 2012, pp. 115–138). Atkinson's speech triggered an extraordinary period of discussion, research, and policy development under BOARS chair Dorothy Perry. Among the products of this work were the holistic-review policy for admissions selection and the Top 4%/ELC policy for eligibility.

In 2002 BOARS issued what was believed to be the first statement of principles by any U.S. university on admissions testing. Among the more important principles was: Admissions tests should measure students' mastery of college-preparatory subjects. Applying these principles, BOARS concluded that curriculum-based achievement tests like the SAT II Subject Tests were the clear choice over tests of general analytic ability or "aptitude" like the SAT and ACT. The decisive consideration for BOARS was not prediction but the educational value of achievement tests and their better alignment with the needs of students and schools. For students, low SAT/ACT scores signaled lack of individual ability, as against broader factors such as unequal access to good schools and well-trained teachers. The message could be damaging to self-esteem and academic aspiration. For schools, norm-referenced admissions tests incentivized test-prep activities outside the classroom. Their implicit message was that test-taking skills learned outside the classroom could override achievement in school.

Achievement tests, in BOARS' view, created better alignment between instruction and assessment. On achievement tests, the best test-prep was regular classroom instruction. A low score on an achievement test meant that the student had not mastered the required content. This might be due to inadequate instructional resources and inferior teaching—or lack of hard work on the part of the student. Achievement tests focused attention on determinants of student performance that were alterable, at least in principle, and so were better suited to the needs of students and schools:

> Aptitude-type tests send the message that academic success is based in some part on immutable characteristics that cannot be changed and are, therefore, independent of good study skills and hard work. In contrast, a policy requiring achievement tests reinforces the primary message that the University strives

> to send to students and schools (and that is embedded in the recent decision to adopt comprehensive admissions review for all applicants): *the best way to prepare for post-secondary education is to take a rigorous and comprehensive college-preparatory curriculum and to excel in this work*. This is what the University's coursework ("A-G") and scholarship (GPA) requirements articulate. An appropriate battery of achievement tests would reinforce this message–independently and in a way that is consistent across all schools and test-takers (BOARS, 2002, p. iii, italics in original).

The BOARS 2002 statement suggests a possible path for UC today: replace the nationally normed tests with a battery of curriculum-based achievement exams. The SAT Subject Tests remain one possibility, but another possibility has emerged in the years since 2002: employing K–12 standards-based exams in university admissions.

The best examples of pure achievement tests now available are employed not in U.S. higher education but in our K–12 public schools: standards-based assessments developed by the various states as part of the movement to articulate clearer curriculum standards, teach to the standards, and assess student achievement against those standards. The schools are well ahead of colleges and universities in this regard.

In 2014, California adopted one such exam, the Smarter Balanced Assessment, as part of its effort to align K–12 assessment and accountability policies with newly adopted Common Core curriculum standards. Smarter Balanced includes an 11th-grade summative exam, and sufficient time has now passed for an initial look at whether that exam might also prove useful for purposes of university admissions. Preliminary results are quite positive. Smarter Balanced performs as well as the SAT in predicting both first-year grades and second-year persistence at UC, yet produces a more socioeconomically and racially diverse applicant pool (Kurlaender & Cohen, 2019).

The idea of adapting K–12 achievement tests for use in college admissions has obvious attractions. In the ideal case, such exams could serve the dual purpose of certifying both achievement in high school and UC eligibility. The burden on students and the testing time they must endure could be greatly reduced. College entrance criteria would be directly aligned with high school curricula, and the signal to students would be clear and unequivocal: Working hard and performing well in one's high school coursework is the most direct route to college.

This is surely an attractive vision. Yet a key question remains unanswered. Standards for what is expected of entering freshmen at highly selective institutions like UC are different and usually much more rigorous than K–12 curriculum standards. They overlap, to be sure, but they are not the same, and it is unclear whether any one exam can serve both institutional purposes equally.

4. Eliminate SAT/ACT Scores in Admissions Selection

A final path is to eliminate use of test scores in admissions decisions. This is not as draconian a step as might first appear. Eliminating tests in admissions need not mean eliminating them entirely. Test scores are employed at two key decision points at UC. *Eligibility* involves assessing whether students are qualified for the UC system, if not their campus of choice. *Admissions selection* involves selecting from among qualified students at oversubscribed UC campuses that have more eligible applicants than places available.

Were the SAT/ACT eliminated in admissions selection, standardized tests could continue to be used in determining students' eligibility for the UC system. Unlike the test-optional approach, all UC applicants would still be required to submit test scores. But scores would be removed from the applicant files reviewed by admissions readers, in the same way that race was removed from admissions files after Proposition 209 took effect in 1998. Admit decisions would be based on the 13 other selection criteria that UC employs.

Discontinuing standardized tests in admissions selection but continuing their use in eligibility might permit a natural experiment at one or more UC campuses. Though not used for admissions purposes, test-score data would be available for all applicants and admits at those campuses. This would facilitate in-depth analysis of the impact of the change on both the quality of admissions decisions and the demographic composition of the admitted pool. Should the experiment prove unsuccessful, it would be a relatively straightforward matter to reintroduce SAT/ACT scores into the campus admissions process.

BOARS's 2002 testing policy implies a change not only in the *kinds* of tests that UC employs but *how* tests are used and for what purpose. Norm-referenced exams like the SAT or ACT are designed to compare and rank applicants. Criterion- or content-referenced exams like Smarter Balanced, on the other hand, are designed to assess whether students have mastered prerequisite subjects and skills. As James Crouse and Dale Trusheim (1988) put it in their classic brief, *The Case Against the SAT*, standardized tests are much more effective as a tool for "certifying competence"—assessing whether students are academically qualified—than for rank-ordering them on their predicted probability of earning a higher freshman GPA. Tests are much better at certification than prediction.

The clear implication of BOARS's 2002 statement in favor of curriculum-based "achievement" exams is that standardized tests are more appropriate for UC eligibility than for admissions selection. In fact, neither norm-referenced exams like the SAT/ACT nor content-referenced exams like Smarter Balanced possess sufficient predictive validity to justify their adverse socioeconomic and racial impact in admissions selection. Though content-referenced exams have less adverse impact than the SAT/ACT, that impact is still considerable, and predictive validity is too weak to draw fine distinctions among applicants without unwarranted adverse impacts on low-income, first-generation, and underrepresented minority applicants. Simply replacing the SAT/ACT with content-referenced exams in admissions selection is not necessarily the answer. Moving to content-referenced assessments, and using them primarily for purposes of certification, is the logical conclusion of BOARS's testing principles.

Since Proposition 209 took effect two decades ago, the University of California has taken extraordinary steps to mitigate the adverse effects of the national admissions tests on underrepresented minority applicants. In addition to class-based admissions preferences, those steps have included holistic review and Eligibility in the Local Context. They have proven only partially successful. The next step is to replace or eliminate SAT/ACT scores in admissions selection.

NOTES

1. California is predominantly an "SAT state." Fewer students take the ACT than the SAT, although that number has grown in recent years. Like UC, most American colleges and universities accept both tests and treat SAT and ACT scores interchangeably. Both are norm-referenced assessments designed to tell admissions officers where an applicant ranks in the national test score distribution.

2. A recent feature article in the *New York Times* found that underrepresentation of Hispanics in the UC system is more pronounced than in any other state, although underrepresentation of African Americans is slightly improved relative to their share of college-age population: "Even With Affirmative Action, Blacks and Hispanics Are More Underrepresented at Top Colleges Than 35 Years Ago" (Ashsenas, Park, & Pearce, 2017).

3. Due to very small sample sizes and attendant concerns about confidentiality of student records, the data provided to the author by the UC president's office do not allow separate identification of American Indian applicants. For this reason, all data on underrepresented minority applicants shown here exclude American Indian or Native American students, who account for less than one percent of all UC applicants.

4. Some researchers hold out hope that better measures of wealth (as opposed to income) might account for the remainder of the test score gap, but this remains unproven. See, e.g., Kahlenberg, 2014a; Wilson, 1998.

5. The Board of Admissions and Relations with Schools, known as BOARS, is the university-wide faculty committee responsible for formulating UC admissions policy.

6. To those unfamiliar with UC admissions, the superiority of high school GPA over standardized test scores in predicting UC student performance may seem odd, given that grading standards vary widely among schools. Despite this, high school GPA in college-preparatory coursework has long been shown to be the best overall

predictor of student outcomes at UC, irrespective of the quality or type of high school attended. One reason may be that test scores are based on a single sitting of 3 or 4 hours, whereas high school GPA is based on repeated sampling of student performance over a period of years. And college preparatory classes present many of the same academic challenges that students will face in college–quizzes, term papers, labs, final exams–so it should not be surprising that prior performance in such activities would be predictive of later performance.

7. See Atkinson & Geiser (2009) for an extended discussion of the preferability of criterion-referenced over norm-referenced assessments in university admissions.

8. The College Board introduced yet another revision of the SAT in 2016, but no change was expected in test validity.

9. Validity studies conducted at UC similarly show that SAT/ACT scores are very weak predictors of graduation rates (Geiser & Santelices, 2007).

10. Compare regression models 17 and 22 in Agronow & Studley, 2007, Table 1.

11. Some have criticized DIF as a measure of item bias. DIF assesses the fairness of individual items by their correlation with test performance among students with similar abilities, which is measured by overall test scores. But if the overall test is itself biased, DIF may not necessarily detect item bias even when present (Kidder & Rosner, 2002).

12. Santelices and Wilson's main finding was that DIF was inversely related to item difficulty. Surprisingly, score differences between Latinx and Black students and others was greater on *easier* rather than on more difficult SAT items.

13. The two-tiered admissions selection process ended in 2001, when the UC regents, on the recommendation of the faculty and the president, mandated comprehensive review for all UC applicants.

REFERENCES

Agronow, S. & R. Studley. (2007, November 4). *Prediction of college GPA from new SAT scores – A first look. A paper presented at the annual meeting of the California Association for Institutional Research.* Retrieved from cair.org/wp-content/uploads/sites/474/2015/07/Agronow.pdf.

American Educational Research Association (AERA), American Psychological Association (APA), & National Council on Measurement in Education (NCME). (2014). *Standards for Educational and Psychological Testing*. Washington, DC: American Educational Research Association.

Ashsenas, J., Park, H., & Pearce, A. (2017, August 24). Even with affirmative action, Blacks and Hispanics are more underrepresented at top colleges than 35 years ago. *New York Times*, p. 1.

Atkinson, R. C. (2001, February 18). *Standardized tests and access to American universities.* The 2001 Robert H. Atwell Distinguished Lecture, delivered at the 83rd annual meeting of the American Council on Education, Washington, DC. Retrieved from rca.ucsd.edu/speeches/satspch.pdf

Atkinson, R. C., & Geiser, S. (2009). Reflections on a century of college admissions tests. *Educational Researcher, 38*(9), 665–676. doi.org/10.3102/0013189X09351981

Board of Admissions and Relations with Schools (BOARS). (2002). *The use of admissions tests by the University of California. Executive summary*. Retrieved from senate.universityofcalifornia.edu/_files/committees/boars/testsummary.pdf

Bowen, W. G., Chingos, M. M., & McPherson, M. S. (2009). *Crossing the finish line: Completing college at America's public universities*. Princeton, NJ: Princeton University Press.

Brown v. Board of Education, 347 US 483 (1954).

Bryn Mawr College. (2009, June 3). Bryn Mawr adopts new testing policy promoting greater flexibility and emphasis on subject mastery. Retrieved from news.blogs.brynmawr.edu/2009/06/03/bryn-mawr-adopts-new-testing-policy-promoting-greater-flexibility-and-emphasis-on-subject-mastery/

Card, D., & Rothstein, J. (2006). *Racial segregation and the Black–White test score gap* (NBER Working Paper No. 12078). Cambridge, MA: National Bureau of Economic Research. Retrieved from www.nber.org/papers/w12078

Carnevale, A., & Haghighat, E. (1998). Selecting the strivers: A report on the preliminary results of the ETS "Educational strivers" study. In D. Bakst (Ed.), *Hopwood, Bakke, and beyond: Diversity on our nation's campuses* (pp. 122–128). Washington, DC: American Association of Collegiate Registrars and Admissions Officers.

Cook, M., & Evans, W. (2000). Families or schools? Explaining the convergence in White and Black academic performance. *Journal of Labor Economics, 18*(4), 729–54.

Corcoran, S., & Evans, W. (2008). The role of inequality in teacher quality. In K. Magnuson & J. Waldfogel (Eds.), *Steady gains and stalled progress: Inequality and the Black–White test score gap* (pp. 212–249). New York, NY: Russell Sage Foundation.

Crouse, J. & D. Trusheim. (1988). *The case against the SAT*. Chicago, IL: University of Chicago Press.

Douglass, J. A. (2007). *The conditions of admission: Access, equity, and the social contract of public universities*. Stanford, CA: Stanford University Press.

Espenshade, T. J., & Chung, C. Y. (2012). Diversity outcomes of test-optional policies. In J. A. Soares. (Ed.), *SAT wars: The case for test-optional college admissions* (pp. 177–200). New York, NY: Teachers College Press.

Fisher v. University of Texas, 579 U.S. ___ (2016).

Geiser, S. (2015, October). *The growing correlation between race and SAT scores: New findings from California* (Research & Occasional Paper

Series: CSHE.10.15). . Berkeley, CA: Center for Studies in Higher Education. Retrieved from cshe.berkeley.edu/publications/growing-correlation-between-race-and-sat-scores-new-findings-california-saul-geiser

Geiser, S. (with Studley, R.). (2002). UC and the SAT: Predictive validity and differential impact of the SAT I and SAT II at the University of California. *Educational Assessment, 8*(1), 1–26.

Geiser, S., & Santelices, M. V. (2007, June). *Validity of high-school grades in predicting student success beyond the freshman year: High-school record vs. standardized tests as indicators of four-year college outcomes* (Research and Occasional Paper Series: CHSE.6.07). Berkeley, CA: Center for Studies in Higher Education. Available at cshe.berkeley.edu/publications/validity-high-school-grades-predicting-student-success-beyond-freshman-yearhigh-school

Haveman, R., Sandefur, G., Wolfe, B., & Voyer, A. (2004). Trends in children's attainments and their determinants as family income inequality has increased. In K. Neckerman (Ed.), *Social inequality* (pp. 149–188). New York, NY: Russell Sage Foundation.

Haveman, R., & Wolfe, B. (1995). The determinants of children's attainments: A review of methods and findings. *Journal of Economic Literature, 33*(4), 1829–1878.

Jencks, C., & Phillips, M. (1998). Introduction. In C. Jencks & M. Phillips (Eds.), *The Black–White test score gap* (pp. 1-51). Washington, DC: Brookings Institution Press.

Kahlenberg, R. D. (2014a). Introduction. In R. D. Kahlenberg (Ed.), *The future of affirmative action: New paths to higher education diversity after Fisher v. University of Texa*s. New York, NY: Century Foundation Press.

Kahlenberg, R. D. (2014b, March 11). No longer Black and White: Why liberals should let California's affirmative-action ban stand. *Slate*. Retrieved from slate.com/news-and-politics/2014/03/california-affirmative-action-ban-why-liberals-should-let-it-stand.html

Kidder, W. C., & Rosner, J. (2002). How the SAT creates built-in headwinds: An educational and legal analysis of disparate impact. *Santa Clara Law Review, 43*(1/3), 131–211. Retrieved from digitalcommons.law.scu.edu/lawreview/vol43/iss1/3

Kobrin, J. L., Patterson, B. F., Shaw, E. J., Mattern, K. D., & Barbuti, S. M. (2008). *Validity of SAT for predicting first-year college grade point average* (College Board Research Report No. 2008-5). New York, NY: The College Board. Retrieved from eric.ed.gov/?id=ED563202

Kurlaender, M. & Cohen, K. (2019, March). Predicting college success: How do different high school assessments measure up? Retrieved from edpolicyinca.org/publications/predicting-college-success-how-do-different-high-school-assessments-measure-2019

Magnuson, K., & Duncan, G. (2006). The role of family socioeconomic resources on racial test score gaps. *Developmental Review, 26*(4), 365–399.

Magnuson, K., Rosenbaum, D., & Waldfogel, J. (2008). Inequality and Black–White achievement trends in the NAEP. In K. Magnuson & J. Waldfogel (Eds.), *Steady gains and stalled progress: Inequality and the Black–White test score* gap (pp. 33–65). New York, NY: Russell Sage Foundation.

Marcus, A. (1999, August 31). New weights can alter SAT scores: Family is factor in determining who's a 'striver.' *Wall Street Journal*, pp. B1, B8. Retrieved from info.wsj.com/classroom/archive/wsjce.99nov.casestudy.html

McDermott, A. B. (2008, September 25). Surviving without the SAT. *The Chronicle of Higher Education*.Retrieved from www.chronicle.com/article/Surviving-Without-the-SAT/18874

Meyers, M., Rosenbaum, D., Ruhm, C., & Waldfogel, J. (2004). Inequality in early childhood education and care: What do we know? In K. Neckerman (Ed.), *Social inequality* (pp. 223–270). New York, NY: Russell Sage Foundation.

Orfield, G., & Ee, J. (2014, May 14). Segregating California's future: Inequality and its alternative 60 years after Brown v. Board of Education. In *The Civil Rights Project / Proyecto Derechos Civiles*. Retrieved from civilrightsproject.ucla.edu/research/k-12-education/integration-and-diversity/segregating-california2019s-future-inequality-and-its-alternative-60-years-after-brown-v.-board-of-education/

Pelfrey, P. A. (2012). Entrepreneurial president: Richard Atkinson and the University of California, 1995–2003. Berkeley, CA: University of California Press.

Phillips, M., & Chin, T. (2004). School inequality: What do we know? In K. Neckerman (Ed.), *Social inequality* (pp. 467–520). New York, NY: Russell Sage Foundation.

Phillips, M., Crouse, J., & Ralph, J. (1998). Does the Black–White test score gap widen after children enter school? In C. Jencks & M. Phillips (Eds.), *The Black–White test score gap* (pp. 229–272). Washington, DC: Brookings Institution Press.

Rothstein, J. M. (2004). College performance predictions and the SAT. *Journal of Econometrics*, *121*, 297–317.

Rothstein, R. (2014). The racial achievement gap, segregated schools, and segregated neighborhoods—A constitutional insult. *Race and Social Problems,* 6(4). Retrieved from www.epi.org/publication/the-racial-achievement-gap-segregated-schools-and-segregated-neighborhoods-a-constitutional-insult/

Santelices, M. V., & Wilson, M. (2012). On the relationship between differential item functioning and item difficulty: An issue of methods? Item response theory approach to differential item functioning. *Educational and Psychological Measurement,* *72*(1), 5–36.

Soares, J. A. (Ed.). (2012). *SAT wars: The case for test-optional college admissions*. New York, NY: Teachers College Press.

Steele, C., & Aronson, J. (1995). Stereotype threat and the intellectual test performance of African Americans. *Journal of Personality and Social Psychology, 69*(5), 797–811.

Studley, R. (2004). Inequality, student achievement, and college admissions: A remedy for underrepresentation. In R. Zwick (Ed.), *Rethinking the SAT: The future of standardized testing in university admissions* (pp. 321–343). New York, NY: RoutledgeFarmer.

Wilson, W. (1998). The role of the environment in the Black–White test score gap. In C. Jencks & M. Phillips (Eds.), *The Black–White test score Gap* (pp. 501–510). Washington, DC: Brookings Institution Press.

CHAPTER 2

Wealth's Influence on College Enrollment and Completion

Paul Fain

Critics of the ACT and SAT have consistently drawn attention to the way these tests serve as proxies for economic class. There is a linear relation between family income and test scores: At the top side of test scores there are disproportionate concentrations of youths from high-income families, and at the bottom end of scores there is an overwhelming representation of youths from low-income families. Test score selection provides a partial disguise of the way a college degree remains in America a privileged good, more enjoyed by the top 20% of America's income class than the bottom 20%. It is important to understand how higher education is an unequal landscape where a youth's attainments are powerfully determined by her or his family's socioeconomic status (SES). This chapter provides an overview as of 2019 of the stratification of higher education by family SES.

The federal government on May 22, 2019, released a wide range of updated and new data on postsecondary education, including broader measures of college completion and several indicators that show how much family wealth contributes to college students' odds of enrolling and graduating (NCES, 2019a). For example, among people who were 9th-graders a decade ago, those from the highest quintile of socioeconomic status (parental education and occupations and family income) were 50 percentage points more likely to be enrolled in college in 2016 than were their peers from the lowest quintile—78% compared to 28%.

Money also played a big role in which college and level of degree program students enrolled in, according to the new report from the U.S. Department of Education's National Center for Education Statistics (NCES) (see nces.ed.gov/programs/coe/indicator_tbe.asp). Students from the lowest quintile who attended college were more likely to first pursue an associate degree (42%) than a bachelor's degree (32%). Their peers from the wealthiest quintile, however, were much more likely to first seek a 4-year degree (78%) than a 2-year degree (13%). Likewise, the percentage of higher-income students who first enrolled at a highly selective college or university (37%) easily outpaced that of lower-income students (7%).

Wealthier students also were much more likely to enroll at a 4-year college than at a community college or for-profit institution. More than half of students from the top quintile first enrolled at a public 4-year institution (54%), while 26% enrolled at a 4-year private college. The report found that 18% enrolled at a community college while less than 2% attended a for-profit. Among students in the lowest quintile, however, 51% first enrolled at a community college (or program length of shorter than 2 years) compared to 28% at a 4-year public, 8% at a 4-year private, and roughly 13% at a for-profit college.

The NCES report found that lower-income students from that 9th-grade class of 2009 were less likely to enroll in college within one year of graduating from high school. Roughly one-third of students from the lowest quintile of that cohort enrolled within one year of graduating high school and were still in college or had earned a credential by 2016, compared to 79% of students from the top quintile. Likewise, 53% of students from the lowest quintile either never enrolled or delayed their enrollment by more than a year, compared to roughly 11% from the top quintile, and 88% from this group enrolled in college within one year after high school. "These numbers are sobering," said Amanda Bergson-Shilcock, director of upskilling policy at the National Skills Coalition, who called the new report an "affirmation of how diverse the higher education cohort is, and how different the college-going experience can be."

The NCES report arrived as the higher education sector has been rocked by scrutiny of its role in perpetuating economic inequality, thanks to a high-profile admissions scandal (Fain, 2019) and unflattering data on social mobility (Lederman, 2017b). As with the so-called Varsity Blues scandal, the federal numbers pull back the curtain on how higher education is stacked in favor of White and wealthy students, said Phil Martin, a spokesman for the Education Trust. "Students from the least affluent families who enrolled in college were more than three times as likely to start at a community college than their wealthier peers. Community colleges are starved for resources. No surprise their outcomes aren't great," Martin said. "Students from the most affluent families were about five times as likely to enroll in a selective college as students from the least affluent families. Selective colleges are typically the ones with lots of resources. So the wealthiest students get the richest campus experience" (personal communication, May 22, 2019).

The NCES report, dubbed "The Condition of Education 2019," features updated and improved measures of student success. Some of those indicators can be broken out by the relative wealth, race, and other characteristics of students, including whether they attended college full-time or part-time. As was the case with students' enrollment patterns, socioeconomic status had a big impact on outcomes, according to the data. For example, the report includes updated completion rates for Pell Grant recipients (data that did not become available until the department recently broadened its completion metrics). The federal grants are need-based and represent a subset of lower-income students within the general undergraduate population, the report said. Completion rates after 8 years for the 2009 cohort were lower for Pell recipients who attended 4-year colleges across all levels of selectivity except for open-admissions institutions (see nces.ed.gov/programs/coe/indicator_ctr.asp). For colleges that accepted 90% or more of applicants, the new federal completion rates were about 12 percentage points lower for Pell recipients than for nonrecipients (35% compared to 47%). Among colleges that accepted less than a quarter of applicants, completion rates for Pell recipients lagged by 10 percentage points (79% compared to 89%).

NCES recently began publishing college completion rates that include part-time students, an improvement from the much-criticized previous limitation of tracking graduation and transfer rates only for full-time students who attend college for the first time (Lederman, 2017a; Fain 2018). "This provides the clearest picture yet of how colleges are doing in providing all of their students a credential," said Michael Itzkowitz, president of the Edvisors Group, a consulting firm, and a former Education Department official during the Obama administration. "This is much more representative of all students who are attending college today." For example, the report said just 22% of students attended public colleges on a full-time, first-time basis, compared to 42% who attended part-time and had previously enrolled at another postsecondary institution. Yet the addition of part-time students to colleges' completion report card doesn't make them look better. The full-time, first-time rate was the "most generous" measure, Itzkowitz said. The new report found that most institutions have 8-year graduation rates of less than 50%, he said, although those numbers improve substantially when transfer numbers are added. "The typical institution leaves students with a mere 50–50 chance of graduating from the institution where they started," he said, adding that a high percentage of part-time students are "leaving without any credential in hand."

The "nontraditional" student is the norm for the 2-year sector, with three-quarters of the 4.7 million community college students who enrolled in 2009 attending either part-time or not for the first time, meaning they were not included in traditional graduation and retention rates. Graduation rates for students who enrolled at a community college in 2009 were higher among those who attended full-time (30% of first-time students and 38% of non-first-time students earned a credential at that college within 8 years) than for part-time students (16% for first-time students and 21% for their non-first-time peers). Transfer rates for community college students 8 years after entry were higher among students who had previously enrolled elsewhere (37% for part-time students and 30% for full-time students) than among their first-time peers (24% for both full-time and part-time).

Part-time students also make up large shares of enrollments at 4-year institutions. The report found that 44% of students who enrolled at a 4-year public college in 2009 attended full-time and first-time, as did 57% of students at 4-year private colleges. Part-time students at 4-year colleges were unlikely to graduate within 8 years. Just 19% of part-time, first-time students who enrolled at a 4-year public or private college graduated within 8 years, according to the report, compared to 32% of part-time students at public colleges who previously attended another institution and 43% at private colleges. (In most cases, similar portions of those students transferred to another college.) The report should be a call to action for policymakers, said Martin. "Students from low-income families are underserved at every level of the U.S. education system," he said. "That's obviously not the kind of system anybody would set up if the goal was equal opportunity."

NOTE

This chapter was adapted from www.insidehighered.com/news/2019/05/23/feds-release-broader-data-socioeconomic-status-and-college-enrollment-and-completion

REFERENCES

Fain, P. (2018, December 5). Broader college completion data from the feds. *Inside Higher Ed*. Retreived from www.insidehighered.com/quick-takes/2018/12/05/broader-college-completion-data-feds

Fain, P. (2019, March 25). Varsity blues, higher ed's image and federal policy. *Inside Higher Ed*. Retrieved from www.insidehighered.com/admissions/article/2019/03/25/democratic-lawmakers-join-chorus-critics-higher-education-engine

Lederman, D. (2017a, October 12). The new, improved IPEDS. *Inside Higher Ed*. Retrieved from /www.insidehighered.com/news/2017/10/12/new-federal-higher-ed-outcome-measures-count-part-time-adult-students

Lederman, D. (2017b, October 31). Understanding why some colleges create economic mobility. *Inside Higher Ed*. Retrieved from www.insidehighered.com/news/2017/10/31/elevating-economic-mobility-agenda-higher-education-leaders

National Center for Education Statistics (NCES). (2019, May). *The Condition of Education 2019* (NCES 2019-144). Washington, DC: U.S. Department of Education. Retrieved from nces.ed.gov/pubsearch/pubsinfo.asp?pubid=2019144

CHAPTER 3

How the SAT Creates "Built-In Headwinds"

An Educational and Legal Analysis of Disparate Impact

William C. Kidder and Jay Rosner

> With the end of affirmative action, it is more apparent than ever that the old-time preferences for folks who are privileged by race and class have never died.
>
> —Charles R. Lawrence III (2001)

INTRODUCTION

In *Griggs v. Duke Power Co.* (1971) the Supreme Court declared that Title VII of the 1964 Civil Rights Act extends to acts of unintentional discrimination. The Court held that Duke Power's reliance on graduation requirements and standardized test scores as hiring and transfer criteria violated Title VII because these requirements invidiously discriminated against African Americans and yet were unrelated to actual job performance. Griggs was the case of first impression in which the Court established a framework for assessing "disparate impact" discrimination, criticizing the unwarranted reliance on standardized tests that operate as "built-in headwinds" against minority groups.

This chapter analyzes the SAT's disparate impact and demonstrates how "built-in headwinds" are designed into the actual process of selecting and developing SAT questions. Although this process may appear facially neutral and nondiscriminatory, the SAT unfairly exacerbates the test's already significant disparate impact on African American and Chicanx test takers. This first section provides an overview of standardized tests in relation to recent affirmative action litigation and admissions policy changes. We challenge the conventional wisdom that the SAT accurately measures merit and fairly reflects group differences in educational attainment.

The next two sections provide evidence of the existence of racial and ethnic bias on the SAT. "Analysis of Sample SAT Questions" analyzes previously undisclosed data about SAT questions and demonstrates that a substantially higher proportion of White test takers correctly answer virtually all questions on the scored sections of the SAT. Contributing to the larger educational debate about test bias, reliability, and construct validity in the next section, "Educational Analysis," our findings indicate that the test development process unintentionally, but consistently and predictably, increases the disparate impact of the SAT. Moreover, traditional methods of rooting out biased questions are ineffective and are based on a dubious premise. A more effective method to lessen disparate impact can be achieved by means of Golden Rule–style techniques for selecting test questions. This part also addresses criticisms of our proposed bias reduction method and some practical difficulties in implementation of this method.

The fourth section, "Legal Analysis," provides a detailed analysis of the law governing standardized tests, university admissions, and Title VI disparate impact claims. Over the past couple of decades, there are shrinking legal opportunities to enforce federal Title VI disparate impact civil rights laws. While the evidence in the second and third sections focuses on racial/ethnic bias in the SAT test construction process, independent of this evidence it remains the case that many universities could be vulnerable to disparate impact challenges or administrative complaints over their use of the SAT for reasons discussed in the fourth section . Many universities may not be able to meet their "educational necessity" burden because they knowingly use the SAT in ways that have not been validated, as is the case with rigid cut-off scores. Even more institutions may have difficulty establishing educational necessity because the SAT only incrementally improves the prediction of college grades and is even less helpful in forecasting graduation rates or contributing to colleges' institutional goals. Even when educational necessity is established, a plaintiff in cases challenging use of the SAT may still prevail by demonstrating that percentage plans or SAT-optional admissions are less discriminatory alternatives that are equally effective in meeting the educational goals of a university.

The last section, "Conclusion," discusses the consequences of ending affirmative action at public and private universities. While it remains unclear how long the Supreme Court will continue to uphold higher education affirmative action programs, either way there are steps that can be taken in the test construction process to lessen the SAT's disparate impact on African Americans and Chicanx without compromising the test's validity. Since test producers have been extremely resistant to the kinds of test development changes advocated in this chapter, we conclude that ending reliance on the SAT, or making the test optional, may be the most pragmatic strategies for fostering equity and fairness in university admissions. This chapter's purpose is to document the ways in which the current SAT development process amounts to covert racial gerrymandering in favor of Whites, thereby exacerbating disparate impact against students of color.

The SAT and Affirmative Action

The SAT has long been a key gatekeeper of higher education. Among the millions of American high school graduates in 2017, 1.7 million took the SAT (many taking it two or more times). In addition, 2.0 million high school students took the ACT, the alternative college admissions test. About half of all college-bound seniors in 2016 who took the SAT were students of color, an all-time record. Yet at the same time, public universities in many of the states are prohibited from considering race as a plus factor in admissions. The Supreme Court has affirmed the educational benefits of diversity in the university setting in *Grutter v. Bollinger* (2003) and *Fisher v. University of Texas* (2013, 2016), though the changing composition of justices on the Court potentially threatens those precedents in the not-to-distant future.

The struggle over the future of affirmative action is closely linked to the debate about how to define fairness in the meritocracy, with its current emphasis on standardized tests. The *Gratz v. Bollinger* (2003) and *Grutter v. Bollinger* cases highlight how divergent views of standardized testing inform the opposing efforts to dismantle or defend affirmative action. In both the *Gratz* and *Grutter* cases, the principal evidence of "reverse discrimination" presented by the Center for Individual Rights (CIR) on behalf of White plaintiffs consisted of comparisons, by racial/ethnic group, of the different admission odds for applicants with similar test scores and grade point averages.[1] Thus CIR litigation theory assumes that scores on the SAT and LSAT are a fair and adequate basis for determining who should be entitled to admission at selective colleges and universities. Given the centrality of test scores to the evidence proffered by CIR in Gratz and Grutter, and other efforts by conservative think tanks like the Center for Equal Opportunity to posit SAT score differences as "incontrovertible evidence of racial preferences," affirmative action opponents are treating standardized test scores as dispositive criteria for assessing claims under the Equal Protection Clause.

Does the SAT Accentuate or Reflect Racial and Ethnic Differences?

A core issue underlying the Grutter and Gratz cases as well as state "Percentage Plan" admissions based on high school GPA, such as the Ten Percent Plan in Texas, is whether standardized tests are a neutral reflection of racial and ethnic differences in educational attainment. The positions taken by many scholars and policymakers in response to this question do not correspond with their stances generally in the affirmative action debate. Rather, as will be demonstrated, a powerful conventional wisdom bridges ideological fault lines, and it is precisely this accepted wisdom that we wish to critically investigate in this empirical study.

Several nonprofit corporations develop and market the major university undergraduate, graduate, and professional admissions tests used in American higher education, including ETS (for the SAT and GRE), the College Board (for the SAT), the Law School Admission Council (for the LSAT), and the American Association of Medical Colleges (for the MCAT). These organizations generally adopt liberal positions on major educational policy issues, including support for race-conscious affirmative action in higher education admissions.

Former College Board president Donald Stewart (1998) vigorously argued against calls at the University of California (UC) to eliminate the SAT:

> It is unfortunate, as the new millennium approaches, that race, ethnic background, or family income can still limit students' educational future. Getting rid of the SAT or any other standard is not going to change that fundamental fact. Instead of smashing the thermometer, why not address the conditions that are causing the fever? (p. A48)

Similarly, UC–Santa Barbara professor Rebecca Zwick (1999), who spent many years as a researcher at ETS, argued that racial and ethnic gaps on the SAT are substantially equivalent to gaps in high school grades.

As with testing industry insiders, a range of conservative scholars defend the SAT and other standardized tests as neutral measures of differences in educational achievement. For example, Jennifer Braceras (2002), author of an article defending standardized testing, concludes:

> The achievement gap between Black and Latino students, on the one hand, and their White peers, on the other hand, has been found to be present across tests and across assessment devices. Thus, data from the national Assessment of Educational Progress (NAEP), the National Educational Longitudinal Survey (NELS), and the SAT all confirm the results of state educational assessments: African-American and Latino students lag behind their peers from other ethnic groups at every educational level. And it is not just standardized test scores that reveal this learning deficit. Grade point averages, graduation rates, and class rankings of students across the country are, regrettably, also consistent with this pattern, indicating that claims of bias are, at best, exaggerated.

Similarly, Stephan and Abigail Thernstrom (1997), influential opponents of affirmative action, reviewed evidence on class rank, grade point averages, and course selection, and concluded that the SAT gap is no larger than the gap on other measures of achievement.

Braceras's argument—that standardized tests are not biased because gaps in achievement are also present in other measures—is artfully imprecise and it misses the point. Few would argue that there are no disparities in educational measures, for what else could be expected given America's history of unequal educational opportunities? However, it hardly follows that, merely because racial/ethnic educational gaps exist in grades and class rank, standardized tests are not biased. Rather, the crucial questions raised in this chapter are, given the consistent finding that the magnitude of racial/ethnic disparities in SAT scores surpasses that of other measures, why might this occur, and what are the legal and social policy implications?

ANALYSIS OF SAMPLE SAT QUESTIONS

Data Samples of SAT Questions

Representatives of the College Board and ETS often proclaim that the SAT is the single most studied test in the world. Although they are purportedly willing to provide outside researchers information about the SAT, much of the relevant data is difficult to access. This chapter analyzes hard-to-access data in a fresh, original way.

Our primary database was generated by ETS, and consists of a nationally representative sample of 100,000 test takers who took the October 1998 SAT. That 1998 version of SAT consisted of 138 test questions in its six scored sections: 60 math items and 78 verbal items. Out of 138 items, 128 are multiple-choice and 10 are student-produced response questions in math called "grid-ins." (There was also an experimental section used to pretest future SAT questions. This seventh, unscored section was either a math or verbal section that looked just like a scored section, so students could not be sure which section was unscored.)

We also analyzed a second ETS database for the October 2000 SAT, similar to the data set just described, again for a nationally representative sample of 100,000 students who took that test. That database had almost identical disaggregated results for its 138 test questions.

To further address whether the October 1998 SAT was typical with respect to racial/ethnic group performance on math and verbal items, we also analyzed a database with 580 questions taken from four SATs administered during 1988 and 1989. This second supplemental database includes approximately 209,000 test takers from New York State. While New York is not representative of the country's overall demographics, for our purposes it was sufficient that it included substantial proportions of African Americans (8.8%) and Latinx (5.7%) in the data set. Because the 1988–1989 database is older than our current sample and makes for a less representative population, this data sample was used to confirm broad conclusions about disparate impact. New York's unique Truth in Testing law compelled ETS to disclose these data.

Disparate Impact of SAT Questions

Our inquiry is quite straightforward: For each of the 138 items in the scored sections of the October 1998 SAT, what were the percentages of White, African American, and Chicanx test takers answering the question correctly? The *impact* of each question is defined as the difference between the correct responses by Whites and these racial minorities. For example, if 50% of Whites, 35% of Chicanx, and 30% of African Americans correctly answer a particular SAT verbal question, that item has a Black–White impact of 20% and a Chicanx–White impact of 15%. The third section of this chapter will establish that this definition of item impact is widely used by both ETS researchers and testing critics. Item impact is often associated with the Golden Rule procedures that emerged from a settlement between ETS and plaintiffs who sued over discrimination in the test construction process on one of ETS's standardized licensing exams.

In adopting this definition of impact, it is not necessary to (and we do not) assume that all racial and ethnic differences in performance on SAT items are entirely a product of cultural bias on top of already existing disparities in preparation for higher education. Rather, our central empirical and policy question is one of degree: How much of the Black–White and Chicanx–White SAT score gap can be reduced by the use of impact reduction techniques in the test development process, while still maintaining reasonable psychometric standards?

In the following sections, we describe our findings regarding the magnitude of Black–White and Chicanx–White impact on the 78 verbal and 60 math items on the October 1998 SAT. In the last few years African Americans trailed Whites on the SAT by an average of about 95 points on the verbal section and 105 on the math section, whereas Chicanx trailed Whites by approximately 75 and 70 points respectively. Both the math and verbal sections are scored on a 200–800 scale, with a standard deviation of about 110 points.

Given a Black–White SAT average gap of approximately one standard deviation, and a Chicanx–White SAT gap of about two-thirds of a standard deviation, it is hardly surprising that the percentage of Whites correctly answering each question would exceed that of African Americans and Chicanx on a substantial majority of SAT items. The consistency of the pattern, however, may be surprising: African Americans or Chicanx did not outperform Whites on any of the 78 verbal and 60 math questions. Overall, on the 78 verbal items, Whites correctly answered an average of 59.8% and African Americans correctly answered an average of 46.4% of the items. This results in an average impact of 13.4%. Zero verbal questions displayed greater African American correct response rates than White rates, and less than a tenth (7/78) of the items had differences of 5% or less. Over one-third (29/78) of the verbal questions had Black–White differences of 15% or more, and one-sixth of the items (13/78) had gaps of 20% or more.

On the October 2000 SAT, there was one solitary verbal question on which Chicanx test takers slightly outperformed Whites, and none on which African Americans outperformed Whites. The White and African American verbal correct answering averages were nearly identical to those above: 60% and 46%, respectively.

The pattern of disparate impact for Chicanx is similar to that for Blacks, although the disparity is smaller. The overall average Chicanx correct response rate was 48.7% (a similar 48% rate is found on the October 2000 SAT) meaning that the average Chicanx–White disparate impact of the 78 items was 11.1%. Out of 78 items, only one question had no adverse impact on Chicanx, and just over a tenth (9/78) of the items had a disparity of 5% or less. Nearly one-fifth of the items (15/78) had gaps of 15% or greater, and three items had gaps of 20% or greater.

Black–White disparities were somewhat larger on the math section than on the verbal section. Overall, the average White correct response rate was 58.4% on the 60 math items, and the African American average correct response rate was 42.0%, for an average impact of 16.4%. The respective rates on the October 2000 SAT were 61% and 45%, both approximately 3% higher. One sixth (10/60) of the items had a disparate impact under 10%. Nearly three out of 10 items (17/60) had a disparity of 20% or more, and two items had an impact of 30%.

The disparities for Chicanx were greater on the math section than on the verbal section. Overall, the average Chicanx correct response rate was 46.5%, for an average disparity of 11.9% as compared to White test takers. Similar to the White and African American rates on the October 2000 SAT, the Chicanx rate on that test was 49%, almost 3% higher. Interestingly, however, results were not as varied (at both the low and high ends) in the math section as on the verbal section. This pattern may be partly attributable to bilingualism. Chicanx tend to perform relatively better on verbal questions with vocabulary words that contain Latin root words, and they tend to perform relatively worse on verbal items with root words that are "false cognates," which are words that appear to have Latin root words but in fact do not (see Pennock-Roman, 1988, pp. 40–41). Only one math item had a disparity under 5%. Nearly one-third of the items (19/60) had a disparate impact of 15% or more, and the item with the greatest disparity had a 20% gap.

The disparate impact of the items on the October 1998 SAT was slightly greater than that found in the 1988–1989 New York SAT database. Of the 580 questions in the New York data set, the Black–White average disparate impact was 13.2%. Specifically, for these 580 questions, Whites were more likely to answer 574 of them correctly, five items had no Black–White differences, and Blacks scored higher than Whites on one question. On the 1998 October SAT, the average disparate impact was 14.7% for the 138 items. Moreover, Whites outperformed Blacks on all of the 138 items.

To better understand the disparate impact of each SAT item, it is helpful to examine actual SAT questions. Compare two 1998 SAT verbal sentence completion items in Figure 3.1 with similar themes: The item correctly answered by more Blacks than Whites was discarded by ETS, whereas the item that has a higher disparate impact against Blacks became part of the actual SAT. On one of the items, which was of medium difficulty, 62% of Whites and 38% of African Americans answered correctly, resulting in a large impact of 24%. The other item was pretested on the experimental section of the SAT in 1998, but it was deemed psychometrically flawed and was removed from the test. On this second item, 8% more African Americans than Whites answered correctly and 9% more women than men answered correctly.

The item on the left (with C as the correct answer) is the one that 8% more African Americans than Whites answered correctly. This item was omitted from the actual SAT.[2] In contrast, the item on the right (with D as the correct answer) was answered correctly by 24% more Whites than African Americans and was included on the actual test.

After presenting this question at several academic conferences, we found that most people cannot readily identify which item favors Whites as opposed to Blacks. As we argue at length in the section "Educational Analysis," the facially neutral SAT test construction will have a strong tendency to eliminate items (such as the one on the left side above) on which African Americans and Chicanx outperform Whites.

The disparate impacts of two SAT verbal items are compared in Figure 3.2. Whites correctly answered 59% of both items, whereas African Americans answered one of the items correctly 49% of the time, and the other 37% of the time. Can you tell which item will have a lower disparate impact of 10% and which will have a higher impact of 22%?

The item on the left (with B as the correct answer) had a Black–White disparate impact of 22%. The item on the right (with D as the correct answer) had a disparity of 10%, even though White test takers found each item to be equally difficult. This chapter argues that a meaningful number of lower impact items can be substituted for higher impact problems without significantly compromising the psychometric properties of the SAT.

With respect to the SAT math section, especially with items that do not include too many words or applied situations (i.e., word problems), it is difficult for many people to conceptualize how such items could be either biased against or in favor of a particular group. We argue that this difficulty is actually the point. The lack of a patently observable bias falsely implies a neutrality that does not exist. Given that educationally sound items testing similar mathematical concepts can have varying levels of disparate impact on African Americans and Chicanx, does sufficient a priori justification exist for preferring items that display relatively larger racial/ethnic disparities? We argue that the legitimacy of such a policy is sorely lacking, yet this is

Figure 3.1. Rejecting Similar Verbal Items for the SAT

Which item appeared on the SAT and which item was rejected?
Is either item (or both) noticeably biased?

The actor's bearing on stage seemed _____; her movements were natural and her technique _______. a. unremitting . . . blasé b. fluid . . . tentative c. unstudied . . . uncontrived d. eclectic . . . uniform e. grandiose . . . controlled	The dance company rejects _____, preferring to present only _______ dances in a manner than underscores their traditional appeal. a. invention . . . emergent b. fidelity . . . long-maligned c. ceremony . . . ritualistic d. innovation . . . time-honored e. custom . . . ancient

precisely what ends up happening on the real SAT and other standardized tests required for higher education admissions.

For example, of the two items shown in Figure 3.3, one is from a scored SAT and was answered correctly by 11% more Whites than African Americans. The other item was on the experimental SAT math section in 1998, but was not included in a scored section of the SAT. This experimental item was answered correctly by 7% more African Americans than Whites. Is it easy to distinguish the item with a disparate impact of 11% favoring Whites from the item with an impact favoring African Americans by 7%?

The item on the right side (with C as the correct answer) was answered correctly by a greater percentage of African American test takers than Whites. The item on the left side (with B as the correct answer) was answered correctly by a higher percentage of Whites. Would it shortchange America's high school seniors if items like that on the right appeared on the scored SAT in addition to or instead of items like that on the left? While the content of both items is ostensibly neutral, can it be said that the SAT is truly unbiased if, time and time again, the test construction process tends to prefer (for statistical reasons) items like the one on the left (that favors Whites), and rejects items like the one on the right (that favors African Americans)?

EDUCATIONAL ANALYSIS

The Devilish Details of Disparate Impact

At the outset, we wish to make clear that neither our results nor other evidence suggests that ETS intends to construct the SAT and other standardized tests to ensure African Americans and Chicanx score lower than Whites. Indeed, it appears that a large majority of ETS staffers believe strongly in increased educational access for students of color and support affirmative

Figure 3.2. Comparing Black–White Disparate Impact of SAT Verbal Items

Which item will have a greater Black–White disparate impact?	
The singer now performs a more _______ repertoire of songs than in the past, when he sang only traditional ballads. a. sentimental b. experimental c. mellow d. customary e. wary	Ann Wickham's marriage seemingly ______ her art because, a few years after her wedding, she began to write prolifically. a. quelled b. construed c. consumed d. invigorated e. sated

action. We do not doubt that those involved in the development of the SAT strive for scrupulous fairness; nor do we contest that blatantly culturally biased questions (such as those rewarding familiarity with regattas, pirouettes, and so on) are by far the exception and not the rule. Good intentions aside, facially neutral test construction has, for purely statistical reasons independent of discriminatory animus, the ultimate effect of contributing to—even guaranteeing—the lower performance of African Americans and Chicanx on the SAT. Obviously, our counter-intuitive and rather startling claim requires explanation.

Before any item is included in a scored section of the SAT, it must first pass through a rigorous, multistep test construction process. The psychometricians who develop norm-referenced standardized tests such as the SAT generally adhere to two primary requirements when selecting items for the final version of the test: (1) items must be reliable, meaning that each item is internally consistent with the other items on the same test; and (2) items must meet particular specifications for level of difficulty (some questions are relatively easy, others are hard) so that the final version of the test will differentiate between test takers of different ability levels (Linn & Drasgow, 1987, p. 13).

While test reliability is operationalized by means of mathematical models with forbidding names like *item response theory* (IRT), the underlying concept is simple: A "reliable" item is one that people of "high ability" tend to answer correctly and people of "low ability" tend to answer incorrectly (Rosner, 1993, pp. 14, 16). The requirements for reliability on the SAT, LSAT, GRE, and similar tests do not depend on an independent, external measure of ability. Rather, item reliability is assessed by the correlation between performance on that item and performance on the test overall (or the entire portion of a test within a defined content domain). If, after pretesting, the correlation between an item and the larger test set drops below about 0.30, that item is typically flagged as a poor, unreliable question that can be excluded from the final version of the test (at least in its current form).

Figure 3.3.Rejecting Similar Math Items for the SAT

Which item appeared on the SAT and which item was rejected?
Is either item (or both) noticeably biased?

If the area of a square is $4x^2$, what is the length of a side?	If $\sqrt{2x}$ is an integer, which one of the following must also be an integer?
a. x	a. $\sqrt{x}$
b. 2x	b. x
c. 4x	c. 4x
d. x^2	d. x^2
e. $2x^2$	e. $2x^2$

To show how a seemingly neutral, innocuous process of selecting test questions creates an unnecessary adverse impact for students of color, imagine a pool of 1,000 pretested SAT verbal sentence-completion questions in which White students, on average, score higher than Black and Chicanx students. Next, assume that among these 1,000 items, 100 items slightly favor Whites and 100 items slightly favor African Americans and Chicanx. As evidenced in the results section, the direction (and the causes) of favoritism will seldom be readily apparent, even to expert sensitivity. After well-intentioned psychometricians calculate the correlations between each of the 1,000 items and total test scores, the key issue is which items will be accepted for an actual SAT and which items will be rejected.

Consistent with our empirical findings, we argue in this hypothetical that questions that are "biased" in favor of Whites have a fair chance of making their way onto a scored section of the SAT; ones that are "biased" against Whites have virtually no chance of appearing on a real SAT section (Loewen, 1993, pp. 85–86). Note that nothing is conspiratorial about our claim; it follows mathematically from the application of facially neutral tools of test construction. If Whites score higher overall on the set of 1,000 questions, then it must be true that "race-blind" item analysis will often detect robust and positive correlations for the items biased in favor of Whites, and weakly positive or even negative correlations for the items biased in favor of Blacks and Chicanx. In other words, item bias favoring Whites will tend to spuriously appear as reliable, whereas item bias favoring African Americans and Chicanx will, on balance, artificially appear as unreliable. The imposition of this White-preference standard of test reliability necessarily follows, because the benchmark of reliability is simply the sum total of all biased and unbiased questions—meaning that there is a "tyranny of the majority" dilemma inherent in the way reliability is constructed.

While skeptics of our analysis may criticize it as too speculative, empirical evidence supports our claims. Rachelle Hackett and other ETS researchers (Hackett, Holland, Pearlman, & Thayer, 1987) studied the issue of disparate impact of test items by assembling two tests from a pool of experimental GRE items: The first was intended to minimize Black–White differences and the second was designed to maximize Black–White differences. Hackett et al. found that the "maximum impact" test sections had item–test correlations that were just as high as the control group. Equally troubling, the ETS researchers found that the maximum impact sections typically exhibited higher correlations with the operational (real) sections of the GRE than did the control sections.

It is even more disconcerting that the disparate impact attributable to SAT reliability requirements is self-perpetuating. The process of developing new SAT questions is an ongoing feedback loop that includes writing, pretesting, analyzing, and finally administering scored questions. Test writers, regardless of their background, obviously strive for maximizing the number of "reliable" items they construct, and minimizing the wasted time associated with developing items that will later be tossed away as "unreliable." Thus this subtle White preference standard may become an imbedded social norm over the course of successive test administrations. Such a bias tends to be obscured because Whites have historically scored higher on the SAT than African Americans and Chicanx. The entire score gap is usually attributed to differences in academic preparation, although a significant and unrecognized portion of the gap is an inevitable result of the flaw in the development process.

Our second, more concrete example also sheds light on the consequences of developing standardized test items around traditional notions of reliability. Over the years, one of us (Jay Rosner) provided pro bono legal services to students in disputes with standardized test producers. One such student, Chris Laucks, took the LSAT in 1981 when it included math problems similar to those appearing on the SAT or GRE today. On a particular geometry problem, ETS mistakenly omitted a right angle marker. With the marker, one answer would have been mathematically correct, but in the absence of the marker, a different answer was mathematically correct. Unfortunately, Laucks picked the answer he knew to be mathematically correct instead of the answer he suspected ETS wanted.

After Laucks received his LSAT score with this geometry question marked incorrect, he wrote a complaint to the Law School Admission Council (LSAC) and attached a flawless mathematical proof of his answer. Oddly enough, LSAC confirmed that Laucks was correct, but it would not give him credit for his correct answer. Strict adherence to correlation requirements accounts for LSAC's peculiar stance. In its view this item was defective, because in pretesting, "high-ability" students picked the other, incorrect answer. Thus to give Laucks points for this question (and to penalize those picking the other answer) would violate a sacrosanct principle of test reliability. Accordingly, ETS wrote a letter to test takers explaining why the item was pulled from scoring (rather than crediting Laucks and others who picked (D) as the correct answer), in which it stated:

> As was noted above, the credited response to the question was (C). Statistical results from a trial administration of the question indicated that the question, with (C) as the answer, was functioning as intended. If the question had been keyed (D) in the trial administration, the statistics would have shown that it did not function properly, and it would not have been used in the LSAT. ("Letter from ETS to LSAT test-takers," 1984)

Chris Laucks learned the hard way that traditional psychometric methods will not allow the "right" people to get the answer wrong and the "wrong" people to get the answer right, even if this is what in fact happened. Critical race theorist Richard Delgado (2001, p. 599) has criticized standardized tests for their "epistemological fascism" because of the ways such tests reward particular thinking styles and punish other styles. Laucks' Alice in Wonderland experience with the LSAT—if the highest scorers pick "A" as their answer, and it is later proven that "B" is the correct answer, then the question, and not the answer key, is deemed to be defective—is certainly consistent with Delgado's criticism.

While test producers vigorously defend item–test reliability as an essential tool of sound test construction, examples such as Laucks's raise the point that the overzealous pursuit of test reliability can actually undermine the construct validity of the SAT and similar standardized tests. For example, psychology professor Stuart Katz and his colleagues at the University of Georgia gave SAT reading comprehension questions and answers to students without the actual reading passages. Katz found that because of factors such as outside knowledge and test-wiseness, honors students correctly answered 47 of the 100 questions on average, and a broader mix of students answered 38 questions correctly, whereas random guessing would result in about twenty correct responses (Katz, Lautenschlager, Blackburn, & Harris, 1990, pp. 123, 125). However, SAT reading comprehension sections were altered in the 1990s to include fewer but longer passages with more questions, and reading comprehension increased from 29% of the verbal score to 51%. Despite these revisions to the SAT, Katz found that students in introductory psychology courses could still answer 36% of the new reading comprehension items correctly without access to the reading passages (Katz, Johnson, & Pohl, 1999, p. 1158; see also Katz, Marsh, Johnson, & Pohl, 2001). We suggest, based partly on this line of research, that reliability requirements likely play a role in undermining the construct validity of SAT reading comprehension. If savvy test taking is more helpful than actually understanding the reading passages, then the SAT's construct validity is suspect, and the hypertrophied virtue of item reliability may be contributing to the degradation of construct validity.

Does Differential Item Functioning Eliminate or Exacerbate Item Bias?

Our principal claim—that SAT reliability requirements can facilitate test item bias against Black and Chicanx students—would be weakened if ETS and other test developers used methods that dependably rooted out biased items in the first place. Differential item functioning (DIF) is a statistical technique for identifying specific test items that are disproportionately more difficult for members of a race or gender group among test takers with equivalent overall test scores.[3] The Mantel–Haenszel statistic and "standardization" are two very similar methods, and are used by ETS, LSAC, and other test developers to measure DIF.

ETS promotional materials suggest that DIF is a sound method for flagging items that can unfairly penalize minorities. Sydell Carlton of ETS states:

> Matching students according to their test scores and then examining how they did on individual test questions helps us to determine whether the test questions themselves may be creating problems for a particular group. . . . By using the DIF procedure, paired with the Test Sensitivity Review procedure, ETS helps ensure that its examinations provide a level playing field for all who take them.[4]

As with claims about the SAT not having a disparate impact relative to other educational measures, ETS's public stance with respect to DIF does not withstand careful inspection. Put simply, DIF does not and cannot, as Carlton argues, "provide a level playing field." Continuing with this same metaphor, DIF techniques actually assume an overall level playing field, then proceed to look for an unusual pothole that might unfairly trip up one team or another, so to speak. If, for example, the playing field favors the home team by allowing them to run downhill to score a goal and forcing the away team to run uphill to score, this obvious bias would be undetected by DIF. The ETS "level playing field" argument is misleading and circular; by controlling for total test score before looking for potentially biased items, it is not possible for DIF to remove aggregate bias or lessen the overall racial and ethnic score gaps on the SAT.

ETS and other researchers even argue that since DIF does not decrease racial disparities, this is further corroboration that SAT items were unbiased all along. Needless to say, we find this logic unconvincing. As James Loewen (1993) aptly put it, "DIF removes the adverse impact before looking for adverse impact!" (p. 85). A close look at the educational measurement literature reveals that several esteemed psychometricians, including many working for ETS and other test producers, acknowledge that DIF cannot identify and eliminate systematic item bias against a minority group because controlling for total test score means there is no external fairness standard (see Angoff, 1993, pp. 3, 17; Shepard et al., 1981, p. 321).

Group test averages cannot be changed by DIF, which creates the foregone conclusion that questions biased "against" a group are counterbalanced by questions "in favor" of that group (see Camilli, 1993, pp. 397, 409). Some experts even argue that DIF can exacerbate rather than eliminate item bias against students of color because many questions favoring Whites would not stand out statistically after controlling for overall test score.

Martha Stocking and other ETS researchers revisited the issue of item bias reduction techniques on populations of women, African Americans, and Latinx.[5] Their findings, consistent with our findings and earlier research, were that accounting for group differences when assembling SAT test forms can lessen the adverse impact of the test without compromising construct validity and with only minor effects on test reliability.

Practical Considerations: Consequences for AAPIs and for Women?

SAT disparate impact reduction procedures raise thorny policy questions about race, ethnicity, gender, and other categories. Which groups should be included in efforts to reduce adverse impact on standardized test questions, and what are the consequences of excluding certain groups from Golden Rule–style adjustments? We will briefly discuss two key considerations: (1) the impact on Asian Americans and Pacific Islander (AAPI) test takers; and (2) the feasibility of simultaneously reducing adverse impact for African Americans, Latinx, and women.

Because of the role that education plays in America's opportunity structure, it is particularly important to attend to interracial and intersectional conflicts that could potentially arise from our approach to impact moderation on the SAT. Some readers may have legitimate concerns about whether using item bias reduction techniques in order to produce a "fairer" SAT for African Americans and Latinx might unintentionally cause harm to AAPIs taking the SAT. AAPIs comprised 8% of those taking the SAT in 1991, and this grew to 10% in 2001. Over that decade AAPIs scored about thirty points lower on average than Whites on the verbal section of the SAT and about thirty-five points higher than Whites on the math section.

Stocking et al.'s (2001) ETS study of impact moderation on the SAT indicates that attempts to reduce Black–White and Latinx–White test score gaps will not adversely affect AAPIs. In a sample of 5,863 Asian Pacific American test takers, the four methods of moderating the verbal section of the test resulted in an average increase in the gap favoring Whites by 0.015 standard difference units, and the six methods of moderating the math section resulted in increasing AAPIs' advantage by 0.083 standard difference units. In practical terms, this would translate to a net gain for AAPIs of approximately five points on the SAT. In fact, the verbal section that resulted in the best impact reduction for Blacks and Latinx also most effectively decreased AAPIs' disadvantage on the verbal section, whereas the section that increased disparate impact for Blacks and Latinx negatively affected AAPIs as well. Likewise, the math section that most effectively reduced impact for African Americans and Latinx also increased AAPIs' advantage on the math section vis-a-vis Whites. These findings suggest no inherent conflict between impact reduction techniques and AAPI performance on the SAT.

In summary, we are confident in concluding that Golden Rule–style impact moderation techniques would not create a barrier to opportunity for AAPI college applicants. Standardized tests usually have a modest disparate impact on women, as it is well documented that women perform slightly less well than men (both overall and within racial/ethnic groups) on the SAT, GRE, GMAT, MCAT, and LSAT. This pattern occurs despite the fact that women consistently obtain better grades than men in high school, college, and most graduate school programs. Consequently, higher education standardized tests are frequently criticized for being gender biased (e.g., see Kidder, 2000; Leonard & Jiang, 1999; Rosser, 1989).

Fortunately, ETS research by Stocking et al. (2001) repeatedly demonstrates that it is possible to simultaneously moderate racial/ethnic item bias and gender item bias. This win–win scenario is, in part, a statistical byproduct of the fact that 59% of African American and 58% of Latinx SAT test takers are women (compared to 54% of Whites)—meaning that efforts to moderate gender impact will necessarily reduce racial/ethnic impact to some degree, and vice versa.

LEGAL ANALYSIS

This section analyzes the law governing standardized tests and Title VI disparate impact claims, including the prospects of enforcing the U.S. Department of Education disparate impact regulations through section 1983 of the Civil Rights Act of 1871. This section also examines the possibility of lodging complaints with the Office for Civil Rights. Because ETS, the College Board, and similar test producers are not recipients of federal financial assistance and are not subject to these civil right statutes, suing colleges and universities on a disparate impact theory over their use of the SAT in admissions is the only judicial remedy.[6]

Title VI Disparate Impact Regulations

The Supreme Court ruled, in *Regents of the University of California v. Bakke* (1978), that Title VI of the Civil Rights Act of 1964 prohibited only the same forms of purposeful discrimination that are forbidden by the Equal

Protection Clause. Similarly, in *Guardians Association v. Civil Service Commission of the City of New York* (1983), five justices (in four separate opinions) held that Bakke compelled, as a matter of stare decisis, that the terms of section 601 of Title VI required proof of discriminatory intent.

The Bakke/Guardians Title VI intentional discrimination requirement has not been overturned in subsequent cases. However, the U.S. Department of Education regulations interpreting Title VI (34 C.F.R. 100.3(vii)(2)) prohibit both intentional discrimination and criteria or practices that have an unwarranted disparate impact on a protected class. This continues to be so as of 2019 under the Trump administration, which as of the time of this writing has not rescinded the aforementioned disparate impact regulations notwithstanding other overtures and changes in enforcement priorities (Congressional Research Service, 2019).

Title VI disparate impact regulations were dealt a serious blow in *Alexander v. Sandoval* (2001), in which the Supreme Court ruled that there is no private right of action to bring a disparate impact suit to enforce Title VI regulations. This was a marked departure from what had been a settled body of jurisprudence, including the unanimous view of the nine circuit courts that addressed the issue.

Post-Sandoval Options for Enforcing Disparate Impact Regulations

One option in the aftermath of *Sandoval* was noted by Justice Stevens in his dissenting opinion in *Alexander v. Sandoval*:

> To the extent that the majority denies relief to the respondents merely because they neglected to mention *42 U.S.C. 1983* in framing their Title VI claim, this case is something of a sport. Litigants who in the future wish to enforce the Title VI regulations against state actors in all likelihood must only reference 1983 to obtain relief. (532 U.S. at 299–300)

Section 1983 originated with the Civil Rights Act of 1871, a statute intended to enforce Fourteenth Amendment protections amid efforts by the Ku Klux Klan and other southern White supremacists to deprive Blacks of their nascent rights after the Civil War (Pettys, 1998, pp. 55–56). The Supreme Court has not definitively addressed this question, but several federal circuit courts have rejected the use of section 1983 to enforce Title VI disparate impact regulations.[7]

That leaves perhaps three other options. One is litigation in state court to enforce state law counterparts to federal disparate impact law, such as California's Government Code 11135 that includes prohibitions on using "criteria or methods of administration that have the . . . effect of" discrimination. A second is filing disparate impact administrative complaints with the Office for Civil Rights (OCR) of the U.S. Department of Education (as noted earlier, under the Trump administration these regulations have not been rescinded thus far, though uncertainty remains). A third option, and one that is a tall order politically, would be congressional repudiation of the *Sandoval* case akin to the way that the 1991 Civil Rights Restoration Act (105 Stat. 1071 (1991) reined in the Court's decision in *Wards Cove Packing Co., Inc. v. Antonio* (490 U.S. 642 (1989).

Elements of a Disparate Impact Claim

After overcoming the private enforcement hurdle through section 1983, the actual requirements for establishing a disparate impact case are relatively straightforward. In Title VI disparate impact analysis, the plaintiffs bear the initial burden of establishing that the challenged test or test use has a demonstrated disparate impact by race and ethnicity. After this prima facie showing has been made, it is the defendant's burden of proof to establish that the challenged test or test use is educationally justified. If the defendant meets this burden, plaintiffs may still prevail upon a disparate impact theory if plaintiffs can convince the court that there is an equally effective and less discriminatory alternative (see U.S. Department of Justice, 2019). This three-part burden-shifting framework mirrors the requirements for Title VII employment discrimination disparate impact cases. Courts confronting Title VI disparate impact challenges therefore often rely on Title VII cases, particularly since the case law is much more extensive in the employment context. There is a paucity of Title VI standardized testing cases challenging college and university admission practices, even prior to the Court's *Alexander v. Sandoval* ruling.[8] This may reflect the availability of affirmative action as a counterbalance to disparate impact, and it may also reflect a recognition on the part of plaintiffs' attorneys that Title VI disparate impact cases are difficult to win and may have even less viability in the future.

Determining Disparate Impact. In the Title VII employment context, the Supreme Court declared that there is "no rigid mathematical threshold" to overcome a facially neutral practice as long as statistical disparities are sufficiently large to raise an inference that the challenged practice caused the disparate results.[9] Courts have essentially adopted the same requirement for Title VI disparate impact claims. Plaintiffs' initial prima facie burden of establishing disparate impact is usually less onerous than contesting educational necessity or providing a workable, less discriminatory alternative.

Determining Educational Necessity. After the plaintiff establishes a prima facie case of disparate impact, the defendant has the burden of justifying its use of a standardized test by proffering evidence of "educational necessity." This standard of "educational necessity" is similar to "business necessity" in Title VII disparate impact litigation.

A university defending its use of the SAT in admissions would undoubtedly rely upon the large body of studies produced by ETS and College Board researchers purporting to validate the SAT as a predictor of first-year college grades (e.g., see Bridgeman, McCamley-Jenkins, & Ervin, 2000; Willingham, Lewis, Morgan, & Ramist, 1990). This position hardly demonstrates educational necessity, however. Scholarly critics of the SAT have for many years pointed out that combining the SAT with high school grades only incrementally improves the prediction of freshman grades compared to high school grade point average (HSGPA) alone.

For example, researchers at the University of California Office of the President studied 78,000 freshmen who entered seven UC campuses between 1996 and 1999 (Geiser, 2002). The authors found that HSGPA explained 15.4% of the variance in freshman grades among enrolled students at UC campuses, HSGPA combined with SAT scores explained 20.8%, HSGPA combined with the SAT II subject-specific achievement tests explained 22.2%, and HSGPA, SAT, and SAT II combined explained 22.3%. Based on these results, if UC were sued over the disparate impact of the SAT, it would be difficult to advance "a substantial legitimate justification" for the SAT when the test improves the percentage of variance explained by a statistically insignificant 0.1% above that explained by HSGPA and the SAT II, and when the SAT only adds 5.4% to the variance explained by HSGPA alone. At UC–Berkeley, UCLA, and UC–San Diego—the most selective campuses, and the ones most likely to be named as defendants in a disparate impact lawsuit—the relative contribution of the SAT was even lower than it was for the UC system overall. To summarize, the SAT imposes a substantial adverse effect on underrepresented minority students, yet its contribution to the prediction of freshman grades is quite modest. Moreover, the UC system's educational necessity position was most likely undermined when UC President Richard Atkinson, who himself is a cognitive psychologist steeped in the testing literature, suggested that the UC system could discontinue using the SAT in favor of another test that it might develop.

More importantly, the ability to predict freshman grades in college is hardly dispositive for a defendant university attempting to meet its educational necessity burden in a Title VI disparate impact claim. A strong argument can be made that college graduation is of greater ultimate importance than freshman GPA, and the educational necessity of the SAT is even more questionable considering available data on graduation patterns. U.S. Department of Education research analyst Clifford Adelman (1999c) argues:

> The justification for using SAT scores in admission decisions is that they are a decent predictor of first-year college grades. True, but so what? That criterion has nothing to do with the principal goal of students at four-year colleges and their families: completing a bachelor's degree. Nor do state legislatures give a

> hoot about grades when they judge the performance of public universities: Performance means graduation rates. (p. B4)

Using the U.S. Department of Education's comprehensive national database, Adelman found that, after controlling for major background characteristics of students, the quality and intensity of high school academic curriculum was a far better predictor of degree completion than SAT scores (see Adelman, 1999a; 1999b, pp. 42, 48). Another major national study by UCLA professor Alexander Astin (1993) looked at longitudinal data for a sample of 38,000 from the Cooperative Institutional Research Program (CIRP), and found that the SAT only correlated 0.27 with graduation rates, meaning that the SAT only explained 5% of the variance in graduation rates.

Do SAT scores have a stronger association with graduation rates at highly selective universities, which are by and large the institutions at issue in the affirmative action debate? According to Abigail and Stephan Thernstrom, prominent critics of affirmative action, UC–Berkeley graduation rates "correlated perfectly with SAT scores." However, more reliable information is presented in *The Shape of the River*, in which William Bowen and Derek Bok (1998), the former presidents of Princeton and Harvard, respectively, extensively studied the College and Beyond (C&B) database of 28 (mostly private) elite colleges and universities. Bowen and Bok found that, after controlling for school selectivity, high school grades, socioeconomic status, and other characteristics, SAT scores bore little relationship to graduation rates (and no relationship above scores of 1000). Students with SAT scores under 1000 had graduation rates of 83%, students in the 1000s had rates of 86%, those in the 1100s had rates of 88%, those in the 1200s had rates of 86%, and those above 1300 graduated 87% of the time. The SAT findings contrasted with school selectivity, which continued to be associated with graduation rates after controlling for other factors. Bowen and Bok also report that at the most selective C&B schools African Americans with SAT scores under 1000 had graduation rates of 88%, whereas in the least selective C&B schools even African American students with SAT scores over 1300 had graduation rates of 75%. In summary, the C&B data suggest that factors other than the SAT—those having to do with institutional resources (endowment size, class size, the availability of support programs,and so on)—are much more influential determinants of graduation rates.

The Bowen and Bok data should also remind researchers that much of the SAT–graduation rate correlation reported in other large-scale studies may be an artifact of combining data from different schools, while failing to acknowledge that the most well-endowed elite private schools simultaneously have greater institutional resources, as well as higher graduation rates and higher SAT scores. For example, a study by Burton and Ramist of the College Board summarized eight studies of SAT and graduation rates, and reported a 0.33 correlation between these two measures. Yet, Burton and Ramist acknowledge that their estimate may be too high because they could not account for institutional effects (Burton & Ramist, 2001, p. 16).

The SAT's correlation with family/parental income levels for 2016 college-bound seniors is displayed in Figure 3.4 (see p. 70). The relationship between income and other measures of socioeconomic status and institutional resources tends to artificially boost the correlation between graduation rates and SAT scores when combining Harvard and Hayward data. Consequently, when Warren Willingham of ETS studied SAT–graduation relationships within each of nine colleges, the correlation coefficient dropped to only 0.15.[10] Recent research by Saul Geiser (2017) reinforces concerns about the relationship between SAT scores, family background characteristics including income, and race/ethnicity.

In analyzing whether "a substantial legitimate justification" exists for overreliance on the SAT despite its disparate impact, a key consideration is that there must be a fit between a university's mission and its admission practices. In a report on standardized tests, the prestigious National Academy of Sciences recommended that "admissions policies and practices should be derived from and clearly linked to an institution's overarching intellectual and other goals" and that the "use of test scores in the admissions process should serve those institutional goals" (Beatty, Greenwood, & Linn, 1999). While these recommendations may seem like common sense, universities espousing lofty institutional missions frequently fail to carefully consider whether or not their admission criteria are well suited to serve important goals.

Evidence suggests that the SAT and other standardized tests are particularly weak predictors of potential contributions to community service and similar "public-spirited" institutional goals. For example, Bowen and Bok found that within the C&B database, African American graduates, many of whom received affirmative action consideration, and who had average SAT scores over 200 points lower than Whites, were nonetheless significantly more likely than their White classmates to become the leaders of civic service organizations, including those in law, medicine, business, and other professions (Bowen & Bok, 1998, pp. 29–31, 160–168). A large and growing number of institutions actually find that making the SAT optional allows them to better fulfill their institutional mission,and has the added bonus of broadening and deepening their applicant pool (Soares, 2012).

CONCLUSION

In this chapter we attempted to identify and analyze one important expression of privilege: racial bias on standardized tests like the SAT. While higher education inequities and standardized test score differences undoubtedly stem from a number of social forces—residential/educational segregation's contribution to inferior K–12 schooling for students of color is a salient example—we argue that the SAT also creates "built-in headwinds" in its own right. We combined empirical evidence with a review of the educational literature to argue that the SAT's test construction process unintentionally exacerbates the disparate impact of the test. Moreover, test assembly/item construction is only one manifestation of racial bias in standardized testing and its surrounding milieu (e.g., another is stereotype threat).

If the SAT contains racial bias, the question remains, where should American higher education go from here? Certainly affirmative action programs can help to counteract the negative impact of racial bias in standardized tests. In addition, we argued in this chapter that the SAT test construction process can be altered to decrease the disparate impact of the test on African Americans and Chicanx. While the majority of psychometricians would most likely disfavor our recommended changes, we should point out that our position is not entirely outside of the mainstream. For example, in the *Standards for Educational and Psychological Testing* (1999), jointly produced by the American Educational Research Association, the American Psychological Association, and the National Council on Measurement in Education, Standard 7.11 states that it can be appropriate to take account of disparate impact: "When a construct can be measured in different ways that are approximately equal in their degree of construct representation and freedom from construct-irrelevant variance, evidence of mean scored differences across relevant subgroups of examinees should be considered in deciding which test to use" (p. 83).

We anticipate that opponents of our recommended SAT item bias reduction procedures will criticize us for advocating "race-norming" in the test assembly process. We conclude by reminding readers that, based on our empirical findings and review of the educational measurement literature, the process currently used to construct the SAT, LSAT, GRE, and similar tests unintentionally operates to select questions with larger racial and ethnic disparities (favoring Whites). Thus the argument that lessening disparate impact in SAT test assembly amounts to unfair racial gerrymandering ignores the current manner in which standardized tests are developed—which incorporates significant behind-the-scenes racial gerrymandering. We believe that the costs of reifying this status quo standardized testing regime (a system that is far from "race-neutral") are too high for America's educational future, particularly for many students of color.

Critics of our proposed changes on the SAT will likely argue that modifying the test assembly process to take cognizance of item impact will degrade the predictive validity of the SAT. Yet, for mathematical reasons having to do with the relationship between reliability and predictive validity, ETS researchers such as Stocking acknowledge that "substantial room" exists to lessen disparate impact without compromising the SAT's ability

Figure 3.4. Family Income Level and SAT Scores (2016)

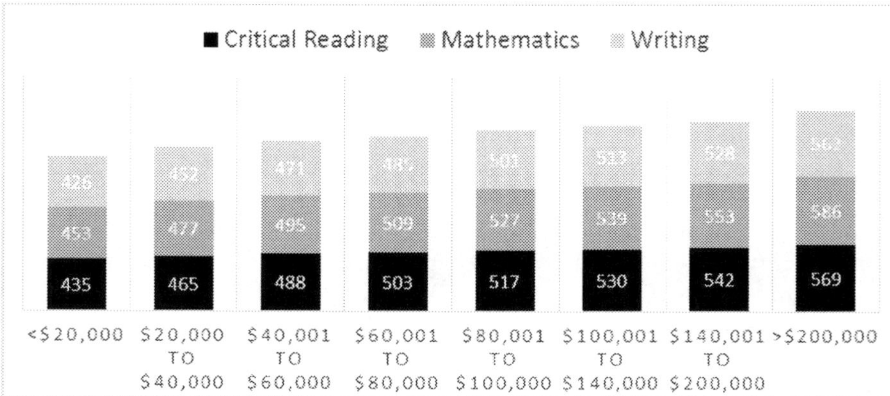

Note. The data are from *2016 College-Bound Seniors: Total Group Profile Report* (p. 4, Table 10), by College Board, 2016.

to predict college grades; indeed, by removing construct-irrelevant variance associated with race and ethnicity, the changes we advocate may even create the "win–win" situation of a less biased SAT that has higher predictive validity than the current form.

Finally, as a pragmatic matter, ETS and the College Board are very unlikely to adopt impact reduction techniques in connection with the SAT unless outside pressure is so substantial as to impact the SAT marketplace. Thus it may be practical to focus energy on urging colleges and universities either to not use the SAT or at least give applicants the choice of whether or not they want it to be considered in admissions decisions.

NOTES

This chapter is a significantly shorter and slightly updated version of the following article: "How the SAT Creates Built-in-Headwinds: An Educational and Legal Analysis of Disparate Impact," by W. C. Kidder and J. Rosner (2002), *Santa Clara Law Review, 43*(1/3), 131–211 (available at digitalcommons.law.scu.edu/lawreview/vol43/iss1/3). Our original article includes far more detailed citations to supporting scholarship. We thank Professor Joseph Soares for the invitation to publish this book chapter, and we thank the following scholars for their helpful reviews of the original article: Vikram Amar, Angelo Ancheta, Richard Delgado, Lani Guinier, William Henderson, Bradford Mank, David Oppenheimer, Peter Sacks, Gerry Spann, Sam Spital, and David M. White. We also appreciate the assistance of Martin Shapiro in transforming our SAT data into a useable form.

1. See William C. Kidder (2001, p. 177) for a summary of the standard testing evidence presented at trial by CIR in *Grutter v. Bollinger*; Kinley Larntz (1999) for

testimony at the trial; and Jodi S. Cohen (2001) for a summary of Larntz's trial testimony.

2. This item and a couple of others noted in our chapter were reported in an article in *The Wall Street Journal* by Amy Dockser Marcus (1999).

3. For an in-depth discussion of DIF techniques, see *Differential Item Functioning*, edited by Paul W. Holland and Howard Wainer (1993).

4. See Educational Testing Service, "What's the DIF? Helping to Ensure Test Question Fairness," at www.ets.org/research/dif.html (available in the Internet Archive: web.archive.org). This claim is not atypical of ETS and other test developers.

5. See Martha Stocking et al. (2001). While the authors of this study did not disclose the particular math and verbal test they studied, the details of their study—including the racial, ethnic, and gender gaps on the test, as well as the size of the populations taking each of the test forms and the size of the item pools—strongly suggest that this was a study of the SAT. (Cf. id. at 7 tbl.1.)

6. See *National Collegiate Athletic Association. v. Smith*, 525 U.S. 459 (1999): ruling that the mere fact that the NCAA received funds from schools that, in turn, received federal financial assistance does not expose the NCAA to lawsuits pursuant to Title IX of the Education Amendments of 1972; and *Cureton v. National Collegiate Athletic Association*, 198 F.3d 107, 114-19 (3d Cir. 1999): holding in part that Title VI disparate impact regulations are program specific, and finding that the NCAA could not be sued over the alleged disparate impact of its minimum SAT score eligibility requirement under the theory that the NCAA has "controlling authority" over colleges and is therefore an indirect recipient of federal assistance.

7. See, for example, *Johnson v. City of Detroit*, 446 F.3d 614, 629 (6th Cir. 2006) (overruling *Loschiavo v. City of Dearborn*, 33 F.3d 548 [6th Cir. 1994]); *Save Our Valley v. Sound Transit*, 335 F.3d 932, 944 (9th Cir. 2003); *South Camden Citizens v. New Jersey Department of Environmental Protection*, 274 F.3d 771, 774 (3d Cir. 2001). See also Kimberly West-Faulcon (2009, p. 1123).

8. Linda Hamilton Krieger (1998): "Although various lower federal courts have followed *Guardians* and permitted Title VI plaintiffs to proceed under a disparate impact theory in actions to enforce the regulations, no reported case has ever challenged the use of either the SAT, the LSAT, the Graduate Record Exam (GRE), or the Medical College Admissions Test (MCAT). Indeed, as of the writing of this Article, I have been unable to find a single reported Title VI or Title IX case in which college or graduate school admissions criteria have been challenged. Thus, unlike employers, whose selection procedures have for years been subject to challenge under Title VII, institutions of higher education have been left to define and assess merit in admissions decision making in an atmosphere utterly devoid of legal contest." (pp. 1300–1301).

9. *Watson v. Fort Worth Bank and Trust*, 487 U.S. 977, 994-95 (1988); see *Wards Cove Packing Co., Inc. v. Antonio*, 490 U.S. 642, 656-57 (1989).

10. See Burton & Ramist (2001), p. 17, citing Warren W. Willingham, *Success in College: The Role of Personal Qualities and Academic Ability*.

REFERENCES

Adelman, C. (1999a). *Answers in the tool box: Academic intensity, attendance patterns, and bachelor's degree attainment.* Short, web-based version retrieved from www.ed.gov/pubs/Toolbox/; full publication (ERIC No. ED431363) available at eric.ed.gov/?id=ED431363

Adelman, C. (1999b, Jan.–Feb.). The rest of the river. *University Business, 2*, 43–46.

Adelman, C. (1999c, Nov. 5). Why can't we stop talking about the SAT? *Chronicle of Higher Education*, p. B4.

Alexander v. Sandoval, 532 U.S. 275 (2001).

American Educational Research Association, American Psychological Association, & National Council on Measurement in Education. (1999). *Standards for Educational and Psychological Testing.* Washington, DC: American Educational Research Association.

Angoff, W. H. (1993). Perspectives on differential item functioning methodology. In P. W. Holland & H. Wainer (Eds.), *Differential item functioning.* Hillsdale, NJ: Lawrence Erlbaum.

Astin, A. W. (1993). *What matters in college: Four critical years revisited.* San Francisco, CA: Jossey-Bass.

Beatty, A., Greenwood, M.R.C., Linn, R. L. (Eds.). (1999). *Myths and tradeoffs: The role of tests in undergraduate admissions.* Washington, DC: National Academy Press.

Bowen, W. G., & Bok, D. (1998). *The shape of the river: Long-term consequences of considering race in college and university admissions.* Princeton, NJ: Princeton University Press.

Braceras, J. C. (2002). Killing the messenger: The misuse of disparate impact theory to challenge high-stakes educational tests. *Vanderbilt Law Review, 55*(4), 1111–1203.

Bridgeman, B., McCamley-Jenkins, L., & Ervin, N. (2000). *Predictions of freshman grade-point average from the revised and recentered SAT I: Reasoning test* (College Board Research Report No. 2000-1; ETS RR 00-1). New York, NY: College Entrance Examination Board.

Burton, N. W., & Ramist, L. (2001). *Predicting success in college: SAT studies of classes graduating since 1980* (College Board Research Report No. 2001-2). New York, NY: College Entrance Examination Board.

Camilli, G. (1993). The case against item bias detection techniques based on internal criteria. In P. W. Holland & H. Wainer (Eds.), *Differential item functioning.* Hillsdale, NJ: Lawrence Erlbaum.

Civil Rights Act of 1871. Pub.L. No. 42–22, 17 Stat. 13 (1871).

Civil Rights Act of 1964. Pub.L. No. 88–352, 78 Stat. 241 (1964).

Civil Rights Restoration Act, 105 Stat. 1071 (1991).

Cohen, J. S. (2001, Jan. 18). Witness: Odds lean to U-M minorities. *Detroit News.*

College Board. (2016). *2016 College-bound seniors: Total group profile report.* Retrieved from secure-media.collegeboard.org/digitalServices/pdf/sat/total-group-2016.pdf

Congressional Research Service. (2019, April). Civil rights at school: Agency enforcement of Title VI of the Civil Rights Act of 1964. Retrieved from crsreports.congress.gov/product/pdf/R/R45665

Delgado, R. (2001). Official elitism or institutional self-interest? 10 reasons why UC–Davis should abandon the LSAT (and why other good law schools should follow suit). *UC Davis Law Review, 34*(3), 593–614.

Dockser Marcus, A. (1999, Aug. 4). To spot bias in SAT questions, test maker tests the test. *The Wall Street Journal.* Retrieved from www.wsj.com/articles/SB934210072325180723

Educational Testing Service. (n.d.). What's the DIF? Helping to ensure test question fairness. Retrieved from www.ets.org/research/dif.html (available in the Internet Archive: web.archive.org).

Fisher v. University of Texas, 570 U.S. ___ (2013).

Fisher v. University of Texas, 579 U.S. ___ (2016).

Geiser, S. (with Studley, R.). (2002). UC and the SAT: Predictive validity and differential impact of the SAT I and SAT II at the University of California. *Educational Assessment, 8*(1), 1–26.

Geiser, S. (2017, December). *Norm-referenced tests and race-blind admissions: The case for eliminating the SAT and ACT at the University of California* (Research & Occasional Paper Series: CSHE.15.17). Retrieved from cshe.berkeley.edu/sites/default/files/publications/2.rops.cshe.15.2017.geiser.testsrace-blind_admissions.12.18.2017.pdf

Gratz v. Bollinger, 539 U.S. 244 (2003)

Griggs v. Duke Power Co., 401 U.S. 424 (1971).

Grutter v. Bollinger, 539 U.S. 306 (2003).

Guardians Association v. Civil Service Commission of the City of New York, 463 U.S. 582 (1983).

Hackett, R. K., Holland, P. W., Pearlman, M., & Thayer, D. T. (1987). *Test construction manipulating score differences between Black and White examinees: Properties of the resulting tests* (ETS Research Report No. RR 87-30). Princeton, NJ: Educational Testing Service.

Holland, P. W., & Wainer, H. (Eds.). (1993). *Differential item functioning.* Hillsdale, NJ: Lawrence Erlbaum.

Katz, S., Johnson, C., & Pohl, E. (1999). Answering reading comprehension items without passages on the SAT-I. *Psychological Reports, 85*(3), 1157–1163.

Katz, S., Lautenschlager, G. L., Blackburn, A. B., & Harris, F. H. (1990, March). Answering reading comprehension items without passages on the SAT. *Psychological Science, 1*(2), 122–127.

Katz, S., Marsh, R. L., Johnson, C., & Pohl, E. (2001). Answering quasi-randomized reading items without the passages on the SAT–I. *Journal of Educational Psychology, 93*(4), 772–775.

Kidder, W. C. (2000). Portia denied: Unmasking gender bias on the LSAT and its relationship to racial diversity in legal education. *Yale Journal of Law & Feminism, 12*(1), 1–42. Retrieved from digitalcommons.law.yale.edu/yjlf/vol12/iss1/2/

Kidder, W. C. (2001). Affirmative action in higher education: Recent developments in litigation, admissions and diversity research. *Berkeley La Raza Law Journal, 12*(2), 173–230.

Kidder, W. C., & Rosner, J. (2002). How the SAT creates built-in headwinds: An educational and legal analysis of disparate impact. *Santa Clara Law Review, 43*(1/3), 131–211. Retrieved from digitalcommons.law.scu.edu/lawreview/vol43/iss1/3

Krieger, L. H. (1998). Civil rights perestroika: Intergroup relations after affirmative action. *California Law Review, 86*(6), 1251–1333.

Larntz, K. (1999). *Expert report of Kinley Larntz, PH.D.*, concerning Barbara Grutter v. Lee Bollinger, et al. *Michigan Journal of Race & Law, 5*(1), 463–557. Retrieved from repository.law.umich.edu/mjrl/vol5/iss1/2

Lawrence, C. R., III. (2001). Two views of the river: A critique of the liberal defense of affirmative action. *Columbia Law Review, 101*(4), 928–976.

Leonard, D. K., & Jiang, J. (1999). Gender bias and the college predictions of the SATs: A cry of despair. *Research in Higher Education, 40*(4), 375–407.

Letter from ETS to LSAT test-takers, April 30, 1981. (1984). In D. M. White, *The effects of coaching, defective questions, and cultural bias on the validity of the Law School Admission Test* (Appendix A). Berkeley, CA: National Conference of Black Lawyers.

Linn, R. L., & Drasgow, F. (1987). Implications of the Golden Rule settlement for test construction. *Educational Measurement: Issues and Practice, 6*(2), 13–17.

Loewen, J. W. (1993). A sociological view of aptitude tests. In U.S. Commission on Civil Rights, *The Validity of Testing in Education and Employment* (pp. 73–91), Washington, DC: U.S. Commission on Civil Rights.

Pennock-Roman, M. (1988). *The status of research on the Scholastic Aptitude Test (SAT) and Hispanic students in postsecondary education* (ETS Research Report No. RR 88-36). Princeton, NJ: Educational Testing Service.

Pettys, T. E. (1998). The intended relationship between administrative regulations and section 1983's "laws." *George Washington Law Review, 67*(1), 51– 99.

Regents of the University of California v. Bakke, 438 U.S. 265, 287 (1978).

Rosner, J. (1993, Sept.–Oct.). Discrimination is built into standardized aptitude tests. *The Long Term View, 1,* 14, 16.

Rosser, P. (1989). *The SAT gender gap: Identifying the causes.* Washington, DC: Center for Women Policy Studies.

Shepard, L., Camilli, G., & Averill, M. (1981). Comparison of procedures for detecting test-item bias with both internal and external ability criteria. *Journal of Educational Statistics,* 6(4), 317–375.

Soares, J. A. (Ed.). (2012). *SAT wars: The case for test-optional college admissions.* New York, NY: Teachers College Press.

Stewart, D. M. (1998, Jan. 30). Why hispanic students need to take the SAT. *Chronicle of Higher Education*, p. A48.

Stocking, M. L., Lawrence, I. M., Feigenbaum, M., Jirele, T. J.. Lewis, C., Van Essen, T. (2001). *An empirical investigation of impact moderation in test construction* (ETS Research Report No. RR 01-04). Princeton, NJ: Educational Testing Service.

Thernstrom, S., & Thernstrom, A. (1997). *America in Black and White: One nation, indivisible.* New York, NY: Simon & Schuster.

U.S. Department of Justice. (2019, March 18). *Title VI legal manual* (updated). Retreived from www.justice.gov/crt/fcs/T6manual

Wards Cove Packing Co., Inc. v. Antonio, 490 U.S. 642 (1989).

West-Faulcon, K. (2009). The river runs dry: When Title VI trumps state anti-affirmative action laws. *University of Pennsylvania Law Review, 157(4)*, 1075–1160. Retreived from scholarship.law.upenn.edu/penn_law_review/vol157/iss4/3

Willingham, W. W., Lewis, C., Morgan, R., & Ramist, L. (1990). *Predicting college grades: An analysis of institutional trends over two decades.* Princeton NJ: Educational Testing Service.

Zwick, R. (1999). Eliminating standardized tests in college admissions: The new affirmative action? *Phi Delta Kappan, 81*(4), 320–324.

CHAPTER 4

The "Landscape" or "Dashboard Adversity Index" Distraction

A Clumsy Attempt at Damage Control

Joseph A. Soares

Hoping to reverse its declining share of the standardized test market, the College Board spent a minimum of 2 years (2017–2019) at considerable expense creating what was called an "Environmental Context Dashboard," or "adversity index." It supposedly would allow "admissions officers to see all students' strengths relative to where they live and learn, in a new, consistent, data-driven way" (College Board, 2019a). The dashboard/adversity index would provide social environmental context for scores on the SAT achieved by individual youths. College admissions staff would be given a number on a 100-point scale, with 50 representing the average, signaling attributes of the neighborhood (such as median family income) and high school (such as average SAT scores of college students from that high school) in which a student did her or his work (College Board, 2019b). The admissions staff could use this score as providing the background context of adversity or privilege facing a student.

In the spring of 2019, when the adversity index was widely picked up by the press, it generated "a storm of criticism from parents and educators" (Hartocollis, 2019b). The response of the College Board was to blow the bugle of retreat, even though it was more a case of regrouping than of abandoning the field. As reported by the *New York Times*, "David Coleman, chief executive of the College Board, said on Tuesday [August 27, 2019] that the board had heard the criticism and was bowing to it. He said that the company had always believed that students should be judged by more than a number, whether a test score or a disadvantage score. . . . . 'I think it is a retreat from the notion that a single score is better,' Mr. Coleman said. 'So in that sense, we've adopted a humbler position. That's admitting that the College Board should keep its focus on scoring achievement'" (Hartocollis, 2019b).

We should pause at this point to reflect on two parts of Coleman's comment to the *New York Times*. If neither "disadvantage" nor "achievement" can be measured by one number, then why isn't the SAT getting abandoned along with the adversity index? And in what sense is the SAT a score of achievement? The SAT was introduced in the 1920s as an aptitude test (Soares, 2007) with pretentions of being a measure of academic IQ. Tests that capture what a student has "achieved" in the course of studying a subject at school were precisely what the SAT was not supposed to be; that's what high school grades are all about. Early on, the SAT was called the "scholastic aptitude test." David Coleman's statements do little to dispel the suspicion that the adversity index is more of an exercise in pleasing the consumer than it is about fairness and science, or even in providing a consistent story line.

As it turns out, the College Board's public relations retreat did not go very far. They are calling the humbler position "Landscape," where two numbers, one for the school and one for the neighborhood, will be reported instead of just one adversity index score. The board's presumption that two numbers, given a different label, will quiet its critics is in line with the same cluelessness that launched the original design of the adversity index.

Regardless of whether it is a single score adversity index or Landscape's two scores, the College Board has fatally undermined, no doubt unintentionally, the pretense that the SAT is a meritocratic equalizer, providing a valid standardized prediction of a student's performance in college. As Bob Schaeffer of FairTest said, "Test makers long claimed that their products were a 'common yardstick' for comparing applicants from a wide range of schools. . . . This latest initiative concedes that the SAT is really a measure of 'accumulated advantage,' which should not be used without an understanding of a student's community and family background" (quoted in Jaschik, 2019a). If test scores should be interpreted in light of one's social context, then any particular SAT score or percentile ranking cannot stand alone.

The College Board's Landscape or adversity index is just a diversion, one of many in recent years, from the test's fundamental flaws. New versions of the test have been rolled out in 2005 and 2016, with minor changes to the way scores were reported introduced in 2009. The SAT has been on the defensive ever since the president of the University of California, Richard Atkinson, in 2001 threatened to drop the test (Schemo, 2001). In 2005 a new SAT was released in a maneuver to keep the University of California on board. The 2005 changes may have protected the SAT's market share in a multibillion dollar industry, but substantively the revisions were cosmetic. After 2005, pressure on the test continued to come from the rise of test-optional colleges, which rejected the idea that a student's fate should be determined by a standardized test score. In response, the College Board in 2016 attempted to prop up the validity of the test and protect its market position through yet another new version of the SAT. As Todd Balf writing in the *New York Times Magazine* put it, president of the College Board "[David] Coleman had to grapple with what it meant for the College Board as a business to have the credibility of the SAT called into question. A growing number of colleges and universities, frustrated by the minimal change to the SAT when it was revised in 2005 and motivated by a report issued in 2008 by the National Association for College Admission Counseling (NACAC), began to eliminate the SAT and its competitor, the ACT, as admission requirements" (Balf, 2014). With more than 43% of America's 4-year degree-granting institutions no longer insisting on SAT/ACT scores from student applicants, the test-optional admissions movement was fast approaching a tipping point.

The main narrative that the College Board has been pushing for decades in defense of the SAT is that the test is fair even if life is not; contrary to the findings of its critics, the Board sees the test as a better proxy for brain power than bank accounts. At Yale, where the dashboard was given a test drive, the admissions dean, Jeremiah Quinlan stated, "There's nothing wrong with the SAT score. . . . It [the dashboard] just helps contextualize the SAT score for us" (quoted in Hartocollis, 2019a). The College Board hopes that the Landscape scores will focus attention on the unfairness of life, instead of the test. But neither Landscape nor the adversity index have been put to any serious tests for scientific validity.

For Landscape or adversity index scores to be scientific, they must have explanatory and predictive power. If the scores given to schools and neighborhoods do not predict anything, they are just numbers that provide more distracting noise than explanatory signal. What does a score of 63 versus a score of 73 really mean? For an index to matter, it needs to be correlated with very particular outcomes. It should enable scientists to predict relevant outcomes based on a precise score. Let me illustrate this with the National Institute of Health (NIH) "stroke scale." Each NIH index or scale is derived from multivariate regression analyses designed to verify that each variable used in the scale or index matters and precisely how much each matters to a particular outcome. For example, the "risk of stroke index" allows health care professionals to know that "for men, each point on the index corresponded to a 12% relative risk increase [over the baseline rate]. . . . For women, each point corresponded to a 14% relative risk increase" over the baseline (Manuel et al., 2015). Do the Landscape scores or the adversity index scores correlate with or predict any particular educational outcome? Do they predict high school grades, standardized test scores, college GPA, and/or crossing the finish line and receiving a degree in 4 years? What does each numeric point correspond to? If a score does not predict any particular outcome, the index is a con job, presenting a precise number as though it explains something when it does not. Without precise guidelines on what the numbers predict, admissions staff are left just guessing at what a score means. The College Board's cavalier attitude is testified to by its failure to take responsibility for instructing college admissions staff on how to use the scores. An *Inside Higher Ed* article by Scott Jaschik (2019a) reported, "The College Board noted that individual colleges will have to decide what, if anything, to do with the information."

Originally, the College Board took the indefensible position that the scores would be kept secret from students and the public. When they dropped the single-score adversity index in favor of Landscape's two scores, they announced that students would be provided with those numbers starting in 2020 (Jaschik, 2019b). If the College Board delivers on that promise, they will regret it. To publish contextual scores will be to invite lawsuits from affluent families who object to the metric as diminishing the value of their offspring's scores. If top-income, elite-educated families cannot claim that their children's high SAT scores are deserved, they will file lawsuits about punitive discrimination. Landscape's scores will be seen as a form of affirmative action in college admissions subject to judicial review and possible overturn. Families of privilege will defend their offspring's besmirched meritocratic credentials with the same legal teams and deep pockets that have pushed lawsuits at Texas, Harvard, and UNC Chapel Hill against any consideration of race in college admissions.

If there are lawsuits linking the Landscape scores to reverse discrimination, they will be ironically on target to draw a connection between those scores and matters of race. If the scores are intended to be a metric of social disparities, then how it is possible to exclude race and ethnicity? Race and ethnicity are attributes of neighborhoods and of schools that are strong determinants of educational outcomes. The College Board's president, David Coleman, is flatly wrong when he excuses the exclusion of race from the metric by claiming that "the tool ignored race because its premise was that race was less of a predictor of success at school than what he called resourcefulness" (Hartocollis, 2019a) What are we to infer from David Coleman's comment that "in America . . . within every racial group—Asian, White, Black, Latino—there are large numbers of people who show resourcefulness within very limited circumstances" (quoted in Hartocollis, 2019a)? If individual resourcefulness is the problem and not structural inequalities and racism, then why bother with social context? Do Blacks and Hispanics do poorly on the test because as individuals they are not being resourceful enough? Or do Blacks and Hispanics perform below par on the SAT because the test is biased and because their neighborhoods and schools are disadvantaged? Coleman's release of a Landscape scale that omits race and ethnicity is at best disingenuous. One can claim it is a political compromise because legislation prevents some public universities from considering race/ethnicity, but that is not a scientific justification for ignoring the effects of race/ethnicity in a quantitative measure of disadvantage. Contrary to Coleman's dismissal of the significance of race, its importance in determining SAT and ACT scores has grown over time. As Saul Geiser's research shows, race explains more about standardized test scores today than it did 25 years ago. Geiser notes that University of California (UC) "data show that race has an independent and growing effect on test scores, after controlling for other socioeconomic factors. . . . Statistically, race has become as important as either family income or parents' education in accounting for test score differences among UC applicants" (see Chapter 1). Race and ethnicity still matter in America, even when household income and parental education are equal; ignoring their effects for the sake of political or courtroom expediency is scientifically invalid.

For colleges who are committed to need-blind admissions, how will this metric affect them? If Landscape provides information on median family incomes in the youth's neighborhood, that information will make it nearly impossible for colleges to do admissions "need-blind." If a college knows a youth is applying from a neighborhood where median family incomes are low or high, that removes any veil of ignorance about ability to pay. Any college pledged to need-blind admission would have to ignore the neighborhood score entirely. Did the College Board think this through and consult with "need-blind" colleges before it decided to create its Landscape scores?

Finally, do these scores make college admissions more scientific than before? With Landscape, will college admissions finally be more science than art? Georgetown's admissions dean does not think so. As reported in the *Washington Post*, "Charles A. Deacon, the veteran dean of undergraduate admission at Georgetown University, said he was skeptical about the value of the score. 'We have so much personal data on all of our applicants that we don't feel the need for a tool like this. In this era of 'data analytics' I guess this is one that could be helpful, but to be honest I still see college admissions as 'an art, not a science' so I'm prone to resist quantifying things too much'" (Anderson & Svrluga, 2019). Georgetown's dean is surely right that admissions are more art than science when multivariate regression models predicting first-year college grades capture just 21% of the variation in outcomes (Zwick, 2017, p. 82).

We should remember that both standardized college admissions tests, the SAT and ACT, were really designed to predict first-year grades, and that is all. The legitimacy of these tests rests on a prediction about grades over two semesters. In its technical literature, the College Board has never claimed that the SAT does a better job in predicting grades than high school grades. The justification for the test rests on the observation that the test, in combination with high school grade point average (HSGPA), gives one a higher r-square than working with just HSGPA alone (Kobrin, Patterson, Shaw, Mattern, & Barbuti, 2008; Morgan, 1989; Zwick, 2017, p. 82).

R-square sounds very technical but it expresses a simple idea: It can be read as a percentage score on how much we understand about an outcome, such as a brain stroke or a college GPA. When one is working with multiple variables at the same time to predict an outcome, the r-square score tells the researcher how much of the variance in the outcome is explained by all of the variables together in the model.

Relevant information about people will always involve more than one attribute; we are all multifaceted beings affected by a vast amount of social, material, and psychological factors. But not everything about our lives is meaningfully related to a particular result, such as a college GPA or a brain stroke. Multivariate regression models enable us to see which attributes matter and how much they matter to something we want to know. If our model gives us a high r-square, then we can say that we really understand the major factors that go into producing an outcome; when we have a low r-square, we may know some factors that matter, but we remain largely in the dark on what really drives a particular result.

The r-squares for multivariate models predicting first-year college grades are not very high. The College Board puts the r-square for its test alone at .12; when the test is combined with high school grades, the r-square goes up to .21 (Zwick, 2017, p. 82). The College Board believes that with both HSGPA and the SAT it can explain 21% of the variance among first-year college grades. One should note that high school grades do not transmit the same high level of social disparities that test scores do (Geiser, 2017). If one wants the strongest, least socially contaminated variable for predicting college grades, one should work with just high school grades, not test scores. But for the sake of argument, if one works with a multivariate regression model that includes both, then one is still left with 79% of what matters unexplained. To jump back to scientific scales on stroke referenced previously, fully 90% of what puts one at risk of a stroke has been identified. Just 10% is left unexplained (O'Donnell et al., 2010). In contrast, we are doing college admissions using test scores produced by a multibillion dollar industry that gives us an r-square for a test that explains by itself just 12% of what matters. When researchers can put together a multivariate regression model that captures at least 50% of what determines first-year grades, then we might be justified in speaking of college admissions as a science, but until then, it remains an art. If one's explanatory punch, using both high school grades and test scores, leaves 79% of what matters unexplained, one doesn't have much license for scientific bragging rights, let alone a multibillion dollar industry. America has been misled at great cost to us, economically, socially, and educationally.

THE RELATIVE VIRTUES OF A STRIVERS INDEX INSTEAD OF LANDSCAPE SCORES

The Landscape is not the first time someone working on behalf of the SAT attempted to take social environment into account. Anthony Carnevale did so back in the 1990s. Carnevale was employed then by the Educational

Testing Service (ETS), which is historically the junior partner with the College Board in the testing industry. Carnevale's argument has been summarized by Richard Kahlenberg (2010) in a Century Foundation book, in the following way: "If admissions officers want to be fair—truly meritocratic—they need to consider not only a student's raw academic credentials, but also what obstacles she had to overcome to achieve them. . . . [Carnevale devised] a program to identify strivers who scored 200 points above their predicted standardized test score based on fourteen factors, including parents' income, education and occupation; . . . and her high school's academic strength and income level" (p. 10). Carnevale had a multivariate statistical regression model that enabled him to do a scientific job of predicting SAT scores based on a youth's demographics and school context. With those predicted scores, he could then identify *strivers* as any youth who outperformed her or his social environment by a margin of 200 SAT points. Once one had this "strivers index," the raw score and the normed percentile ranking would not matter as much as the relative performance of a youth in comparison to her or his peers. The College Board apparently did not want admissions staff to know if a youth was an overperforming striver or an underperformer because it rejected Carnevale's program and forced him to shred his work, leaving no trace behind (Carnevale, 2011). Carnevale's work was erased and his idea was suppressed by the Board. Now, nearly thirty years later, the Board has revived a version of Carnevale's index but without his solid statistical anchor. His index predicted something specific—SAT scores—and could measure the distance, up or down, between a youth's circumstances and her or his score. The College Board's Landscape scores fall far short of the scientific standard set by Carnevale.

Carnevale's work showed the tight correlation between SAT scores and environmental information. It is far easier to statistically predict a youth's SAT score than her college GPA. Using variables like what Carnevale had to work with, we can get an r-square model that predicts over 50% of what goes into a youth's SAT score, in contrast to the modest 12 percentage points we get when using the SAT to predict college grades. We nearly quadruple our statistical power, our ability to predict, when we look at SAT scores as the dependent variable instead of college grades. Clearly, the SAT is tied rigidly to social characteristics, while college grades express a more elastic relation to social origins. By design or default, the SAT tells us more about who you are than what you are able to do in college. The test, due in part to how questions are selected and how the nationally normed bell curve ranks youths into percentile scores, has social inequality built into its algorithm. Grades in high school and in college are both more meritocratic than the socially biased and predictively weak SAT.

THE DATA

Carnevale had a better sense of how to contextualize SAT scores than what the College Board offers today. In the rest of this chapter, I illustrate this by working with data to display the extent to which SAT scores are determined by demographics and environmental context. I do not have Carnevale's data, but I do have a viable alternative database, the National Longitudinal Survey of Freshmen (NLSF), which is entirely suitable for this pilot analysis. It is longitudinal, includes 28 very selective colleges, nearly 4 thousand students, and provides information on them, their families, neighborhoods, and characteristics of high schools. Data on participants in this survey were gathered every spring from 1999 to 2003. Findings from the data have so far been published in two books by Princeton University Press (e.g., Massey, Charles, Lundy, & Fischer, 2003; Charles, Fischer, Mooney, & Massey 2009) and in scores of articles.

This data set is appropriate for a study of "adversity" effects in that it includes variables at at five levels: individual, family, peer group, neighborhood, and school. We can separate the contribution of neighborhood and school effects from individual- and family-level effects to see how much each matters to an outcome such as grades, test scores, college admissions, college grades, choice of major, and years to degree. Inasmuch as the sample is based on colleges with very selective admissions, the range of scores will be more restricted to high SAT scores and the effects of demography and geography will be understated. But this data has already been used successfully to show the impact of segregated neighborhoods on academic performance (Massey & Fischer, 2006), so it should suffice to explore whether or not aggregate-level community and school attributes contribute to measurable academic outcomes.

ANALYTIC STRATEGY

This is an exercise in predicting SAT scores based on grades, courses taken, individual demographic information, family, neighborhood, and school variables. Since the challenge is to shed light on how an SAT score may be affected by a youth's "landscape," I ran three multivariate linear regression models to tease out how much neighborhood and school variables contribute to the prediction of SAT scores. I will present the results as a table on the sociological determinants of SAT scores.

In the first regression model (Model 1), I look at what high school grades and courses taken in high school can tell us; this is a model working with just the high school academic transcript by itself, without any information about the race, gender, or family characteristics of the youth. The second model (Model 2) adds individual and family demographic information to the high school transcript. It includes variables on the youth's race, gender, and family income. The third model (Model 3) includes all of the variables used in the previous two, but adds those variables that would go into an "adversity index," such as racial composition of a school, level of school disorder, neighborhood crime and violence, and rate of home ownership. A look at each model's r-square shows how the introduction of additional variables did or did not alter the statistical significance and relative weight of each variable.

Keep in mind that these regression models are predicting SAT scores, not college grades or some other measure of success in higher education. Irrespective of the findings here, as long as SAT scores remain weak predictors of college performance, the case against using them for college admissions still stands. This is a study of how environment predicts SAT grades, not how SAT grades fail to predict college outcomes.The greater the weight carried by environment and demographics in predicting SAT scores, the more those scores are exposed as proxies for race, gender, and social class. If test scores are strong proxies for social characteristics, then college admissions that rely on test scores are a discriminatory exercise in social Darwinism disguised as academic selection.

FINDINGS AND INTERPRETATION

This study is limited by being based on a cohort of youths who successfully enrolled at highly selective colleges in 1998; this is not a random sample, representative of the entire nation. These youths are sociologically within America's collegiate elite. There is racial and economic diversity among them, but the effects of family and neighborhoods may be diminished by the selection effect of being in a sample of those found desirable by America's elite colleges. It is safe to assume that the main results visible in this data will probably be more pronounced in the general population, and that some of the minor but statistically significant results will be noise that a larger random sample study would filter out. Not everything here that looks like it matters does really matter, and some of the variables that do matter here, may matter a lot more nationwide than these numbers show.

The main story line here is that academic variables (Model 1) explain 28% of the variance in SAT scores, but demographic and local context variables nearly double the explanatory power of the model (Model 3) to 52%. These results strongly support the idea that local context matters to SAT scores. An "adversity index" or "landscape" tally that predicts average SAT scores for a particular student profile, against which actual SAT scores could be compared, would work in a way consistent with Carnevale's plan for a "strivers index" back in the 1990s.

In Table 4.1 the *Constant* in each model presented here is the reference baseline SAT score out of a possible 1600 points; the *Unstandardized Coefficients* are actual score increases or decreases that should be factored in if they are statistically significant. Only those coefficients that have one (*), two (**), or three (***) asterisks next to their score are statistically significant. When the variable is binary, a zero or a one, then the variable adds its coefficient's score to the baseline (constant); for example, in Model 1, having attended a private high school is a yes/no binary variable worth 11 SAT points, raising private school attendees' average scores from 942 to 953. When the variable is on a scale, each step up the scale adds the same number of points as the coefficient displays. For example, in Model 1, if high school GPA is worth 28 points per step up a 4-point scale, at the highest step it would be worth 112 points, raising one's SAT score from 942 to 1054. Another example from Model 1 is years of English or literature classes, which is statistically significant (worth 24 points) and can count four separate times, once for each year of high school, potentially giving a 96-point increase in one's SAT score.

What matters across these three models is often, but not always, intuitive. One's SAT score is reduced the most by the following variables (in decreasing order of negative impact): years of typing class; being Black; being Hispanic; being female; low-income; first-generation college; parental involvement in formation of social capital; being in a high school where students verbally abuse teachers; having a best friend who drinks alcohol; a close friend who had sex; school spirit; years of earth science; or friends who are Black or Hispanic. There are other variables with statistically significant but minor negative impacts that one can see from the table.

It is important to note that racial effects are reduced by nearly 50% once one controls in Model 3 for neighborhood and school effects. On average in this data, being Black reduces one's SAT score by 94 points, but once local context is statistically controlled for, the size of the Black race effect declines to 51 points. The shift in the direct effects of being Hispanic in reducing one's SAT score declines from 40 points to 19 points when local context is known. Approximately half of what appears in Model 2 to be effects of race are community effects, yet half of the impact of race remains regardless. Interestingly, the negative consequences of years of typing is also reduced by about 50% in Model 3, while the effects of gender and first-generation college are reduced by approximately 20% and 15% respectively.

What helps increase one's SAT score the most are the following variables (in descending order of impact): high school grades; years of physics; years of English/literature instruction; years of chemistry; parental involvement in formation of cultural capital; higher family incomes; having a best friend who took illegal drugs; amount of teacher interest in students; valuing the same things as peers; having parents with postgraduate degrees.

It is critical to register what does not seem to matter much, or not at all, for this data sample. The racial composition of neighborhoods does not matter in this data; racial composition of schools matters a tiny bit, negatively when Black, positively for Asian. Being Asian is not statistically significant in any of these models. Neighborhood disorder does not count. School qualities for buildings, classrooms, audiovisual equipment, computers, and libraries do not matter. Parents' postgraduate degrees matter in Model 2, but not at all in Model 3. Once local environment is made equal statistically speaking, parental postgraduate degrees do not predict a higher SAT score for offspring. It is possible that the neighborhood and school characteristics variables that do not rise to the level of statistical significance are due to the highly selected character of this data cohort. We need a proper national study using academic, demographic, and local context variables to shed more light on environmental effects.

On variables that matter in this data, there is the counter-intuitive finding that if one's best friend does illegal drugs, that is worth an increase of 20 points on one's SAT score. There are reasons to believe that if this effect is real, it could derive from a test score correlation with social deviance instead of the doubtful payoff of intoxication. Remember, that if one's best friend drinks alcohol, it hurts one's SAT score, so this is not about altered mental states. Plus, we do not know if this survey score is a reflection of mere bragging or of actual behavior.

It was surprising to see that parental involvement in social capital, the formation of network ties that provide resources for accomplishing goals, hurts SAT scores by as much as minus 29 points. It is possible that social capital is more important as a constraint on undesirable behavior, such as dropping out of school, than it is a means of enhancing standardized test score performance. In contrast, parental cultivation of cultural capital, those highbrow tastes and activities that one associates with art museum and classical music concert attendance, helps a lot. The gain from having a top score on its 44-step scale would be to raise one's SAT score by 50 points.

All three models display higher r-squares than what the College Board can put on the table to justify their defense of the SAT. It has proven easier to statistically predict SAT scores than to predict college grades, and that is all the more reason why a landscape or adversity index that is transformed into a more honest strivers index, that shows how much demography and local context are driving SAT scores, would be justifiable in terms of empirical science. The right choice, however, would be to eliminate the SAT and the ACT entirely, but colleges who insist on imposing that burden onto their students should have the integrity to have a "strivers index" on hand to show the difference between predicted and individual performance.

I can safely predict that the College Board will not provide the world with such an index because to do so would expose what Lani Guinier (2015) of Harvard Law so aptly labels as the "testocracy" for what it really is: the

Table 4.1. Three Models on the Sociological Determinants of SAT Scores (Scores Ranged from 200 to 1600)

Model 1: Academic variables only: grades and classes on transcript

Model 2: Academic variables, plus individual and family variables

Model 3: Academic variables and individual and family variables, plus peer, neighborhood, and school variables

Variable	Unstandardized Coefficients		UnStandardized Coefficients
	MODEL 1	MODEL 2	MODEL 3
(Constant)	942.327***	1061.415***	1029.759***
HSGPA 8 pt scale	28.626***	22.398***	23.000***
HS private (0/1)	11.976***	3.860	-13.754
HS: years of algebra (0–4)	5.520	.642	-2.408
HS: years of geometry	2.772	-8.870	-16.530
HS: years of general math	3.677	2.419	1.699
HS: years of biology	7.953**	7.842**	2.879
HS: years of chemistry	18.316***	12.410***	11.397**
HS: years of physics	27.113***	17.432***	13.491***
HS: years of computer science	.728	2.764	5.374
HS: years of earth science	-8.276**	-6.183*	-8.961*
HS: years of general science or other science	-7.568***	-6.615**	-5.143
HS: years of U.S. history	5.393	2.025	5.673
HS: years of world history	7.315**	5.682*	4.306
HS: years of economics	-8.860**	-6.751*	-1.514
HS: years of English or literature	24.015**	20.377*	36.391**
HS: years of foreign language/lit	11.595	8.647	7.561
HS: years of music	1.531	.673	.477
HS: years of drama	.165	3.280	1.033
HS: years of art	-2.119	-2.288	-3.523
HS: years of typing	-44.554***	-28.693***	-18.178***
Middle income (second 20%)		36.485***	26.531**

Upper middle income (third 20%)	46.116***	28.639*
Upper income (fourth 20%)	36.861**	27.413
Rich (top 20%)	44.223***	30.060*
Female (0/1)	-33.063***	-26.170***
Black (0/1)	-93.775***	-50.947***
Asian (0/1)	9.661	2.978
Hispanic (0/1)	-40.101***	-19.193*
First-generation college (0/1)	-40.690***	-34.645***
Parents' ed.: some college (0/1)	22.888	21.315
Parents' ed.: postgrad (0/1)	22.254***	13.339
Parent owned home/apt (0/1)	1.169	-.849
Parental involvement in human capital formation (0 to 72 scale)	-.528	-.303
Parental involvement in social capital formation (0 to 16 scale)	-1.835*	-2.168
Parental involvement in cultural capital formation (0 to 44 scale)	1.251**	.843
% Black in high school		-.390*
% Hispanic in high school		-.143
% Asian in high school		.817***
HS had foreign language lab (0/1)		1.235
HS had computers for students (0/1)		2.787
HS had theater for drama productions (0/1)		-7.837*
HS had non-teaching guidance counslers (0/1)		-1.811
HS had school psychologist (0/1)		-.109
HS had metal detectors (0/1)		2.155
HS witnessed fights among students (0/1)		-4.009
HS students late for class (0/1)		10.005
HS students cutting class (0/1)		1.401

HS students cutting school (0/1)	-6.010
HS students verbally abuse teachers (0/1)	-16.551***
HS students vandalize school property (0/1)	10.039
HS graffiti on school property (0/1)	-7.515
HS students consuming alcohol (0/1)	2.108
HS students taking illegal drugs (0/1)	-4.690
HS students carrying knives as weapons (0/1)	-1.300
HS: teachers encouraged independent thinking (0/1)	5.193
job during school year (0/1)	.296
hours worked per week	.025
HS: peers cool to study	-8.267
HS: peers cool to ask hard questions	6.066
HS: peers cool to volunteer information in class	-6.536
HS: peers cool to answer teachers' questions	-4.479
HS: peers cool to use creative problem solving	1.057
HS: peers cool to help others with homework	8.203
HS: peers cool to do well in hard classes	-3.252
HS: peers planning to go to college	-3.911
felt comfortable around peers	-2.386
valued same things as peers	12.506**
age 18: # close friends dropped out	-14.536
age 18: # close friends used drugs	.810
age 18: # close friends used alcohol	9.936

age 18: # close friends had sex	-13.951**
age 18: respondent had sex	-.212
% close friends Black	-6.963***
% close friends Hispanic	-6.960*
% close friends Asian	.781
% close friends other (not White)	-5.955
best friend: got good grades	6.901
best friend: interested in school	4.802
best friend: studied hard	-4.109
best friend: attended class regularly	-6.058
best friend: planned to go to college	6.714
best friend: was popular	.418
best friend: played sports	-3.031
best friend: read a lot	7.558
best friend: watched tv a lot	-1.994
best friend: had sex	-3.388
best friend: took illegal drugs	19.977**
best friend: drank alcohol	-14.742*
HS: quality of school buildings	-.094
HS: quality of classrooms	.535
HS: quality of audiovisual equipment	-5.973
HS: quality of library	-2.948
HS: quality of computers for students	-1.292
HS: amount of teacher interest in students	14.349*
HS: amount of teacher preparedness	-.540
HS: strictness of discipline	-7.896
HS: fairness of discipline	-8.512*

HS: school spirit	-11.288**
HS: overall quality of school	11.730
HS: school reputation in community	2.638
% Neighbors Black	.112
% Neighbors Hispanic	-.055
% Neighbors Asian	.229*
% Neighbors other (not White)	-.247
homeless in neighborhood	5.865
Prostitutes in neighborhood	-11.406
drug paraphernalia in neighborhood	.985
people selling drugs in neighborhood	2.740
people using drugs in neighborhood	-2.483
people drinking in public in neighborhood	5.074
graffiti on businesses in neighborhood	4.112
graffiti on homes in neighborhood	3.496
gang members on streets in neighborhood	.755
violence in public in neighborhood	.833
heard gunshots in neighborhood	-6.947
saw stabbing in neighborhood	-12.418
saw shooting in neighborhood	19.894
saw mugging in neighborhood	-10.041

Notes. Dependent variable: SAT Total; *** p = .001,** p = .01,*p = .05

Model 1 r-square = 28; Model 2 r-square = 42; Model 3 r-square = 52

Notes on scoring binary categories. HS private variable: 1 = private high school, 0 = public high school; Female variable: female = 1, male = 0; other categories, 0 = no, 1 = yes.

Notes on missing reference categories. Income: bottom 20%; Race: White; Parents' ed.: college degree (Parents' ed.: Some college = some college but no degree; Parents' ed.: postgrad = parent achieved a graduate or professional school degree—PhD, MA, MD, JD, etc.);

Percentages for racial/ethnic composition of high school, close friends, and neighborhood: White.

inheritors of privilege. The SAT and the ACT help disguise the role privilege plays in educational attainments in America; a strivers index would strip away that facade. Standardized tests stigmatize and relegate unprivileged youths, at the same time as they confer the halo of meritocracy on youths of inherited privilege. The College Board will drop and retire its Landscape scores before it would ever make it into a strivers index.

CLOSING THOUGHTS

The test industry profits from the production of statistical noise. But the larger failing here, shared by the College Board with the "testocracy" and many in academia, is an obsession with high scores. Academics have a legitimate interest in estimating if an applicant is prepared to do college-level work, but the college preparation threshold is brightly displayed by a candidate's high school transcript. What is the point of a high-stakes standardized test that claims to predict, for example, whether a youth will get a 3.5 instead of a 3.0 in their first year of college? Success in college really should be about growth and exploration, about the "value added" by an undergraduate experience. As Rudolph Steiner famously said, "education is a journey, not a race" (quoted in Brookes, 2016). The 2.5 undergraduate may be getting more from her or his education, and may end up contributing more to society, than the 3.7 student. An admissions dean has written to me that "if I enroll a student who just barely graduates (based on GPA) but has engaged with challenging new ideas, has studied abroad, has developed their leadership skills through campus clubs/organizations, has learned how to interact with people from very different backgrounds, and has emerged as an informed, thoughtful citizen—I feel they have had a very successful college experience" (personal communication, August 29, 2019). Is the mission of America's colleges to educate our citizens for the 21st century? Are we best served by selecting for the 3.5 candidate, or by opening wide our doors to the 2.5 youth? Should collegiate prestige be based on how many one excludes at the entry gate or by how many we invite on the journey and by how far we travel with them? Are we helping our society to become better educated or are we just labelling youths with dubious metrics of mental abilities winners and losers? The College Board is in the business of sorting youths, of disguising social Darwinism as meritocracy; but what we need are academics who fully embrace the democratic mission of American higher education.

REFERENCES

Anderson, N., & Svrluga, S. (2019, May 16). Coming soon to the SAT: An "adversity score" offering a snapshot of challenges students face.

The Washington Post. Retrieved from www.washingtonpost.com/education/2019/05/16/coming-soon-sat-an-adversity-score-offering-snapshot-challenges-students-face/?utm_term=.8a899221839a

Balf, T. (2014, March 6). The story behind the SAT overhaul. *New York Times Magazine*. Retrieved from www.nytimes.com/2014/03/09/magazine/the-story-behind-the-sat-overhaul.html

Brookes, A. (2016, April 14). "Education is a journey, not a race –the Steiner approach to schooling. Retrieved from www.teachwire.net/news/education-is-a-journey-not-a-race-the-steiner-approach-to-schooling

Carnevale, A. (2011, January 27). The case for change from the perspectives of educational scholars: What we do, why, and with what results. Session held at CERPP Conference, Los Angeles, California.

Charles, C. Z., Fischer, M. J., Mooney, M. A., & Massey, D. S. (2009). *Taming the river: Negotiating the academic, financial, and social currents in selective colleges and universities*. Princeton, NJ: Princeton University Press.

College Board. (2019a). Environmental context dashboard. Frequently asked questions. Retrieved from pages.collegeboard.org/landscape#faq

College Board. (2019b). Environmental context dashboard. Retrieved from professionals.collegeboard.org/landscape

Geiser, S. (2017, December). *Norm-referenced tests and race-blind admissions: The case for eliminating the SAT and ACT at the University of California* (Research & Occasional Paper Series: CSHE.15.17). Retrieved from cshe.berkeley.edu/sites/default/files/publications/2.rops.cshe.15.2017.geiser.testsrace-blind_admissions.12.18.2017.pdf

Guinier, L. (2015). *The tyranny of meritocracy: Democratizing higher education in America*. Boston, MA: Beacon Press.

Hartocollis, A. (2019a, May 16). SAT's new "adversity score" will take students' hardships into account. *The New York Times*. Retrieved from www.nytimes.com/2019/05/16/us/sat-score.html

Hartocollis, A. (2019b, August 27). SAT "adversity score" is abandoned in wake of criticism. *The New York Times*. Retrieved from www.nytimes.com/2019/08/27/us/sat-adversity-score-college-board.html

Jaschik, S. (2019a, May 20). New SAT score: Adversity. *Inside Higher Ed*. Retrieved from www.insidehighered.com/admissions/article/2019/05/20/college-board-will-add-adversity-score-everyone-taking-sat

Jaschik, S. (2019b, September 3). College Board overhauls "adversity index." *Inside Higher Ed*. Retrieved from www.insidehighered.com/admissions/article/2019/09/03/college-board-overhauls-adversity-index

Kahlenberg, R. D. (2010). *Rewarding strivers: Helping low-income students succeed in college*. New York, NY: Century Foundation Press.

Kobrin, J. L., Patterson, B. F., Shaw, E. J., Mattern, K. D., & Barbuti, S. M. (2008). *Validity of SAT for predicting first-year college grade point average* (College Board Research Report No. 2008-5). New York, NY:

The College Board. Retrieved from eric.ed.gov/?id=ED563202

Manuel, D. G., Tuna, M., Perez, R., Tanuseputro, P., Hennessy, D., Bennett C., . . . Tu, J. V. (2015). Predicting stroke risk based on health behaviours: Development of the stroke population risk tool (SPoRT). *PLOS ONE, 10*(12), e0143342. doi.org/10.1371/journal.pone.0143342

Massey, D. S., Charles, C. Z., Lundy, G. F., & Fischer, M. J. (2003). *The source of the river: The social origins of freshmen at America's selective colleges and universities.* Princeton, NJ: Princeton University Press.

Massey, D. S., & Fischer, M. J. (2006). The effect of childhood segregation on minority academic performance at selective colleges. *Ethnic and Racial Studies, 29*(1), 1–26.

Morgan, R. (1989). *Analyses of the predictive validity of the SAT and high school grades from 1976 to 1985* (College Board Report No. 89-7; ETS RR No. 89-37). New York, NY: College Entrance Examination Board. Available at eric.ed.gov/?id=ED562586

O'Donnell, M. J., Xavier, D., Liu, L., Zhang, H., Chin, S. L., Rao-Melacini, P., . . . Yusuf, S. (2010, July 10). Risk factors for ischaemic and intracerebral haemorrhagic stroke in 22 countries (the INTERSTROKE study): a case-control study. *Lancet, 376*(9735), 112–123. doi:10.1016/S0140-6736(10)60834-3

Schemo, D. J. (2001, February 17). Head of U. of California seeks to end SAT use in admissions. *The New York Times*. Retrieved from www.nytimes.com/2001/02/17/us/head-of-u-of-california-seeks-to-end-sat-use-in-admissions.html

Soares, J.A. (2007). *The power of privilege: Yale and America's elite colleges.* Stanford, CA: Stanford University Press.

Zwick, R. (2017). *Who gets in? Strategies for fair and effective college admissions.* Cambridge, MA: Harvard University Press.

Part II

ADMISSIONS WITHOUT REQUIRING TEST SCORES

CHAPTER 5

The SAT/ACT Optional Admissions Growth Surge

More Colleges Conclude "Test Scores Do Not Equal Merit"

Robert A. Schaeffer

More than 1,050 accredited, bachelor's degree–granting colleges and universities across the United States now will make admissions decisions about all or many applicants without regard to their ACT or SAT scores (FairTest, 2019).

These test-optional institutions range in size and mission from multi-campus public systems, such as the University of Texas, to competitive liberal arts colleges such as Smith College in Massachusetts, Muhlenberg College in Pennsylvania, Lawrence University in Wisconsin, and Pitzer College in California. A growing number of top-ranked private universities including the University of Chicago, Wake Forest University, and Worcester Polytechnic Institute have also eliminated ACT and SAT requirements.

The list of institutions deemphasizing standardized exam results includes more than half of all top-ranked liberal arts colleges, many highly regarded regional schools, and a growing number of state university campuses (U.S. News & World Report, 2019). According to the best-selling *Fiske Guide to Colleges*, "a critical mass has emerged of quality liberal arts colleges and major state universities that are test-optional or test-flexible" (Fiske, 2018, p. xxxviii).

From Maine to California, educators and policymakers are subjecting the SAT and ACT to unprecedented scrutiny. Increasingly, they identify standardized admissions tests as significant barriers to entry for thousands of academically qualified minority, first-generation, and low-income applicants. Often, they have decided that the social and academic costs of continuing to rely on these tests outweigh any possible benefits. By turning away from making decisions based on test scores, these institutions are promoting equity and excellence.

Many 4-year colleges and universities have long had broad concerns about the validity, equity, and educational impact of standardized admissions tests. Bowdoin College in Maine made the decision to go test-optional more than 50 years ago in 1969, recognizing that the entrance exam requirements were unnecessarily restricting its applicant pool. Other institutions, including many land-grant colleges such as the University of Arizona, did not require test scores from their inception, consistent with their founding missions. Many more analyzed their admissions numbers and found that standardized tests were simply not very good predictors of first-year college performance, which the tests purport to predict, let alone more important outcomes such as retention rates and graduation.

Schools that have dropped or sharply restricted the use of the ACT and SAT have generally been very pleased with the results. Regardless of size or selectivity, most test-optional institutions have seen substantial benefits. These include increased diversity, more applicants, and better prepared students as well as positive reactions from alumni, guidance counselors, and the public.

Higher education institutions that reduce their emphasis on standardized admissions tests are sending a strong message that "test scores do not equal merit." For many years, one of the central arguments in favor of the SAT and ACT is that they serve as a "common yardstick." That, supposedly, enables admissions officials to compare students from different high schools and academic backgrounds. However, no one would seriously argue that a 1300 combined reading and math score on the SAT or an ACT composite of 28 at a selective magnet school means the same thing as a similar score at a resource-starved school serving a low-income community. Even the Educational Testing Service, which helps administer the SAT, has criticized the "myth of a single yardstick," arguing that there is "no single, primary ordering of people as 'best-qualified' or 'most meritorious' as simple notions of merit require" (Cole, 1997). In fact, the test's sponsor, the College Board, recently developed an Environmental Context Dashboard now labelled "Landscape" for evaluating SAT scores (College Board, 2018).

Test-optional schools have put into practice a skepticism about the value of scores from largely multiple-choice exams as a significant measure of preparation for undergraduate success. In many cases, schools that join the ranks of "test-optional" colleges are merely making explicit and formal their long-standing admissions practices that depend very little on standardized admissions tests.

If, as test makers acknowledge (Chingos, 2018) and data from many colleges substantiate, high school achievement is the strongest predictor of undergraduate academic performance with test results providing no more than supplemental information, there are only two possible reasons for emphasizing such scores in the admissions process. Both affect the admit/deny decision that would be made in the absence of the test. If information from the ACT and SAT does not alter the fate of applicants, then they are clearly of no use to admissions officers.

The first possible justification for looking at test scores would be to identify students whose academic records indicate they can perform successfully in their first year of college but who are not truly academically qualified because their high school grades and course-taking patterns overstate their preparedness. Such students—disproportionately minority and lower-income—are at the heart of many debates over the reliance on ACT/SAT results for admissions. Strict test score requirements will keep these students out of more competitive institutions, despite their records of achievement in classrooms, extracurricular activities, and community leadership. By dropping or deemphasizing test scores, private colleges open their campuses to these students and thereby promote both equity and excellence. Selective public institutions, often vital gateways to participation in a state's political, business, and community organizations, play down tests so as not to shut out talented and capable minority, low-income, rural, and first-generation college students.

The second justification for continuing use of test scores would be to flag applicants with greater promise than was revealed by their performance in high school. Although this type of discrepancy may occur on occasion, it is unlikely that a significant body of students who had underperformed in high school would suddenly excel in college. A far larger number are likely to be slackers, whose college grades will mirror their weak high school records. In any case, test-optional policies do not hurt these applicants because they can still submit SAT or ACT scores along with an explanation of their classroom performance.

Thus test score–optional policies allow colleges to include many applicants with strong records of academic and other forms of achievement. At the same time, these policies do not exclude students who believe submission of test scores helps demonstrate their academic potential.

THE BENEFITS OF MAKING ACT AND SAT SCORES OPTIONAL

The Tests Do Not Help Colleges

Comprehensive statistical analyses in decades of data-filled studies such as *The Case Against the SAT* (Crouse & Trusheim, 1988) and *Crossing the Finish Line* (Bowen, Chingos, & McPherson, 2009) demonstrate that deemphasizing the SAT in admissions would not harm colleges' abilities to accurately select their incoming classes. The former book concludes, "From a practical viewpoint, most colleges could ignore their applicants' SAT score reports when they make selection decisions without appreciably altering the academic performance and graduation rates of the students they admit"

(Crouse & Trusheim, 1988, p. 68). Similarly, the second book finds, "High school grades are a far better incremental predictor of graduation rates than are standard SAT/ACT tests scores" and "The strong predictive power of high school GPA holds even when we know little or nothing about the quality of the high school attended" (Bowen et al., 2009, p. 226).

More recently, research led by William Hiss, former Admissions Director and Vice President of Bates College, concluded that test-optional policies increase student body diversity without undermining academic quality (Hiss & Franks, 2014). A follow-up study, published in 2018, demonstrated how those positive outcomes were achieved after schools dropped ACT and SAT requirements (Syverson, Franks, & Hiss, 2018).

The practical experience of test-optional schools is fully consistent with the academic research. Having made submission of standardized exam scores optional back in 1969, Bowdoin College has a wealth of experience in admitting highly selective classes. Bowdoin's research shows that, since the test-optional policy was initiated, the academic performance of students who do not submit SAT or ACT results has been comparable to the performance of those students who do submit scores.

In a multiyear study of its test-optional policy, Bates College "found no differences in academic performance or graduation rates between submitters and non-submitters" (20-year Bates college study, 2005). Other highly selective schools report similar findings.

Peter Van Buskirk (2010), Dean of Admissions at Franklin & Marshall College when his school began eliminating its admissions testing requirements, noted another advantage: "The day my former institution went test optional in the admission process was a day of liberation for my colleagues and me. Free from the 'tyranny of numbers,' we were able to admit the students who were most interesting to us."

Of course, these highly selective schools, which receive multiple applications for each spot, must cull their applicant pools. However, most colleges and universities do not need to sort and rank their applicants. According to the Pew Research Center more than half of bachelor's degree–granting institutions admit two-thirds or more of their applicants (DeSilver, 2019).

Deemphasizing Tests Helps Colleges and Universities Diversify Their Student Bodies

At Bates College the test-optional policy resulted in a more diverse student body, with applications and enrollment by minority students more than doubling in the first five years (Hiss, 1990, p. 18). Members of minority groups make strong use of the policy, electing to withhold their ACT and SAT scores at a higher rate than the total applicant pool. Wheaton College in Massachusetts has attracted more minority students since its optional policy went into effect in 1992. When the Texas Higher Education

Coordinating Board (1997) studied ways to promote diversity at the state's public universities, it concluded that "the use of standardized tests unduly limits admissions [and] . . . has had a chilling effect on the motivations and aspirations of underserved populations" (p. 12).

Research by the authors of *Crossing the Finish Line* reached a similar conclusion: "Overly heavy reliance on SAT/ACT scores in admitting students can have adverse effects on the diversity of the student bodies enrolled by universities" (Bowen et al., 2009, p. 226).

Going Test-Optional Helps Students

As more schools eliminate admissions testing requirements or deemphasize the role of the ACT and SAT, applicants will know that they will be evaluated based more on their performance in the classroom. This should encourage greater attention to academics. Removing test scores from the equation will offer particular benefits to low-income, minority, first-generation, rural, female, and older students or, more generally, to students whose performance on tests does not provide a meaningful measure of their academic abilities.

Reducing the role of one-shot tests will result in test coaching having less influence over the admissions process. Commercial test-prep courses cost $1,000 or more and private tutors charge up to $1,500 per hour (Green Test Prep, n.d.) . Some "guarantee" a student's composite SAT score will increase by more than 200 points (Prep Expert, n.d.) and ACT composites by six points or more (Excel Test Prep, n.d.). Yet admissions officers have no way to determine which applicants have taken such courses. Thus they cannot know whose scores were boosted by test-prep "steroids" and whose were not.

As more schools move away from the SAT and ACT, students will feel less pressure to take these expensive and time-consuming courses. William Hiss (1990), the former admissions director at Bates College, noted, "We think coaching distracts a student at precisely the critical moment when young people need to build up confidence and personal steam for critical thinking, effective writing, and developing strong analytical skills" (p. 15). He added that Bates went optional in part as an "attempt to say to these young people, use your time and your energy to create real forward motion in your life" (p. 15).

Students with lower test scores, even with otherwise strong academic records, are often discouraged from applying to colleges with SAT/ACT requirements and higher average test scores for the student body. Many schools report that changing their test score requirements brought in new applicants, some with lower test scores, who have done well after being admitted, but who would likely not have applied had test score requirements been in place.

Test-optional policies also give students greater say in the admissions process. After dropping its test submission requirement, Muhlenberg College included this statement in its "Questions and Answers About Muhlenberg's ACT/SAT Policy:"

"Our hope is that the decision to move to a test-optional admissions policy will give some of the power back to students in the college admissions process. This decision gives students a larger say in how to present themselves, what constitutes their strongest portfolio of credentials, etc. On a number of levels, we hope that this new policy will reinforce the kind of active, thoughtful, engaged, intellectual participation we expect from our students once they are members of the college community" (Muhlenberg College, n.d.).

Societal Benefits of Test-Optional Admissions Policies

A shift away from test-based admissions promotes more widespread access to selective colleges and universities. Students from families with greater household incomes typically post higher scores than those from families with lower incomes. There are still huge gaps in test results between Whites, Asian Americans, and members of historically disenfranchised minority groups, particularly African Americans, Hispanics, and Native Americans (see Tables 5.1 and 5.2).

Heavy reliance on test scores in the admissions process assures that students who have had the greatest opportunities in life are further advantaged in terms of access to higher education. Moving away from policies that rely heavily on SAT or ACT scores opens the doors to academically qualified students whose test scores say more about their family backgrounds than about their capacity to perform well in college.

At the same time, deemphasizing college entrance tests would benefit K–12 public education. Many admissions officers fear that a heavy focus on the ACT and SAT leads many students to invest a great deal of their time and energy on standardized exam scores rather than high school work. It also leads to high schools feeling pressure to devote precious resources to test preparation rather than more meaningful learning. Bill Mason, then Admissions Director at Bowdoin College, claimed, "The natural outgrowth of a system . . . which relies solely on SAT scores" is high schools designing their courses "to accommodate multiple-choice exams." He added: "The message we should be sending to high schools is that admissions offices at selective colleges are capable of making informed decisions without relying heavily or at all on the Educational Testing Service, not that we want them to design their courses to what can be tested by multiple-choice exams. By and large, that isn't the way we evaluate our students. Why should we require that high school students be evaluated in that fashion?" (W. R. Mason, personal communication, August 5, 1987).

ACT and SAT scores are now used for everything from selecting scholarship winners to promoting real estate. The quality of high schools, colleges, and even state education systems are often judged based on test score averages. Yet experts—and the test makers themselves—have long dismissed such comparisons as invalid because of the varying proportion of students taking the test and the differences within student populations. For instance, an increase in the number of students for whom English is a second language taking college entrance tests can alter a high school's average score without revealing anything about the quality of its education. By moving away from reliance on the ACT and SAT, colleges and universities would send a strong message that "test scores do not equal merit."

WHY SOME COLLEGES STILL USE ACT AND SAT SCORES

Over the past 15 years, more than 235 colleges and universities have eliminated their testing requirements. Still, a majority of undergraduate institutions do require most recent high school graduates to submit either ACT or SAT scores. Given all the problems with the exams and the many advantages of test-optional admissions policies, why do these schools still require applicants to submit standardized exam results? Admissions professionals offer three primary explanations.

Marketing

Many colleges fear that dropping their ACT/SAT requirements might signal potential applicants and other important stakeholders that they are lowering academic standards. College rankings, particularly those from *U.S. News & World Report* magazine, which include average test scores in their calculations, help reinforce this concern.

This belief is profoundly mistaken. In fact, the *U.S. News* ranking formula weights ACT or SAT averages for less than 8% of each school's total score (Morse, Brooks, & Mason, 2019). Schools that have made submission of the tests optional have not, on average, suffered either a drop or an increase in their rankings, according to Robert Morse, the Chief Data Strategist for *U.S. News* (personal communication, n.d.). Moreover, the publication's rankings formula actually punishes schools that do not report test scores from at least 75% of their enrollees (Morse, 2016).

Currently, more than half of all *U.S. News*'s top tier of national liberal arts colleges have test-optional policies (FairTest/National Center for Fair & Open Testing, 2019). So do the first- and second-ranked regional universities in the North (Fairfield and Providence), first- and third-ranked in the Midwest (Creighton and Drake) the second- and fifth-ranked in the South (Rollins and Stetson) and the seventh- and eighth-ranked in the West

Table 5.1. 2018 SAT Scores for College-Bound Seniors by Race/Ethnicity

	Reading/Writing	Math	Total
All Test Takers	536	531	1068
American Indian or Alaskan Native	480	469	949
Asian, Asian American, or Pacific Islander	588	635	1223
Black or African American	483	463	946
Hispanic, Latinx, or Latin American	501	489	990
Two or More Races	558	543	1101
White	566	557	1123

Note: Data from www.fairtest.org/fairtest-reacts-2018-sat-scores

Table 5.2. 2018 ACT Scores for College-Bound Seniors by Race/Ethnicity

	Composite Score
All Test Takers	20.8
African American	16.9
American Indian	17.3
Asian	24.5
Hispanic/ Latinx	18.8
White	22.2
Female	20.9
Male	20.8

Note. Data from is The ACT Profile Report, National Graduating Class 2018 (Retrieved from www.act.org/condition2018)

(Mills and Whitworth). A rapidly growing number of highly regarded national universities, such as Chicago, Wake Forest, Brandeis, Worcester Polytechnic, and George Washington, also have test-optional policies (FairTest/National Center for Fair & Open Testing, 2020). Clearly, whatever stigma might have been attached to test-optional schools no longer exists.

Political Pressure

At public institutions, in particular, administrators are subject to decisions made by state and local governments for political purposes. Raising average test scores is an easy way to create the impression that a university is "raising academic standards" and a convenient mechanism to cut the size of entering classes. Over the years, public universities in New York City, Massachusetts, and elsewhere have responded to political pressure to reduce enrollment or improve the appearance of academic quality by boosting ACT and SAT score requirements to restrict access.

At the same time, however, other state university systems, including those in Texas and California, have long maintained diversity and academic excellence by creating admissions pathways that do not depend on test score. The Texas "Top 10%" rule, which has provided automatic entry for in-state students who graduate in the top tenth of their high school classes, having taken a college preparatory curriculum, is widely heralded for preserving diversity in the face of restrictions on affirmative action. To a lesser degree, the University of California's system of Eligibility in the Local Context, which has automatically qualified students in the top 9% of their high schools for state university seats, has had a similar effect.

In recent years, however, more state-funded campuses have eliminated ACT/SAT test requirements. Public institutions with test-optional policies now include Temple in Pennsylvania, Ball State in Indiana, George Mason in Virginia, Montclair State in New Jersey, and the University of Massachusetts at Boston, among others.

Cost

Colleges pay nothing to receive applicants' test scores. Students and their parents bear the entire financial and psychological burden. Test scores are easy to process and require little time on the part of admissions offices. They also come with a vast body of demographic data that can be used for honing recruiting and "yield management" programs. Evaluating a more sophisticated, comprehensive set of admissions criteria does entail more staff time and somewhat higher costs.

The successful records of the more than 1,000 test-optional colleges and universities undermines the purely economic argument. Yes, more time is needed to perform a "holistic" read of an applicant's file than to do a "triage" sort based on ACT/SAT scores. But the benefits from the additional investment are worth it to schools committed to maximizing equity and excellence. They recognize that trying to carry out admissions on the cheap has significant negative consequences in terms of diversity and academic quality.

MAKING THE CHANGE

Colleges and universities seeking to revamp their admissions processes by deemphasizing standardized tests can tap into a diverse set of experiences at public and private 4-year schools that have already taken these steps. Institutions that have gone test-optional have done so for a wide range of reasons and have chosen several different general approaches. No matter what the path, dropping the testing requirement helps promote the twin goals of equity and academic excellence.

Though each college or university must chart its own specific course when redesigning admissions requirements, there is a general process, with roughly similar steps, necessary to develop, implement, and market a test-optional admissions policy.

Conduct a Standardized Test Audit

Before considering how to modify standardized exam admissions requirements, a school must understand how it currently uses ACT and SAT results. There is often widespread misunderstanding about the role test scores play in the admissions process, even among faculty members, senior administrators, trustees, and other key stakeholders. Potential applicants, parents, guidance counselors, and others outside the school may also under- or overestimate how much decisions are driven by the ACT or SAT, often because written descriptions of requirements and policies are intentionally vague. Sometimes repeat calls to the same institution yield different answers about how the test is used in the admissions process. Websites may offer inconsistent information on different pages. At larger universities, individual programs may have different test score requirements, further complicating the picture.

For some schools, adoption of a test-optional admissions policy would have little impact on how selection decisions are actually made, though it might alter the applicant pool. At many others, however, such a shift would likely have an impact in areas ranging from the number and diversity of applicants to the resources needed for the admissions office, to the school's reputation among high school counselors. A school, which currently relies heavily on the ACT and SAT as an initial screen, would have to turn to other methods or, better, give all applications at least a basic, holistic reading. If a university now uses a test score–based admissions index but wants to replace it with a more individualized approach to selection, changes in staffing likely will be necessary.

Some colleges, universities, and university systems continue to use eligibility or admissions formulas with fixed ACT or SAT requirements. Most schools do not publicize these cutoffs because they violate guidelines for proper score use. However, many appear to act as if they have required de facto score minimums that must be met before an application is thoroughly evaluated.

On the other hand, many institutions waive test score submission requirements for applicants who have been out of school for several years, are transferring from other colleges, or have documented learning disabilities. Still others adjust scores for applicants from certain groups. Admissions officers at the Massachusetts Institute of Technology, for example, long used separate test score/grade point average indices to evaluate men and women (Johnson, 1993).

Admissions office practices vary significantly. In some cases, tests are used as an initial screening device but are not scrutinized thereafter. Alternatively, test scores sometimes serve as "tiebreakers," evaluated only when two or more candidates are closely matched in other ways. Test scores might be weighted so that they have more significance than grades and curriculum rigor or given less weight than high school performance.

Finally, and of increasing importance in the admissions process, some schools use standardized test results to make decisions about "merit" scholarship awards and course placement. Because of historic score gaps between demographic groups (see Tables 5.1 and 5.2), such requirements skew tuition aid toward individuals from historically advantaged populations who may not need so much financial assistance to afford higher education.

Any tuition award program that relies exclusively on ACT or SAT scores, with cutoffs, should be restructured since the tests are not meant for such precise use. A minimum score requirement for any financial aid program violates guidelines for proper test use such as the College Board's injunction to "Ensure that small differences in test scores are not the basis for rejecting an otherwise qualified applicant." (See research.collegeboard.org/pdf/guidelines-uses-college-board-test-scores-and-data.pdf) At the same the use of such cut-off scores undermines equity.

Determine Whether Predicting First-Year GPA is a Sufficient Criterion

The College Board and ACT have long justified their products based on their capacity to predict first-year undergraduate grades, a task somewhat better performed by high school grades. With the increased focus on retention and graduation, schools should ask whether first-year grades are truly meaningful outcome criteria.

William Sedlacek (1998), professor emeritus and former testing center director at the University of Maryland–College Park, has identified some of the limitations of relying on first-year grades as the primary criterion for assessing the value of admissions test scores:

> Most scholars who research human abilities agree that the attributes first-year college students need to succeed differ from those they subsequently need. Typically, the first year of any curriculum is more didactic. Students learn facts and basic concepts in different disciplines. In later years, students are required to be more creative and to synthesize and reorganize their thoughts. Many students who do not do well in the first year often shine in the majors and in their later years of studies. (pp. 5–6)

Sedlacek (1998) adds that "standardized tests do not measure motivation, study habits, personal or professional goals, and other factors that can affect academic performance and persistence to graduation" (p. 6). He has long been a leading advocate for incorporating noncognitive factors into the admissions process, noting that "student attitudes and expectations at matriculation are related to graduation five and six years later" (Tracey & Sedlacek, 1986, p. 12).

Research on predictors of undergraduate education sponsored by the Mellon Foundation and published in *Crossing the Finish Line: Completing College at America's Public Universities* found, "High school grades are a far better predictor of both four-year and six-year graduation rates than are SAT/ACT test scores—a central finding that holds within each of the six sets of public universities that we study" (Bowen et al., 2009, p. 113). According to this analysis, applicants' high school GPAs are between three and ten times more powerful a predictor of college graduation than their standardized test scores. The authors conclude, "In short, this analysis reinforces the point that high school grades measure a student's ability to 'get it done' in a more powerful way than do SAT scores—a conclusion that holds, we wish to emphasize, regardless of the high school attended" (Bowen et al., 2009, p. 123).

Look at Diversity and Outreach Issues

A nuanced understanding of how a college is using standardized admissions tests, how well those exams predict performance at the institution, and whether there are alternatives that predict as well or better is, unquestionably, critical. So is engaging in a broader debate about a school's mission, its admissions goals, and how to achieve them.

At some institutions that adopted test-optional admissions, the evaluation of ACT/SAT requirements was embedded in a broader debate about how to make the school more diverse while preserving rigorous academic standards. Elsewhere, as in the case of the University of Texas, the reworking of admissions requirements came in response to court-ordered bans on affirmative action and concerns about keeping campuses accessible to a range of applicants.

Even the best college GPA and graduation prediction equations cannot reveal whether otherwise-qualified students were being deterred from applying by test score requirements. In Texas, higher education officials were deeply concerned with making sure that students from underrepresented groups still felt welcome at the state's public universities after the *Hopwood v. Texas* (1996) case ruling. Many liberal arts colleges wanted to develop more equitable ways of evaluating applicants and, at the same time, signal their openness to students from a wide variety of backgrounds.

To evaluate the potential impact of test score requirements on these outreach and recruitment issues, schools need to know who is applying, who from the pool of potential applicants is not applying and why, and whether the current mix is consistent with the institution's mission and goals. Schools should examine the statistics from high schools, cities, regions, and states that are generating applicants. Are top students from low-income areas turned off from applying? Is a college developing new pools of applicants, especially from historically underrepresented groups?

Changing application and enrollment patterns requires modifications not just of outreach programs and admissions requirements but also of financial aid. Many institutions, including some which are test-optional for admissions, still have ACT or SAT score requirements for so-called "merit" scholarships (Leider, 2011) , a process that also can deter some students from matriculating.

Develop Admissions Alternatives

Schools have deemphasized standardized tests in a variety of ways. The two most common approaches: (1) making submission on ACT/SAT scores optional for all applicants and (2) exempting students with proven high school records of achievement (usually measured by grade point average or class rank) from submitting test score results. Each of these policies has numerous variants and might include requiring applicants who choose the test-optional route to submit a graded research paper or other evidence of academic accomplishment such as a science project.

As the test-optional movement grows and matures, additional alternatives have been developed and implemented. For example, Hampshire College calls itself "test blind." The school's admissions office will not consider ACT and SAT results even if they are included in the application file. A few other institutions—including Hamilton College, Middlebury College, and New York University—are "test flexible." They allow applicants to choose to submit results from an array of standardized exams, such as Advanced Placement, International Baccalaureate, and SAT Subject Tests in lieu of ACT/SAT scores.

As part of its review of admissions testing requirements, each institution needs to determine which policy would best fit its mission, goals, and staffing capability. At most selective liberal arts colleges, admissions officials already review individual applicants and know far more about each student than just their test scores and grades. There the transition to test-optional admissions is not particularly difficult, as dozens of such schools have shown.

For larger universities, which might receive 10,000 or more applications each year, the shift could be more complicated. Additional trained file readers might be needed to assure each student's credentials are carefully reviewed. But the extra investment will pay off in an undergraduate body that is more diverse in every possible way without any sacrifice in academic quality.

Build Support for New Policies

Mechanisms for making decisions about instituting broad admissions policy reforms vary substantially from college to college. In some cases, faculty members will vote on whether to drop tests, while in others reforms may be initiated by the campus president (e.g., Drew University), admissions office staff, revisions in state law (e.g., University of Texas system) or policy changes at the trustee or regents level (e.g., California State University system).

Whatever the process, broad dissemination of information about the current admissions policy and prospective changes will enhance the level of discussion. A report by the admissions office, faculty task force, or commission should provide an overview of the issues connected with standardized testing. It could make note of all current uses of test scores, the impact of such policies on admissions decisions, the effects of test requirements on different groups (by income, ethnicity, gender, and region), predictive data for grades, retention and graduation by subgroup, and any available evidence about the role of test coaching.

Beyond the data, the report should also lay out the ethical issues connected with standardized admissions testing, including impact on high school curricula, psychological and financial costs to students, access to higher education, and societal notions about what constitutes "merit."

In every case, efforts should be made to include all key stakeholder groups. These include faculty, administration, admissions staff, students, alumni, and donors, all of whom benefit from understanding how and why deemphasizing admissions test scores enhances equity and excellence.

Publicize Admissions Reforms

Once new admissions testing criteria have been put into place, it is very important to publicize the details to potential applicants, college counselors, parents, and the wide range of print and Internet guides that list college admissions requirements. For example, FairTest's online lists of test-optional colleges (www.fairtest.org/university/optional) host more than 250,000 unique visitors per year.

Because of the many "flavors" of test-optional policies now in place, it is extremely important that the school's own website include highly visible links with clear language defining which students, if any, must submit test scores, and under which conditions. The same information needs to be incorporated into print materials distributed at college fairs and school presentations, and to campus visitors.

Institutions such as Bates College (20-year Bates College Study, 2005), Ithaca College (Mulugetta, 2013), and Mount Holyoke College (2005), which have conducted and then broadly disseminated the results of internal studies about the impact of test-optional admissions, provide an important service for the broader higher education community. By sharing their experiences, they help define a path that other institutions can follow.

CONCLUSION

The successful experience of so many test-optional schools of all sorts (Syverson et al., 2018) demonstrates that there is life after standardized exams. At the majority of institutions that do not rely heavily on test scores to make admissions decisions, the transition to a test-optional policy can take place smoothly. For admissions offices that already read every admissions file, SAT and ACT can also be dropped or deemphasized easily. Data from the transcript and other items in the application will provide richer information than test scores.

The potential gains for individual schools from deemphasizing the ACT and SAT, in terms of the diversity and quality of applicants, is very clear from the track records of schools that have already adopted such policies. Broader gains, particularly for academically qualified students from underrepresented groups, also accompany moves toward test-optional admissions.

The best admissions policies permit applicants to demonstrate their potential in a variety of ways. Eliminating test score requirements is a proven strategy for maximizing both excellence and equity.

NOTE

This chapter is adapted, revised, and updated from *Test Scores Do Not Equal Merit: Enhancing Equity & Excellence in College Admission by Deemphasizing SAT and ACT Results,* by Charles Rooney (with Bob Schaeffer). (1998). Cambridge, MA: National Center for Fair & Open Testing (FairTest).

REFERENCES

20-year Bates College study of optional SATs finds no differences. (2005, Ocotber 1). *Bates News*. Retrieved from www.bates.edu/news/2005/10/1/sat-study

ACT. (2018). *The condition of college and career readiness: National 2018*. Available at www.act.org/condition2018

Bowen, W. G., Chingos, M. M., & McPherson, M. S. (2009). *Crossing the finish line: Completing college at America's public universities*. Princeton, NJ: Princeton University Press.

Chingos, M. (2018, April). *What matters most for college completion*. Washington, DC: American Enterprise Institution.

Cole, N. (1997, September 19). Merit and opportunity: Testing and higher education at the vortex [Editorial]. *New York Times*, p. A25.

College Board. (2018, October 23). *More than numbers, context matters: A peek at College Board's Environmental Context Dashboard pilot* [Blog post]. In All Access: News for Members [Blog].

Crouse, J., & Trusheim, D. (1988). *The case against the SAT*. Chicago, IL: University of Chicago Press.

DeSilver, D. (2019, April 9). A majority of colleges admit most students who apply. In *Pew Research Center* [Website]. Retrieved from pewrsr.ch/2uDe6gn

Excel Test Prep. (n.d.). Score increase guarantees! Retrieved from www.exceltest.com/page/score-increase-guarantees

FairTest, National Center for Fair & Open Testing. (2019). Test score optional list: Schools that do not use SAT or ACT scores for admitting substantial numbers of students into bachelor's degree programs. Retrieved from www.fairtest.org/university/optional

FairTest, National Center for Fair & Open Testing. (2020). "Top tier" schools that deemphasize the ACT/SAT in admissions decisions per U.S. News & World Report *Best Colleges* guide (2019 edition). Retrieved from www.fairtest.org/sites/default/files/Optional-Schools-in-U.S.News-Top-Tiers.pdf

Fiske, E. B. (Ed.). (2018), *Fiske Guide to Colleges 2019*. Naperville, IL: Sourcebooks.

Green Test Prep. (n.d.). Meet the $1,500/hour tutor transforming the SAT & ACT prep industry: Anthony-James Green. Retrieved from greentestprep.com/about/

Hiss, W. C. (1990, September). Optional SATs: Six years later. *Bates: The Alumni Magazine,* pp. 15–19.

Hiss, W. C., & Franks, V. (2014). *Defining promise: Optional standardized testing policies in American college and university admissions*. Retrieved from www.nacacnet.org/globalassets/documents/defining-promise-poster--optional-standardized-testing-policies.pdf

Hopwood v. Texas, 78 F.3d 932, (5th Cir. 1996).

Johnson, E. S. (1993). College women's performance in a math–science curriculum: A case study. *College & University, 68*(2), 74–78.

Leider, A. J. (2011). *The A's & B's of academic scholarships: 100,000 scholarships for top students* (27th ed.). Alexandria, VA: Octameron Associates.

Morse, R., Brooks, E., & Mason, M. (2019, Sept. 8). How U.S. News calculated the 2020 best colleges rankings. Retrieved from www.usnews.com/education/best-colleges/articles/how-us-news-calculated-the-rankings

Mount Holyoke College. (2005). Early results from MHC study reaffirm SAT–optional policy. Retrieved from www.mtholyoke.edu/offices/comm/press/releases/satstudy.shtml

Morse, R. (2016, March 30). How U.S. News accounts for test-optional colleges in our rankings. [Blog post]. *U.S. News Education*. Retrieved from www.usnews.com/education/blogs/college-rankings-blog/articles/2016-03-30/how-us-news-accounts-for-test-optional-colleges-in-our-rankings

Muhlenberg College. (n.d.) Questions and answers about Muhlenberg's test–optional policy. Retrieved from www.fairtest.org/act-sat-optional-colleges-list-soars-280

Mulugetta, Y. (2013, November 9–12). *Going test–optional: Gathering evidence and making the decision at Ithaca College*. Retrieved from www.ithaca.edu/ir/docs/testoptionalpaper.pdf

Prep Expert. (n.d.). SAT prep courses. Retrieved from prepexpert.com/sat–prep–courses/

Rooney, C. (with Schaeffer, B.). (1998). *Test scores do not equal merit: Enhancing equity & excellence in college admission by deemphasizing SAT and ACT results*. Cambridge, MA: FairTest, National Center for Fair & Open Testing. Available at www.fairtest.org/test-scores-do-not-equal-merit-executive-summary

Sedlacek, W. E. (1998, Winter). Multiple choices for standardized tests. *AGB Priorities*, No. 10.

Syverson, S. T., Franks, V., & Hiss, W. C. (2018). *Defining access: How test-optional works*. Available on the website of the National Association for College Admissions Counseling (NACAC) at www.nacacnet.org/news--publications/Research/Defining-Access/

Texas Higher Education Coordinating Board (THECB), Advisory Committee on Criteria for Diversity. (1997, January 16). *Second status report*. Austin, TX: THECB.

Tracey, T. J., & Sedlacek, W. E. (1986). *Prediction of college graduation using noncognitive variables by race* (Research Report No. 2-86). College Park, MD: Counseling Center, University of Maryland.

U.S. News & World Report. (2019). *Best Colleges*. Washington, DC: Author.

Van Buskirk, P. (2010, September 8). Inside the "test-option" opportunity. [Blog post]. Retrieved from www.bestcollegefit.com/blog/archives/1009

CHAPTER 6

Non-Submitter Analysis

A Review of Students Who Did Not Submit Versus Those Who Did

Michael DeWitt and Philip Handwerk

In 2009 Wake Forest University became test-optional, meaning that during the undergraduate admissions process the requirement for submitting a standardized test score (ACT/ SAT) was made optional. Since that time, questions have arisen from both inside and outside the institution as to whether or not there are differences between those who applied with test scores and those who did not (Atkinson & Geiser, 2009; Sternberg, 2010; Zwick, 2017). In an attempt to answer those questions, and possibly provide insights to other universities exploring a move to testing optional admissions, this study investigated differences in the enrolled students' demographics, academic performance, and social interactions while enrolled at Wake Forest by whether or not the students submitted their standardized test scores when they applied.

METHODS

Data

The data used in this analysis were gathered from the applications and subsequent enrollments of Wake Forest University's fall 2010 through fall 2017 first-time, full-time undergraduate cohorts. There were 11,551 students in this study, of whom 29% (n = 3,379) did not submit standardized test scores (i.e., *non-submitters*).

Comparisons of Demographics and Admissions Data

Chi-square tests were performed on demographic and admission indicators for all students. If significant differences between submitters and non-submitters were observed, the effect size differences were indicated. In the case that there was a statistically significant difference between submitters and non-submitters, the effect size difference was shown. Cohen's *d* was used to measure effect size with effect size descriptions as per Cohen (1988) and Sawilowsky (2009).

Outcomes at Wake Forest

Bayesian regression with noninformative priors was used in order to test for the differences between non-submitters and submitters on certain academic and social metrics, seen in Equation 1. Equation 2 models the difference between these two groups on first-year attrition risk, likelihood of studying abroad, likelihood of registering to rush a fraternity or sorority, and likelihood of joining a fraternity or sorority. In each case the model was adjusted by potential confounding variables represented by *X* (socioeconomic status, gender, race, status as a scholarship athlete, and being from North Carolina). The variable of interest was τ, which represents the effect of being a non-submitter.

$$\text{youtcome} \sim N(X\beta + z_{sub\ status\tau}, \sigma) \qquad (1)$$

Where:

$y_{outcome}$ = the given academic or social metric.
$z_{sub\ status}$ = a binary variable of 1 if non-submitter, 0 otherwise

$$P(Y = 1) \sim \text{invlog}(N(X\beta + \text{zsub status}\tau, \sigma) \qquad (2)$$

Where:

$P(Y = 1)$ = probability of specified event occurring[1]
X = a vector of controls (socioeconomic status, gender, race, status as a scholarship athlete, and being from North Carolina)
$z_{sub\ status}$ = a binary variable of 1 if non-submitter, 0 otherwise

Effect size descriptions were added to the regression coefficients using those put forward by Kraft (2018) based on education research benchmarks that tend to reflect smaller criteria than the traditional descriptions in order to capture the noisy nature of educational outcome measures (e.g., a Cohen's *d* of 0.15 would be described as a medium effect size, while in the traditional definitions this would be described as a small effect size).[2] These effect size descriptions were used because this section of the analysis focused on educational outcomes rather than population statistics where the traditional effect size descriptions would be more salient.

Comparison of Cumulative GPA

In this section the cumulative GPA by term for students was examined for the fall and spring semesters. As we are measuring the same student repeatedly over time, a hierarchical linear model was utilized with group effects for the term within each student. This can be interpreted as having a random slope for the term effect for each student, and a random intercept for each student. This formulation, as shown in Equation 3, isolates the variable of interest to τ, which represents the effect of being a non-submitter versus a submitter. This methodology is common in clinical trials and captures the autocorrelation within a given student's results in order to discern the effect of being a non-submitter versus a submitter.[3] Additionally, a control was included to adjust for a student's scholarship athlete status. Student athletes are required to submit standardized test scores to the NCAA for eligibility purposes.[4] Given that 93% of athletes opted to submit test scores, this feature was added as a control.

$$y_{gpa} \sim N(\mu,\sigma)$$
$$\mu_i = \tau + \beta_0,i + \beta_{i,j} \sim \text{term number} + \beta_2 \sim \text{athlete} \quad (3)$$

Where:

i represents the ith student (i = 1, . . ., 11,551)
j represents the jth term (j = 1, . . ., 15)
τ represents the effect of being a non-submitter on GPA

Again, effect size descriptions were added to the regression coefficients using definitions specified by Kraft (2018).

RESULTS

Demographic Comparisons

In the below tables the results from chi-square tests are displayed for categorical, demographic response options. In each table a chi-square test was performed in order to test the hypothesis that the distribution between the non-submitters and submitters were equivalent (e.g., drawn from the same overall population).

First-Generation. A slightly greater percentage of non-submitters than submitters were first-generation college students (see Table 6.1). *First-generation status* was defined as a student whose parents'/guardians' highest level of education was high school (NCES, 1998, p. 100). If one parent or

Table 6.1. Comparison of First-Generation Status

Status	Submitter	Non-submitter
First-generation	7% (561)	12% (420)
Not first-generation	93% (7645)	88% (2960)

guardian had a level of education higher than high school, the student was not considered first- generation. There was evidence of a statistically significant difference between submitters and non-submitters at the 0.05 level and very small (0.18+/-0.02) effect size.

Gender. More non-submitters than submitters indicated being female, when given a choice of binary gender classifications (see Table 6.2). There was evidence of a statistically significant difference between submitters and non-submitters at the 0.05 level and small (0.25+/-0.02) effect size.

Race. Two-thirds of non-submitters reported being White compared to three-quarters of the submitters (see Table 6.3). The U.S. Department of Education's Integrated Postsecondary Education Data System (IPEDS) classification rules are used for the assignment of race (e.g., if a student selected "White" and "Hispanic" they were classified as "Hispanic" or if a student indicated more than one race and did not select Hispanic, they were classified as "Two or More Races"). There was evidence of a statistically significant difference between submitters and non-submitters at the 0.05 level and small (0.25+/-0.02) effect size.

Legacy. There were no differences between non-submitters and submitters by whether or not the student was a legacy (see Table 6.4). Legacy status indicated that an immediate family member attended Wake Forest University (parent, sibling, grandparent, aunt, and/or uncle).

Socioeconomic Status. Non-submitters were slightly more likely to come from lower socioeconomic status homes than submitters (see Table 6.5). Socioeconomic status was defined as low-income if the student received a Pell Grant, medium- income if the student did not receive a Pell Grant but had need based on their Free Application for Federal Student Aid application (FAFSA), and high-income if the student did not demonstrate financial need or did not submit a FAFSA. There was evidence of a statistically significant difference between submitters and non-submitters at the 0.05 level and very small (0.17+/-0.02) effect size.

Admission Type Group. Non-submitters were more likely to apply for early admission than submitters (see Table 6.6). This pattern was observed

Table 6.2. Comparison of Gender

Gender	Submitter	Non-submitter
Female	49% (3997)	62% (2096)
Male	51% (4199)	38% (1277)

Table 6.3. Comparison of Race/Ethnicity

Race/Ethnicity	Submitter	Non-submitter
American Indian / Alaska Native	0% (14)	0% (2)
Asian	10% (841)	10% (321)
Black or African American	5% (431)	9% (312)
Hispanic / Latinx	6% (464)	11% (359)
Native Hawaiian / Pacific Islander	0% (4)	0% (0)
Race and Ethnicity Unknown	0% (7)	0% (5)
Two or More Races	3% (234)	3% (118)
White	76% (6201)	67% (2256)

Table 6.4. Comparison of Legacy Status

Status	Submitter	Non-submitter
Legacy	7% (535)	7% (237)
Not legacy	93% (7678)	93% (3147)

Table 6.5. Comparison of Socioeconomic Status

SES	Submitter	Non-submitter
Low-income	8% (670)	14% (460)
Medium-income	28% (2298)	28% (956)
High-income	64% (5231)	58% (1960)

before and after the FAFSA methodology changed for the 2017–2018 application process to allow applicants to use 2 years of tax returns when preparing the FAFSA application. There was evidence of a statistically significant difference between submitters and non-submitters at the 0.05 level and small (0.24+/-0.02) effect size.

High School Type. Although there was evidence of a statistically significant difference between submitters and non-submitters with regard to type of high school attended (see Table 6.7), the effect size was negligible (0.08+/-0.02).

Table 6.6. Comparison of Admission Type

Admission Type	Submitter	Non-submitter
Early	34% (2702)	46% (1515)
Internationl	7% (561)	7% (242)
Regular	59% (4751)	47% (1556)

Table 6.7. Comparison of High School Type

HS Type	Submitter	Non-submitter
Private	38% (2597)	42% (1151)
Public	62% (4271)	58% (1573)

Table 6.8. Comparison of Geographic Origin

Region	Submitter	Non-submitter
International	8% (620)	9% (299)
Midwest	7% (611)	5% (165)
Northeast	28% (2285)	25% (838)
South	51% (4161)	56% (1908)
West	7% (536)	5% (174)

Geographic Regions. Non-submitters were a little more likely than submitters to come from the South (see Table 6.8). Geographic regions are defined by the U.S. Census Bureau (2013). Additionally, international students are included for comparison. There was evidence of a statistically significant difference between submitters and non-submitters at the 0.05 level and very small (0.14+/-0.02) effect size.

Comparisons by Admissions Variables

Interviewed. More non-submitters than submitters interviewed as part of their application process (see Table 6.9). These interviews could have occurred on-campus or via Skype. There was evidence of a statistically significant difference between submitters and non-submitters at the 0.05 level and small (0.21+/-0.02) effect size.

AP/IB Credits. Submitters, on average, entered Wake Forest with more credits than non-submitters earned via Advanced Placement (AP) or International Baccalaureate (IB) programs (see Table 6.10). For students who take AP classes and/or participate in IB programs during high school, Wake

Table 6.9. Comparison of Interview Status

Status	Submitter	Non-submitter
Did not interview	37% (3040)	26% (878)
Interviewed	63% (5173)	74% (2506)

Table 6.10. Comparison of Average Wake Forest Credits Awarded from AP/IB Scores

Metric	Submitter	Non-submitter	Effect Size
Avg AP/ IB Credits Earned	9.3 (n = 8213; Std = 9.6)	4.5 (n = 3384; Std = 6.1)	Small

Table 6.11. Comparison of Pre-orientation Attendance

Pre-orientation	Submitter	Non-submitter
Attended	25% (1101)	27% (552)
Did not attend	75% (3333)	73% (1494)

Forest course credit may be awarded by the Office of the University Registrar based on the scores a student received in these programs (see newstudents.wfu.edu/academics/academic-success/planning-for-registration/).

Pre-orientation. There was no evidence of a difference between submitters and non-submitters in pre-orientation program participation (see Table 6.11). Pre-orientation programming allows students to engage in campus activities with incoming students prior to enrollment (e.g., a wilderness exploration trip, community service projects). Important to note is that each program has a participation fee (newstudents.wfu.edu/gettingstarted/pre-orientation-programs/). In some cases (e.g., Magnolia Scholars) this fee was waived. These data are only available from the entering cohort for the fall of 2013 forward.

Outcomes at Wake Forest

Wake Forest outcomes such as grades, retention, and graduation rates by whether or not standardized test scores were submitted are presented below. Please note that the 95% highest density intervals (HDI) are shown for each estimate because Bayesian regression was performed. HDIs are the Bayesian version of frequentist confidence intervals (CI), where the interpretation for an HDI is that there is a 95% probability that the true value lies between the upper and lower HDI, given the observed data (e.g., there is a 95% probability that the true difference for Hours Attempted between a non-submitter and a submitter's first fall term is between -0.18 and -0.09 given the observed data).[5]

First Year Outcomes. Non-submitters, when compared to submitters, attempted and earned fewer first semester hours resulting in lower first-year GPAs. They were more likely in their first year to pursue Greek life as well as seek academic and writing assistance. Table 6.12 reflects the differences between those students who did not submit test scores and those who did. Positive values indicate that a non-submitter, on average, scored higher on the given metric (e.g., non-submitters, on average, visited the Office of Academic Advising 0.22 more times in their first fall at Wake Forest than submitters) while negative values indicate that a non-submitter, on average, scored lower on a given metric (e.g., non-submitters, on average, had a GPA that was 0.13 points lower than submitters during their first fall).

First Year Retention Rate. Although there was a statistically significant difference between submitters and non-submitters, the effect size difference in first-year retention rates between the two groups was negligible (0.05+/-0.02) (see Table 6.13). First-year retention rate was defined as a student returning for their second fall at Wake Forest.

Longitudinal GPA. Longitudinal GPA analysis below shows that on average for all students GPA increased 0.01 points for each term (term number). Non-submitters typically had an average, cumulative GPA that was 0.12 points lower than submitters (non-submitter effect; 95% confidence interval 0.14–0.10) (see Table 6.14).

Majors Awarded. While the top 10 majors awarded were the same between those who submitted and those who did not (see Table 6.15), there was a small effect size difference (0.21+/-0.02) in the distribution of the majors between the two groups. Please note that students at Wake Forest can be awarded up to two majors, so some students may have appeared twice in these counts.

Graduation Rates. There was no difference in 4-year or 6-year graduation rates between those students who submitted their test scores and those who did not (see Tables 6.16 and 6.17). Four- and six-year graduation rates were calculated for students using the definitions provided by the IPEDS for normal time to completion (NCES, 2018).

Graduate Education. A comparison of graduate degrees awarded for 2010–2014 entering cohorts, utilizing data from the National Student Clearinghouse, found there were no differences in the earning of graduate degrees between those students who submitted their test scores and those who did not (see Table 6.18).

Table 6.12. Impact of Being a Non-Submitter (Regression Estimates)

Metric	Estimate	Lower HDI (5%)	Upper HDI (95%)	Effect Size (Cohen's d)	Effect Size Description
Likelihood of studying abroad*	0.06	-0.04	0.17	0.03	
Hours attempted first fall	-0.13	-0.18	-0.09	-0.10	Medium
Hours attempted first spring	-0.06	-0.11	0.00	-0.04	
Hours earned first fall	-0.27	-0.33	-0.21	-0.17	Medium
Hours earned first spring	-0.17	-0.25	-0.10	-0.09	Medium
GPA first fall	-0.13	-0.15	-0.11	-0.27	Large
GPA first spring	-0.12	-0.14	-0.10	-0.23	Large
Likelihood of joining Greek System*‡	0.18	0.10	0.25	0.10	Medium
Likelihood of rushing Greek system*†‡	0.20	0.06	0.35	0.11	Medium
Intramural games played first fall	-0.09	-0.22	0.04	-0.03	
Intramural games played first spring	-0.04	-0.14	0.06	-0.02	
Intramural teams first fall	-0.02	-0.05	0.02	-0.02	
Intramural teams first spring	-0.05	-0.08	-0.01	-0.05	Medium
Office of Academic Advising visits first fall	0.22	0.15	0.28	0.16	Medium
Office of Academic Advising visits first spring	0.28	0.21	0.36	0.18	Medium
First year attrition risk	-0.14	-0.33	0.05	-0.08	
Writing Center visits first fall	0.19	0.14	0.24	0.14	Medium
Writing Center visits first spring	0.27	0.21	0.33	0.18	Medium

* Estimates and intervals based on log odds

† Considers only 2015–2017 entering cohorts

‡ Students cannot rush/join the Greek system until the spring of their first year

Table 6.13. Comparison of First-Year Retention

First Year Retention	Submitter	Non-submitter
Did Not Leave WFU	94% (6718)	95% (2892)
Left WFU	6% (414)	5% (138)

Table 6.14. Cumulative GPA Regression Estimates (Fixed Effects)

Metric	Estimate	Lower CI (5%)	Upper CI (95%)	Effect Size Description
Constant	3.31	3.30	3.32	Large
Term Number	0.01	0.01	0.01	Large
Non-submitter Effect	-0.12	-0.14	-0.10	Large
Athlete Status	-0.34	-0.37	-0.30	Large

Table 6.15. Comparison of Majors Awarded

Major	Submitter	Non-submitter
Economics	9% (440)	7% (128)
Finance	9% (413)	6% (110)
Biology	8% (378)	6% (106)
Psychology	8% (364)	9% (164)
Communication	8% (349)	11% (199)
Business and enterprise management	7% (345)	7% (134)
Politics & international affairs	7% (305)	8% (149)
Health & exercise science	5% (213)	7% (120)
English	4% (165)	4% (79)
History	3% (146)	3% (63)
Other	33% (1529)	31% (572)

Table 6.16. Comparison of 4-Year Graduation Rates for 2010–2014 Entering Cohorts

Status	Submitter	Non-submitter
Graduated	84% (2986)	85% (1226)
Did not graduate	16% (560)	15% (209)

Table 6.17. Comparison of 6-Year Graduation Rates for 2010–2012 Entering Cohorts

Status	Submitter	Non-submitter
Graduated	88% (1607)	89% (573)
Did not graduate	12% (211)	11% (74)

Table 6.18. Comparison of Postgraduate Degrees Awarded for 2010–2014 Entering Cohorts

Status	Submitter	Non-submitter
Awarded Graduate Degree	7% (232)	5% (76)
No Graduate Degree	93% (3314)	95% (1359)

CONCLUSION

Examination of Wake Forest University's fall 2010 through 2017 first-time, full-time, undergraduate cohorts found students who did not submit their test scores during the application process, when compared to those who submitted test scores, to be more diverse while progressing through the institution with similar results. Those students who did not submit their test scores were more likely to be female, non-White, applying for early admission, and having fewer AP/IB course credits awarded. While at Wake Forest, when controlling for other characteristics, non-submitters visited the Office of Academic Advising and the Writing Center more often, attempted, then earned, fewer credit hours during their first year, and had slightly lower GPAs (about 0.1 on a 4.0 scale). However, no meaningful differences between non-submitters and submitters were found in first-year retention rates, graduation rates, selection of most popular majors, or graduate degree attainment.

These findings encourage universities exploring a move to testing-optional admissions to consider what changes might be seen on their campus given Wake Forest's experiences. Depending upon existing demographics, an institution could experience changes in student diversity (e.g., racial, gender, and/or socioeconomic status) and academic preparedness. Institutions should contemplate how these shifts may impact the campus and its resource allocations. For example, a similar increase in utilization of academic support services (e.g., Office of Academic Advising and Writing Centers) by non-submitters might require an institution to adjust staffing in order to serve these students.

NOTES

1. In the case of attrition risk, this represented the probability that the student will not be retained after their second year. For the case of participation in the Greek system and studying abroad this represented the probability that a student will participate. In each case the equation is the same.

2. Additionally, the Cohen's d was calculated using the methodology proposed by Sánchez-Meca, Marín-Martínez, and Chacón-Moscoso (2003) where the log odds ratio was converted to Cohen's d for those binomial outcomes (e.g., first-year retention where a value of 1 indicates that the student left and a value of 0 indicates

that the student returned after their first year).

3. See Albert (1999) and Liu, Rovine, & Molenaar (2012) for additional details about this type of modeling approach.

4. The NCAA Clearinghouse requires that all athletes take the SAT or ACT. These scores are then compared with several other metrics (e.g., high school GPA and certain courses) to determine eligibility to participate in NCAA sanctioned sports. See www.ncaa.org/student-athletes/play-division-i-sports for details. As a result, scholarship athletes are not truly test-optional.

5. The key philosophy of Bayesian statistics is that a given parameter of interest, θ, is drawn from a probability distribution and is thus a random variable. Therefore, we can make probabilistic inferences about the true value of θ using the language of probability (e.g., there is a 95% probability that the true value is between 20 and 30). Frequentist methods and associated confidence intervals posit that there is a *fixed* and unknown parameter of interest, θ. As this parameter is fixed, any one particular trial or experiment either captures the true value or does not. Because of this, frequentist methods of inference rely on long-run results (e.g., if one were to repeat this experiment many times, 95% of the associated confidences intervals would contain the true value). See van de Schoot et al. (2013) for more details on Bayesian inference.

REFERENCES

Albert, P. S. (1999). Longitudinal data analysis (repeated measures) in clinical trials. *Statistics in Medicine, 18*(13), 1707–1732. doi.org/10.1002/(SICI)1097-0258(19990715)18:13<1707::AID-SIM138>3.0.CO;2-H

Atkinson, R. C., & Geiser, S. (2009). Reflections on a century of college admissions tests. *Educational Researcher, 38*(9), 665–676. doi.org/10.3102/0013189X09351981

Cohen, J. (1988). *Statistical power analysis for the behavioral sciences* (2nd ed.). Hillsdale, NJ: Lawrence Erlbaum.

Kraft, M. (2018, December). *Interpreting effect sizes of education intervention* (Working paper). Brown University, Providence, RI. Retrieved from scholar.harvard.edu/files/mkraft/files/kraft_2018_interpreting_effect_sizes.pdf

Liu, S., Rovine, M. J., & Molenaar, P. C. M. (2012). Selecting a linear mixed model for longitudinal data: Repeated measures analysis of variance, covariance pattern model, and growth curve approaches. *Psychological Methods, 17*(1), 15–30. doi.org/10.1037/a0026971

National Center for Education Statistics (NCES). (1998). *First-generation students: Undergraduates whose parents never enrolled in postsecondary education* (NCES 98-082). Retrieved from nces.ed.gov/pubsearch/pubsinfo.asp?pubid=98082

National Center for Education Statistics (NCES). (2018). *IPEDS Survey Materials: Instructions.* Retrieved from surveys.nces.ed.gov/ipeds/VisInstructions.aspx?survey=2&id=30084

Sánchez-Meca, J., Marín-Martínez, F., & Chacón-Moscoso, S. (2003). Effect-size indices for dichotomized outcomes in meta-analysis. *Psychological Methods, 8*(4), 448–467. doi.org/10.1037/1082-989X.8.4.448

Sawilowsky, S. S. (2009). New effect size rules of thumb. *Journal of Modern Applied Statistical Methods, 8*(2), 597–599. doi.org/10.22237/jmasm/1257035100

Sternberg, R. J. (2010). *College Admissions for the 21st Century*. Cambridge, MA: Harvard University Press.

U.S. Census Bureau. (2013). *Census regions and divisions of the United States*. Retrieved from www2.census.gov/geo/pdfs/maps-data/maps/reference/us_regdiv.pdf

Van de Schoot, R., Kaplan, D., Denissen, J., Asendorpf, J. B., Neyer, F. J., & van Aken, M.A.G. (2013). A gentle introduction to Bayesian analysis: Applications to developmental research. *Child Development, 85*(3), 842–860. doi.org/10.1111/cdev.12169

Zwick, R. (2017). *Who gets in? Strategies for fair and effective college admissions*. Cambridge, MA: Harvard University Press.

CHAPTER 7

Defining Access

How Test-Optional Works

Steven T. Syverson, Valerie W. Franks, and William C. Hiss

> This Commission wishes to emphasize at the outset that a "one-size-fits-all" approach for the use of standardized tests in undergraduate admission does not reflect the realities facing our nation's many and varied colleges and universities. These institutions differ greatly in size, selectivity and mission. At some, standardized tests are important predictors of students' academic success, while at others, they add little compared to high school grades. (*Report of the Commission on the Use of Standardized Tests in Undergraduate Admission,* National Association for College Admission Counseling [NACAC],2008)

The number of colleges using test-optional policies (TOPs) in higher education admissions has dramatically expanded in recent years. And these colleges have avoided one-size-fits-all policies, finding varied ways to administer TOPs and experiencing varied outcomes. Much of the momentum around test-optional admission is focused on whether the use of standardized tests (specifically SAT and ACT) unnecessarily truncates the admission of otherwise well-qualified students. In particular, there is concern about whether widespread reliance on the use of these tests in the admission process tends to replicate the status quo in social class and opportunity in our American society.

In this study we collected student record–level data from 28 institutions that illustrate the variety among institutions that have adopted a TOP. They ranged in undergraduate enrollments from 1,500 to 20,000 and from15%–90% in admission selectivity, and included long-time users of TOP as well as recent adopters of the policy. In most instances we received four cohorts of student data, in total representing a data set of 955,774 individual applicant records. We focused on interpreting the data using practical significance rather than experimental statistical techniques.

A TOP was described by many of the admission deans of the participating institutions as a tool they employed in the hope of increasing applications from a more diverse range of students, so this report focuses great attention on traditionally underrepresented populations in American higher education. To do so, we used our record-level data to identify the intersectionality of the following underserved populations: first-generation-to-college, students from lower SES backgrounds (Pell recipients as proxy), and students from racial and ethnic groups that have traditionally been underrepresented in college populations (i.e., underrepresented minorities [URM]). We identified students associated with *any* of these three groups and designated them as a single category of "expanded diversity," and when possible, used it in our explorations.

The experiences of institutions in this study provide evidence that the adoption of a well-executed test-optional admissions policy can lead to an increase in overall applications as well as an increase in the representation of URM students (both numeric and proportionate) in the applicant pool and the freshman class. Roughly two-thirds of our TOP institutions experienced URM growth above that of a matched test-requiring peer institution. A similar but smaller magnitude increase was seen among Pell recipients.

Approximately one quarter of the students in this study did not submit standardized test scores with their college application (the *non-submitters*). As noted in earlier studies (Hiss & Franks, 2015), URM, first-generation-to-college, and Pell recipients were more strongly represented among non-submitters. For instance, 35% of Black or African American students chose to be non-submitters (12 percentage points higher than the overall non-submitting rate), as compared to 18% of White students. Similarly, women chose to be non-submitters at higher rates than men.

We also found that non-submitters were often admitted at lower rates than students who did submit standardized test scores (the *submitters*), but, on average, enrolled at substantially higher rates. Their HSGPAs were modestly lower than the submitters, and, upon entering college, their first-year GPAs (FYGPAs) and cumulative GPAs (CumGPAs) were comparably lower. However, they ultimately graduated at rates equivalent to, or marginally higher than, submitters—the ultimate proof of success.

Furthermore, our data indicated that high school GPA had a stronger correlation with college success for non-submitters than the ACT/SAT (for the 27% of non-submitters for whom we had test scores)—both in terms of college cumulative GPA and graduation rate. While test scores had a generally stronger relationship with college GPAs for the submitters, they tended to show a weaker relationship for the non-submitters, essentially underpredicting the college GPA. The test scores continued to most strongly correlate with family income.

A financial analysis, though inconclusive, suggested that some degree of financial investment was required to support the success of a TOP policy. While the proportion of students with need did not necessarily increase after policy adoption, the average demonstrated need and gift aid per capita did.

Non-submitters were generally needier than submitters. They also, however, included a sizable proportion of no-need students (those not requesting financial aid or not qualifying for aid), only modestly lower than that of submitters. We noted that well over half of all no-need students were offered some gift aid, but no-need non-submitters were less likely than no-need submitters to receive gift awards, in spite of the fact that these two groups were shown to graduate at comparable rates.

We cannot lay claim to definitive conclusions about the workings of a test-optional admissions policy. However, our findings suggest that a TOP works well for many types of institutions. It appears to offer a less obstructed path to higher education for this population of students who feel that their scores do not match their ability. We do not argue that institutions should entirely eliminate consideration of the ACT and SAT for all their students; however, we do continue to question whether the added value of testing is large enough to justify the price—time spent, financial cost, and emotional drain—being paid by students due to societal preoccupation with these tests.

We find that there is plenty of room in American higher education for diversity of process, allowing test-optional admissions to contribute to that diversity. Some have asked, "Why ignore a piece of information if it is available?" And we agree. Indeed, when a student chooses to be a non-submitter, that, too, is a valuable piece of information.

OBSERVATIONS ON THE TEST-OPTIONAL MOVEMENT

A rapidly increasing number of colleges and universities have adopted test-optional admissions policies, or TOPs, that allow some or all of their applicants to refrain from submitting standardized test scores. The institutions that officially deemphasize standardized tests in admission now total more than 1,000, including over 100 more not-for-profit institutions[1] in the past 4 years (FairTest, 2019). From early adopter TOP institutions (Bowdoin in 1969 and Bates in 1984) to those recently adopting a TOP (Wesleyan University and Bryn Mawr, both in 2014, George Washington University in 2016, University of Chicago, Bucknell and Colby in 2018, and Colorado College, University of New Hampshire, University of Rochester and Rhode Island School of Design in 2019) some of the institutions choosing a TOP have national reputations for excellence. But TOP is not used just by highly selective private institutions—the FairTest list covers a range of public, regional private, not-for-profit, and also for-profit institutions. A wide variety of institutions have found TOPs to be workable, productive tools to support their enrollment planning. Echoing many of his professional colleagues, an admissions dean from a small private college commented, "We have drawn great pride from how well TOP works for first gen and diversity, and kids with special talents. For us, removing the testing was a big help in looking at everything else."

The momentum of the test-optional movement appears to be fed in part by several overlapping changes in how academic promise and outcomes are being evaluated. Collectively these changes are moving admission decisions away from heavy reliance on measures increasingly deemed to provide a narrow assessment of human potential. Many K–12 schools are moving toward proficiency and standards-based evaluations. Thousands of high schools have stopped providing class rank, as a false or misleading measure. Many colleges and universities are broadly moving to "holistic" admissions philosophies, using TOPs, and versions of "portfolio" admissions with new technologies like the Mastery Transcript that encourage students to provide evidence of individual talents and commitments. Collectively, these changes are decreasing the reliance on test scores and class rank to guide college admission decisions and guidebook rankings. Experiments are drawing on the findings of admissions reform groups like the Institute on Character and Admission, or several ongoing research projects: the Turning the Tide project at Harvard (Weissbourd & Thacker, 2016), the Character Skills Snapshot from the Enrollment Planning Consortium, or the Mastery Transcript Consortium.

As this policy has become more pervasive, researchers have investigated its relative success. A 2015 study out of the University of Georgia (Belasco, Rosinger, & Hearn, 2015) found that, at the aggregate level, selective liberal arts colleges that adopted a TOP (in comparison with those that continued to require SAT or ACT scores) had *not* increased their enrollment of URM students or Pell recipients. But in focusing on these high-level, averaged outcomes, that study may not have been able to discern impact at the institutional level.

There has also been a proliferation of research on standardized testing in admission focused on the predictive value of testing and its fairness relative to various subpopulations of students. (NACAC, 2016; Mulugetta, 2015). Much of the research affirming the value of the SAT and ACT has been conducted by the testing organizations (Kobrin, Camera & Milewski, 2002; Mattern, Shaw & Kobrin, 2010; McNeish, Radunzel, & Sanchez (2015). One such study, a synthesis of recent test score validity studies (Mattern & Patterson, 2014), states that the SAT provides incremental validity above and beyond HSGPA in the prediction of cumulative GPA, retention, and graduation. Their conclusion: The combination of HSGPA and testing will produce the most accurate predictions of college success. Another recent release, a just-published volume of essays, *Measuring Success: Testing, Grades, and the Future of College Admissions* (Buckley, Letukas, and Wildavsky, 2018) is principally a response by the College Board and ACT to the rapid growth of TOPs.

Challenges to the pervasive use of these tests, their actual value, and their negative impact on students have come in a number of books—*Crossing the*

Finish Line: Completing College at America's Public Universities (Bowen, Chingos, & McPherson, 2009); *SAT Wars: The Case for Test-Optional Admissions* (Soares, 2012)—the work and recommendations of the NACAC Commission on the Use of Standardized Testing in Undergraduate Admissions, the ongoing work of FairTest, a thoughtful documentary film released in early 2018 titled *The Test and the Art of Thinking* (Davis, 2018), and a variety of articles and smaller research projects.

In particular, the exhaustive research available in *Crossing the Finish Line* has been centrally important in this discussion. The authors, the late William Bowen and Michael McPherson, the former presidents of Princeton and Macalester, respectively, with their research colleague Matthew Chingos, addressed what characteristics predicted graduation at a group of large public universities. Their data was drawn from institutions that required standardized tests from all students; none of the universities they studied had adopted a "threshold" admissions policy, with automatic admission granted to students who meet cut-off requirements for HSGPA. In the chapter that examined the predictive value of test scores and high school grades, they reported the following results of their research:

> The findings are dramatic. . . . The coefficients for SAT/ACT scores are always less than 0.02, which means that an increase in test scores of one standard deviation is associated with an increase of less than 2 percentage points in six-year graduation rates; this relationship is even negative at the historically Black colleges and universities (HBCUs). . . . The consistency of the results is extraordinary: In all but one of these more than 50 public universities, high school GPA remains a highly significant predictor of six-year graduation rates after taking account of the effects of test scores. . . . Test scores, on the other hand, routinely fail to pass standard tests of statistical significance when included with high school GPA in regressions predicting graduation rates, especially when we leave the realm of the most highly selective public universities. . . . The remaining incremental predictive power of the SAT/ACT scores disappears entirely when we add controls for the high school attended, whereas the predictive value of the high school GPA increases. (Bowen, Chingos, & McPherson, 2009, p. 114)

In 2014 William Hiss and Valerie Franks —two of the three coauthors of this study—released *Defining Promise: Optional Standardized Testing Policies in American College and University Admission* (Hiss & Franks, 2014). It was the first large-scale, multi-institution assessment of the outcomes of optional testing and extended the research done earlier by Hiss and his coauthor Kate Doria in a 25-year look-back study on the outcomes of the policy at Bates College (Hiss & Doria, 2011).

The 2014 research revealed that—when given the option at one of those 33 TOP institutions —roughly a third of enrolled students chose to apply without standardized test scores (non-submitters). These non-submitters went on to graduate at virtually the same rates (a 0.6% difference) and with nearly the same college GPA (0.05 of a CumGPA point) as the submitters, whose test scores were considered in the admission process. Their research also concluded that non-submitters were more likely to be first-generation-to-college, underrepresented minority students, women, Pell Grant recipients, and students with learning differences. And, using large volumes of HSGPA data, their findings underscored the sturdiness of the HSGPA as a predictor of college performance.

This current study highlights an interesting intersection between the testing agencies and that of the counter views. In a recent book titled *Measuring Success* (Buckley et al., 2018) a meta-analysis of studies of "discrepant performance" revealed that "a quarter to a third of tested students exhibit some degree of mismatch between their grades and their test scores" (p. 118). Within this group, approximately half of them have high school grades that are higher than what the tests would predict. Across the studies cited, the range appears to be between 11% and 18% of the sample population.

Another related study by Sanchez and Edmunds (2015) identified the students most likely to have strong HSGPAs and low testing: women, first-generation to college, low-income students, and students who speak a second language at home. Furthermore, those most likely to be discordant with weaker HSGPAs and stronger testing are males, Whites, and those of higher income.

We would emphasize that the results only include those students who took the tests. It is quite plausible that there are other students who might have succeeded in college, had they been encouraged, found the right mentor, or were not so discouraged by the costs. If so, the real "discrepancies" may be even higher.

And it is worth noting the parallels between the proportions noted in the above studies and the median percentage (23%) of students choosing to be non-submitters at the institutions in this study. Does TOP indeed serve this "discrepant" population of students? Does it reduce admission barriers for underserved populations? The following study design continues with the full list of research questions and explains how we went about answering them.

THE STRUCTURE OF THE STUDY

We began this study by reviewing the FairTest list of 1,000 colleges and universites with one form or another of optional testing. We tried to achieve a balance of institutional types, sizes, selectivity, and geography, as well as to have representation from institutions with different approaches to TOP. We approached about one hundred institutions to discuss whether they would consider joining the study. We launched the study with 28 interested institutions that felt they could provide reliable data for the multiple cohorts needed for the study. Among the 28, we achieved most of these balances, though were somewhat overrepresented by private institutions, which largely reflects the pool of test-optional institutions and also some restrictions on public institutions sharing their data.

To provide context, we interviewed the dean of admissions or enrollment VP at each institution in the study about their rationale for adopting a test-optional admission policy as well as commentary about how well they felt it was working at their institutions. In many instances, the current dean had not been at the institution at the time of adoption, so they relayed their best understanding of the circumstances at the time of adoption.

We received a large set of data from the 28 colleges and universities: 955,744 student records, with up to 40 data items in each student record. With any data set of this size, there will be elements that require careful examination and decisions about clarity and reliability. However, all data in this study come from participating colleges and universities or from the U.S. Department of Education's Integrated Post-secondary Education Data System (IPEDS).

The study was not designed to come to a single conclusion about the use of test-optional admissions policies, but to explore as many dimensions around the policy as possible. We began by conducting individual case study analyses for the 28 public and private colleges and universities. They have all been guaranteed anonymity, so this report uses aggregated data from subsets of institutions and avoids institutionally identifiable information. Below each chart or diagram is a description of the number of institutions and records included, along with a brief profile. In every case we have included all the institutions that had reliable data for the analysis being presented. This report is a series of observations, rather than a series of parallel findings on a single set of data.

Principal Research Questions In an effort to shed additional light on the impact of a test-optional admissions policy, this report explores several pertinent questions about test-optional admissions:

- If an institution adopts a test-optional admission policy, does it reduce admission barriers, thereby encouraging more students to apply?
- Does adopting a test-optional admission policy help an institution attract and enroll more traditionally underrepresented minority (URM), first-generation-to-college, and low-SES students?
- How do institutions treat students who have chosen to withhold their scores from the admissions process—in both their admission decisions and their aid decisions?
- Are there institutional financial implications to adopting a test-optional admission policy?

- Who are the non-submitters—the students who use a test-optional policy? How do they perform academically in college compared to students who do not use the policy? This portion of the study is a retesting of the findings from *Defining Promise* (Hiss & Franks, 2014), with a largely different group of institutions, but a parallel methodology.

We are conscious of, and accept, the responsibility to have this study examine both the ethical issues like access and diversity, and the strategic issues of enrollments, and potential financial impact on the institution.

Types of Institutions and Policies Represented We focused our participant recruitment on 4-year, degree-granting, IPEDS-submitting, public and private not-for-profit institutions in the United States. We then investigated the breadth of test-optional policy (TOP) types employed by institutions in the United States. There is no standard definition of "test-optional admissions," leaving institutions to define and implement a variety of policies. We organized the various versions of the policy in common categories, and we found, in approximate numbers, the primary types of TOP used by institutions (in rank order of frequency they were observed): Academic Threshold, Optional for All, Optional Plus, Optional for Some, and Test Flexible. The most commonly used policies—Optional for All and Academic Threshold—were of particular interest, as was the Optional Plus policy. Institutions with Test Blind and Test Flexible policies were not considered for inclusion in this study. While considered, no Optional for Some institutions were included in the study due to small numbers of non-submitters.

Below is a brief description of the principal forms of TOP policies with their width of use and representation in this study.

- *Optional for All* allows most or all students to choose whether or not to submit test scores as part of their application. The most common exceptions are home-schooled or international students being required to submit some form of tests. Optional for All is used by approximately 39% of the institutions in the FairTest list. Seventeen of the 28 institutions in this study have an Optional for All policy.
- *Optional Plus* requires non-submitters to submit additional application materials, such as having an interview, or submitting an additional essay, writing samples or a graded paper. This policy is used by 9% of the FairTest list, and by 9 of the institutions in this study.
- *Optional for Some* allows some students to apply as non-submitters, but requires testing from others. Commonly, under an Optional for Some policy, it might be required for students applying

for special scholarships, in certain academic fields such as nursing or engineering, or required to supply tests for NCAA athletic policies, or for out-of-state applicants to public universities. It is used by 5% of the FairTest list.

- *Academic Threshold Policy* requires non-submitters to meet a published academic threshold, such as HSGPA or class rank. It is more commonly (but not exclusively) used by public universities. It is used by 48% of the institutions on the FairTest list, and by 2 institutions in this study.
- *Test Flexible Policy* allows students to submit other forms of testing (International Baccalaureate, Advanced Placement, SAT II, Regents) in place of SATs or ACTs. It is only used by 1% of institutions on the FairTest list.
- *Test Blind* means an institution will not consider any test scores in the evaluation, even if submitted. It is used by only a tiny handful of institutions.

Some institutions (including many public universities) have a required HSGPA or class rank for non-submitters, often a requirement from a state education agency or the legislature. We have referred to this form of TOP as Academic Threshold, in that the students must meet the HSGPA required for automatic admission. Shaped largely by the ability of particular threshold institutions to provide data, our research in the 2014 study had more of these "threshold" public institutions than this 2018 study. The best known of these are the "Texas Top 10" policy at all Texas public universities and the GPA requirement at the California State University system. Those requirements often become a self-fulfilling prophecy of student success in college. While sometimes contentious, a number of these policies have been in place for many years and seem to work successfully to open these public universities to a wider pool of applicants.

For this study, we sought to include institutions of a variety of sizes, levels of selectivity, and geographical locations. We sent initial inquiries to the deans of admissions at about one hundred TOP institutions and followed up with those who responded to our initial inquiry. Not all that wanted to participate were able to provide the volume of data we were requesting of them. However, the 28 institutions that are included in our study represent a diverse group of institutions (see Figure 7.1)

Collection and Use of Data. Each institution supplied record-level data, consisting of 40 variables for every applicant from 2 cohort years prior to adoption of their test-optional policy and 2 cohort years after adoption of the policy. The exceptions to this form of data gathering were the four institutions that had adopted a TOP prior to 2004 and were unable to submit data from years prior to their adoption of TOPs, and three of the five most

Figure 7.1. Participating Institution Profile

Category	Count of Institutions
Control	
Private not-for-profit	24
Public	4
Institution Size Category*	
1,000 - 4,999	17
5,000 - 9,999	7
10,000 - 19,999	1
20,000 and above	3
Carnegie Classification: Basic	
Baccalaureate Colleges	14
Master's Colleges & Universities	7
Doctoral Universities	7
Selectivity	
<30%	4
30%-50%	10
51%-70%	9
>70%	5
Endowment per FTE**	
<$20,000	6
$20,001-$50,000	5
$50,001-$100,000	4
$100,001-$200,000	9
>$200,000	4
Geography	
Far West	2
Great Lakes	3
Mid East	8
New England	12
Plains & Southeast	3
URM Enrollment	
<10%	4
10%-20%	15
21%-30%	7
31%-40%	2
US News "National" or "Regional" Ranking	
National	20
Regional	8

Notes. The first seven sections of data are drawn from IPEDS data 2016, the last section from USNWR rankings, 2018.

*The institutional sizes here reflect total enrollments, including graduate programs, whereas the sizes referred to in our report refer solely to undergraduates.

** FTE (Full Time Equivalent) is a measurement equal to one student enrolled full time for one academic year, calculated using total reported credit and/or contact hours divided by a factor to determine full-time equivalence of students.

Among our participating institutions, the proportion of non-submitters at each institution ranges widely—from 2% to 52%. Excluding the Academic Threshold institutions, the mean is 21.5% and the median non-submitter rate is about 23%.

recent adopters that could provide data for only one cohort subsequent to their adoption of a TOP.

All data for the study was submitted on a "blind crosswalk" basis, where the institution created a random record ID number for each student record, and only the institution kept that "crosswalk." The study received no identifiable individual information, and we guaranteed confidentiality and anonymity to the institutions in the study, as they shared a great deal of data with us. At the conclusion and publication of this study, each institution can decide if they wish to announce that they were participants.

A primary focus is on exploring the impact of adoption of a test-optional admission policy on the size and composition of a college's admission funnel—from applicant pool, through admitted students, to enrolled students. The funnel's shape reflects the numbers of students as they move through consideration of a college or university. Much student and family attention is given to the Admissions Office decision, to admit, deny or waitlist. But while the institution chooses once, the students choose four times: to become an inquiry, to visit the campus, to apply, and then to enroll. Test-optional policies certainly can change the patterns of institutional Admissions decisions, but this study also provides evidence of how dramatically a test-optional policy can shift student decisions, principally to apply and enroll. Additionally, we have explored the differences between the non-submitters and submitters at each stage of the funnel. This conceptual framework underpinned our approach to gathering, organizing, and analyzing the data.

The traditional admission funnel includes prospects, inquirers, applicants, admitted students, and matriculants. For the purposes of this study (see Figure 7.2.) we collected data beginning with applicants and added a layer of assessment we have labeled Decision Rendered (DR), asking the institutions to identify each candidate for whom they actually rendered a decision (admit, deny, waitlist). Thus the number of DR applicants excludes applicants who remained incomplete and those who withdrew their applications prior to receiving a decision (e.g., made an Early Decision commitment elsewhere). This gave us insight into the inner workings of the policy, for instance, identifying whether non-submitters were completing applications at rates equivalent to submitters.

In addition to the funnel data, institutions provided the following categories of information on each student: racial and ethnic student identification, high school GPA data, standardized test score data, financial aid data (expected family contribution (EFC), total gift aid dollars, Pell Grant recipient, merit aid recipient), first-year college GPA (FYGPA), most recent (or final) CumGPA, major designation, current student enrollment status, and an up-to-date same-school graduation status for all students who enrolled, and a range of IPEDS data on test-requiring institutions:

Figure 7.2. The Admission Funnel Framework

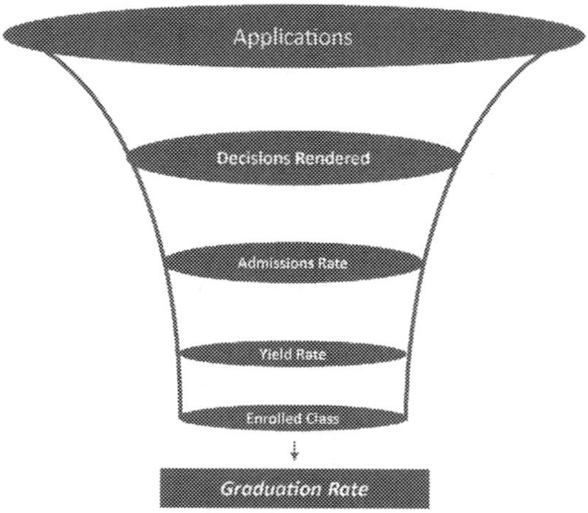

Note. For the purposes of this study the admission funnel has been expanded to include a category of Decisions Rendered and concludes with a category of Graduation Rate (as a measure of student success).

- Racial and ethnic student identification. IPEDS-defined categories of racial/ethnic identification.
- High school GPA data. HSGPAs were reported to us as recorded by the institution's admissions or institutional research offices. We did an extensive individual analysis of the GPAs reported by each of the 28 institutions in the study, using whatever scales that institution provided, and allowing for the GPA scales to exceed the traditional 4-point scale. No imputations were used in analysis. For the analyses in this combined report, we truncated all HSGPAs at 4.0.
- Standardized test score data. ACT and/or SAT scores were gathered and a concordance table (College Board, 2009) used to convert ACT scores to SAT scores. For simplicity, all references in the report refer to them simply as SATs. The new SAT had not been taken by most[2] of the student cohorts in this study (College Board, 2016). 27% of all non-submitter records contained a test score. Some institutions keep in a blind file test scores submitted by students before they decided to become non-submitters, while other institutions try to collect test scores after students enroll, both for later research purposes. Much of the data in this study comes from these retained or collected-after-enrollment test scores.
- Financial aid data. The data was categorized into segments using the following financial aid numbers:

    - » Expected family contribution (EFC). At some institutions this was the federal EFC, and at others it was an institutionally determined EFC. Because we were attempting to assess aid award differences between submitters and non-submitters at the individual institution, we sought whatever EFC they used to determine the need for aid.
    - » Total gift aid. We requested the total gift aid (from any source) received by the student.
    - » Pell Grant recipients. We asked institutions simply to identify any student receiving a Pell Grant, but did not ask for the specific amount of the Pell Grant.
    - » Merit aid recipients. We asked them to identify any student to whom they had awarded non-need-based, "merit" gift aid.
- Academic outcome data. First-year college GPA (FYGPA), most recent (or final) CumGPA, major designation, a current student enrollment status, and an up-to-date same-school graduation status for all students who enrolled. We used graduation status as our ultimate measure of student academic success. The data was collected in 2016.
- Data from test-requiring institutions. IPEDS data for both the TOP institutions and their test-required policy (TRP) peers for each of the matched cohorts of students. To try to examine how a test-optional policy can change the application funnel, we matched each TOP institution with a TRP peer institution that was similar in size, applicant pools, and overall level of admissions competitiveness. We were able to see some patterns of change more commonly in TOP than in TRP institutions.

We also wanted to examine data from institutions that had varying years of experience with the policy, so there is a range of policy adoption time frames represented in the study. Four institutions adopted their policies prior to 2004, five adopted their policies very recently, and the remaining institutions adopted the policy between 2004 and 2014. With the exception of the earliest adopters, each of them provided data for two cohorts just prior to adoption of their policies, and two cohorts after policy adoption.

We asked institutions to submit the first cohort after they adopted the policy, to allow for a full cycle of trial before starting the policy analysis. Seven submitted post-TOP data beginning with the first cohort immediately after they adopted the policy, and the other institutions submitted data ranging from 2 to 6 years after adoption to align data for a 4–5 year graduation rate comparison. Out of necessity, our subset of most recent adopters provided data beginning with the year they adopted the policy.

Analysis and Summaries of Data We compiled a large set of data with many different facets. At the institutional level we focused on the differences

Figure 7.3. Illustrative Summary of the Admission Funnel Activity for One Institution for One Cohort Year

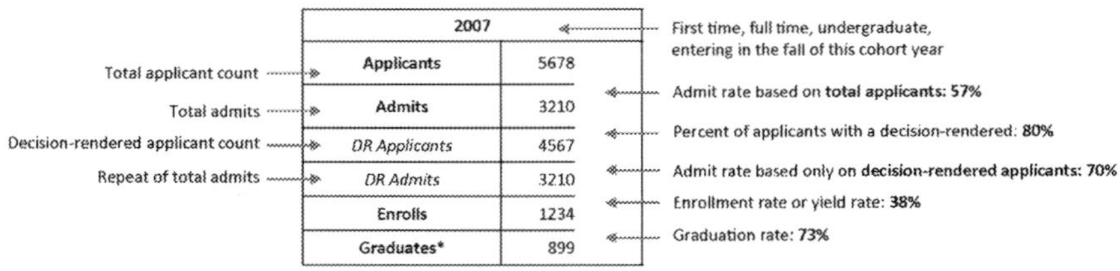

*For "Graduates," participating institutions submitted an updated status on all students as of June 2016.

between submitters and non-submitters at various stages in the funnel. The funnel activity was summarized in a chart for each institution for each cohort year submitted (see Figure 7.3 for an example).

Then the data was averaged across pre-policy years and across post-policy years. After that, it was filtered by the demographic and admission behavior data we collected: gender, race/ethnicity, athletic participation, high school type, early decision usage, family financial status, and first-generation-to-college status.

Limitations of the Research This study is a case study exploration into the role of testing in college admissions. Its very strength is in the attention paid to unique scenarios at each institution, following through to detailed understanding of admission and enrollment patterns. However, there are limitations that come along with this case study approach:

- While we were able to recruit a wide range of institutions to volunteer participation in the study, and we learned quite a bit about each one, the sample size was not large enough to be considered definitively representative of institution or policy type.
- Each institution in the study maintained different record-keeping practices, data definitions, and data governance policies. Our very detailed data request form and data transformation approach mitigated many of these differences. However, we rarely received identically comprehensive data sets from any two participating institutions. This led us to declare certain aspects of some data submissions as unavailable, unreliable, or irreconcilable. We have made notes in each figure description to this effect.
- Working with historical data meant that there were sometimes inconsistencies across cohorts at individual institutions due to

changes in computer systems or data coding schema. Similarly, the current staff were often not those who were at the helm during the time of policy adoption. Therefore, our understanding of context surrounding the policy (e.g., motivation for adoption, concurrent initiatives, and financial aid packaging strategies) was not always clear.

- The nature of our study inherently dealt with self-selection bias, both at the institution level (e.g., each institution made the decision to adopt TOP) and at the student level (e.g., all but two of the institutions—those with threshold policies—had policies that allowed students to choose to withhold test scores in the admission process). There are a number of underlying motivations and demographic and psychographic elements that we cannot account for in this study, rendering the determination of causation more difficult.

PRINCIPAL FINDINGS

We open our findings with an homage to the variability of institutions. We present two case studies of institutions that effectively realized the goals they set for their test-optional policy. While trying to provide a clear picture of the institutions, in order to protect their anonymity, we have kept some of the descriptive information broad (see box descriptions, Institution A and Institution B).

Effects of a Test-Optional Policy

Does a TOP encourage more students to apply? All institutions saw an application increase, but just over half saw application growth greater than that of a matched test-requiring peer (TRP peer).

We interviewed the admissions dean at each of the 28 participating institutions about the impetus and the goals behind their institution's adoption of a TOP. They had not all been in their roles at the time the policy was adopted, but the recurring theme was that a major goal had been to increase applications, particularly among underrepresented student groups.

Not surprisingly, our data reveals that participating institutions saw application increases after policy adoption. The overall average increase in applications was 1,926 (and a median of 1,234), with an average increase of 29% at the private institutions in the study and 11% at the public institutions. Note that these application increases represent various spans of time from the date an institution adopted a TOP to the date of the latest cohort they submitted for the study. These time spans range from 1 year to 6 years, collected during the period of 2004–2016.

Institution A

Large, urban, private, not-for-profit

This institution described TOP as a means of formalizing what they had been doing all along, namely, to "give students a choice about how they might want to present themselves."

They described the process of transitioning to TOP as largely uneventful, requiring a few more temporary readers to aid the transition because without testing "you typically need to look more closely at the high school record, the rigor of the curriculum, and the school profile for context."

After adopting TOP, the institution drew a smaller than average proportion of non-submitters, students who did not submit testing (9% vs. 23%). And, although applications increased, they grew proportionately more slowly than their matched TRP peer.

It was a different story for URM students. The institution enrolled substantially more of these students (15 percentage points more) than they did prior to adopting TOP, which was proportionately a 76% greater gain than their TRP peer. So, in spite of having their applicant pool grow at a slower pace than their TRP peer, they were able to make substantially greater gains in enrolling URM students (and to a slightly lesser extent, Pell recipients and first-generation-to-college students).

Compared to the pre-policy cohorts, the enrolled TOP cohorts saw a 12 percentage point rise in the proportion of students with need, and although this institution did not submit data on gift aid, it likely had to increase aid commitments to support this growth.

Once enrolled, submitters had a marginally higher CumGPA than non-submitters, but both the overall population and the URM population graduated at virtually identical rates.

These universal increases are not surprising, as most institutions posted gains during this period. The critical question is whether our TOP institutions fared better or worse than peer institutions that still required standardized tests of their applicants. A 2015 study out of the University of Georgia (Belasco et al., 2015) sought to answer this question and concluded that, in the aggregate, selective liberal arts colleges that adopted a TOP (in comparison with those that continued to require SAT or ACT scores) had not increased their enrollment of URM students or Pell recipients. But in focusing on the averaged outcomes, that study may not have been able to discern impact at the institutional level.

Recognizing that there is great variation among institutions in selectivity, size, financial resources, and geographical markets, and that not all test-optional admissions policies are the same, nor pursued with the same vigor, it seemed appropriate to apply a more institutionally focused approach to

Institution B

Small, suburban, private, not-for-profit

This institution was motivated to adopt TOP because they thought the test requirement was preventing some students from applying.

After the institution adopted TOP, their applicant pool grew proportionately faster than that of the TRP peer (proportionately 40% more growth), with non-submitters comprising 19% of the overall pool—a slightly lower proportion than the majority of the institutions in the study.

Their percentage of enrolled URM students was 17 points higher after they adopted a TOP, which was proportionately a 75% greater gain than their TRP peer. As with most of our institutions, they admitted non-submitters at a substantially lower rate than submitters (15 percentage points lower), and the non-submitters enrolled at a substantially higher rate (23 percentage points higher).

At this institution, the post-policy cohorts included a lower proportion of students with need (11 percentage points lower), than the pre-policy cohorts, but non-submitters were, on average, $4,000 needier. To the detriment of higher need students, though, this institution seemed to favor low and no-need students in its awarding strategy.

Once enrolled, submitters had a marginally higher FYGPA and CumGPA (+0.09 and +0.07, respectively) than non-submitters. There are mixed results from the two graduating cohorts, with non-submitters graduating at a higher 4-year rate (8 points higher) than submitters, but lower from the earlier cohort with a 5-year graduation rate (4 points lower). We offer no speculation on the difference other than that perhaps as they refined their review process for non-submitters, they got better at it! For both the 4-year and 5-year cohorts, the URM non-submitters graduated at a consistently higher rate (7 points higher) than the URM submitters.

answering this question. We asked the admissions dean at each of our participating institutions to identify their top three "peer competitors"—the institutions they felt were most like their institution, and were in most direct competition for their students (i.e., not an "aspirational" institution, but one with which they had a fairly even win–loss ratio with students admitted to both institutions). Then we identified institutional match criteria to finalize the selection of the single, most comparable, test-required policy (TRP) peer match[3] for use in our analysis. Comparisons are made using data from the same cohort years for the test-required peer as were submitted to us by the test-optional institution, but for these comparisons, all data for both institutions was drawn from IPEDS to ensure consistency in the comparison.

Comparing application growth rather than raw numbers between TOP and TRP institutions (to compensate for the varying sizes of institutions (enrollments range from approximately 1,500 to about 20,000)[4] we observe that 13 of 23 (57%) of the TOP institutions in our study experienced greater proportionate growth in overall applications than their TRP peers during the same time period. This in contrast to only six (26%) TOP institutions experiencing less application growth than their TRP peers. Four experienced essentially the same level of growth (within +/- 3%).

Does a TOP help institutions enroll more traditionally URM and low-SES students? For the majority of the TOP institutions in the study, yes. Almost all these institutions saw a rise in URM applications after TOP, and two-thirds of them saw that rise correspond to URM enrollment growth above that seen by a matched TRP peer institution. Half experienced Pell enrollment growth above a TRP peer.

Based solely on the raw counts of URM applicants and enrollees, the data shows that all but one of our TOP institutions experienced an increase in URM applications after TOP adoption. The overall average increase in application count was 835, with a slightly higher median of 938. Similarly, all but three of them increased their enrollment of URM students after adoption of a TOP.

It is important to try to assess whether offering the option to apply as a non-submitter actually increased the proportion of underrepresented students who chose to apply and enroll at an institution, or did it have no real impact on the composition of the class? A Hispanic female from rural Texas commented in a documentary film on test-optional policies: "I looked at the average test scores of colleges, and if my scores didn't fit that range, I just nixed them. That was the first time that I was presented with the idea that SATs could be optional; I didn't know. I would never have thought to apply to liberal arts schools in the Northeast" (Davis, 2018).

Given that this time frame coincided with a period of rapid growth in the diversity of college applicants, we used the matched TRP peers to assess any true differences. There were 14 of 23 (61%) of the TOP institutions that achieved proportionately greater increases in enrollment of URM students than their TRP peers; one was essentially the same (within +/- 3%); and eight (35%) fared less well than their TRP peers. Enrollment of Pell recipients was more evenly split, with 11 of 22 (50%) of the TOP institutions increasing the proportion of Pell recipients more than their TRP peers, three enrolling roughly the same proportions, and eight (36%) losing ground in comparison with their TRP.

Finally, to summarize the pre- to post-policy analysis, we completed a statistical test to compare the institutional averages between our TOP institutions and their TRP peers. This indicates that our TOP institutions experienced greater application and URM enrollment growth than their matched peer institutions. Using a statistical measure of effect size (Cohen's d), we find a medium effect size (.4) between the proportionate differences in the mean application growth and the mean URM enrollment growth for the TOP institutions versus their matched TRP peers. There is only a small effect size (.1) seen for Pell recipient enrollment proportions.

Although there were differences between the TOP institution and its TRP peer in the amount of improvement on each characteristic, all of the TOP institutions had increases in the actual number of applications. All but one received an increased number of applications from URM students. All but two enrolled more URM students. And all but one enrolled more Pell recipients.

Some additional observations in these growth comparisons are worth noting here:

- The institution that had the least growth (in comparison to its TRP peer) in applications, also had the least growth in Pell recipients, but had strong growth in URM enrollment, suggesting that this institution many have focused its recruitment and enrollment efforts on this population.
- In a similar flip-flop, the institution with the lowest comparative growth in URM had high comparative growth in applications overall.
- Three of the four public institutions in the study were included in this part of the analysis, and it is interesting to note that all three of them were among the eight that increased less than their TR peers in enrolling URM students.
- A small subset of institutions repeatedly appeared as outliers "in the negative" compared to their TRP peer in our analysis. We will provide some additional perspective on these cases in the section "How do the academic outcomes compare with those of 'Defining Promise' (2014)?" later in this chapter.

So it is clear that, in comparison to their TRP peer institutions, TOP institutions have varied outcomes relative to the characteristics we assessed. However, the overall comparison suggests a positive relationship between TOP policy adoption and application growth, URM enrollment growth, and slightly less so, Pell enrollment growth.

Does a TOP negatively impact the patterns seen in admissions, from selectivity to enrollment rates? The answer is no. All of the institutions that provided consecutive cohort years pre-policy to post-policy data saw overall application growth, and all but one saw URM application growth. A few institutions saw an increase in selectivity.

A major concern about making a significant change in an admissions policy is whether doing so will in some way have a negative impact on the quantity, quality, or composition of the applicant pool and, ultimately, on the enrolled student body. While we cannot isolate the impact of the adoption of the policy from the impact of other changes occurring concurrently, by limiting the comparison to the 13 institutions that submitted data from the cohorts immediately preceding and immediately following their adoption of a TOP, we were able to observe the changes that were synchronous with the policy adoption.

At the applicant stage we found that all 13 of these TOP institutions had increases in the number of applications ranging from trivial to twice as many in the 5-year period. And all but one of them experienced substantive gains in the number of applications submitted by URM students (see Figure 7.4).

Similarly, the applicant pools do not appear to have suffered subsequent to adopting the policy. For this group of 13 institutions, we compared aspects of the admissions funnel for all students in the cohorts during the pre-policy (test-required) years against those of the ensuing post-policy (test-optional) cohorts, and the decision to adopt a TOP has not had a negative impact on their admission funnels. One Dean of Admissions from a large private university commented, "After several years of essentially no growth in African-American enrollments, our first year of TOP had a dramatic increase in African-American, Hispanic, and International apps." To illustrate the impact, we chose a "box and whisker" style of chart for a number of comparisons (Figures 7.6–7.7) as it provides a multidimensional visual representation that allows the reader to simultaneously view the complete range, the middle 50%, the mean and the mode, as well as any outliers, thereby illustrating the sometimes-wide variation between institutions and their experiences with TOP. (For a brief guide to interpretation of box and whisker charts, see Figure 7.5.)

The funnel patterns of the pre-policy cohort years are very similar to the post-policy cohort years. The mean and median admit rates are marginally lower, as are the enrollment rates, or yield rates. But as applicant pools increase in size, it is not unusual for the institutions to become somewhat more selective. Similarly, yield rates at colleges have tended to decline over the past couple of decades as students, on average, have applied to an increasing number of colleges. One study offered the opinion that colleges were becoming test-optional, not to increase diversity, but to appear more selective (Belasco et al., 2015). As readers will see later, the admit rate for non-submitters is modestly lower, but the modest differences in overall admit rates from pre- to post-TOP do not offer much credence to the argument that colleges are recruiting non-submitters only to turn them down.

The admission funnel focusing exclusively on URM students displays similar, but more exaggerated patterns (see Figure 7.6.).

The median admit rate and the quartile span during the test-optional years is lower and wider —from 16% to almost 60%—compared to the test-required years. The Decision Rendered proportion is equivalent, but with some significantly lower institution outliers. However, the enrollment rate quartile range has a distinctly wider span, indicating that some institutions saw a significant rise in yield, while others experienced a drop.

Figure 7.4. Growth of All Applications and URM Applications, by Institution

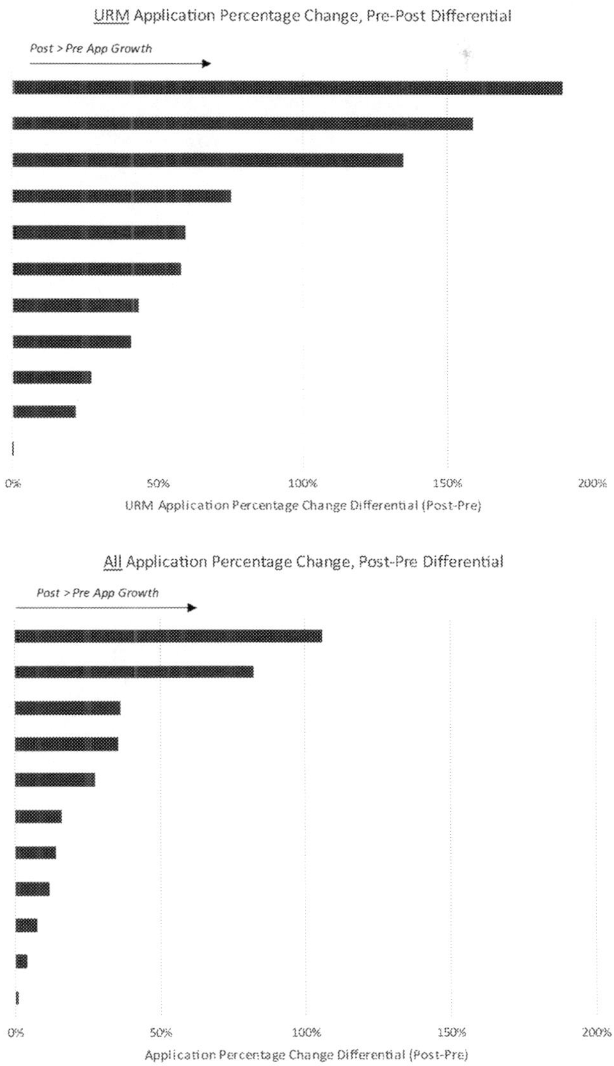

Note. The institutions represented include 13 public and private TOP institutions in the study that provided cohorts immediately preceding and immediately following their adoption of a TOP.

Exclusions: 4 policy early adopters and 2 institutions with unreliable URM data

All applicants: 13 institutions | 656,491 records

URM applicants: 13 institutions| 138,482 URM records

Enrollment = 2,000–10,000 (4,000 M) | Endowment per FTE = $4,000–$250,000 ($60,000 M) | Admit rate = 20%–80% (45% M)

Figure 7.5. Pre- and Post-Policy Overall Admission Funnel

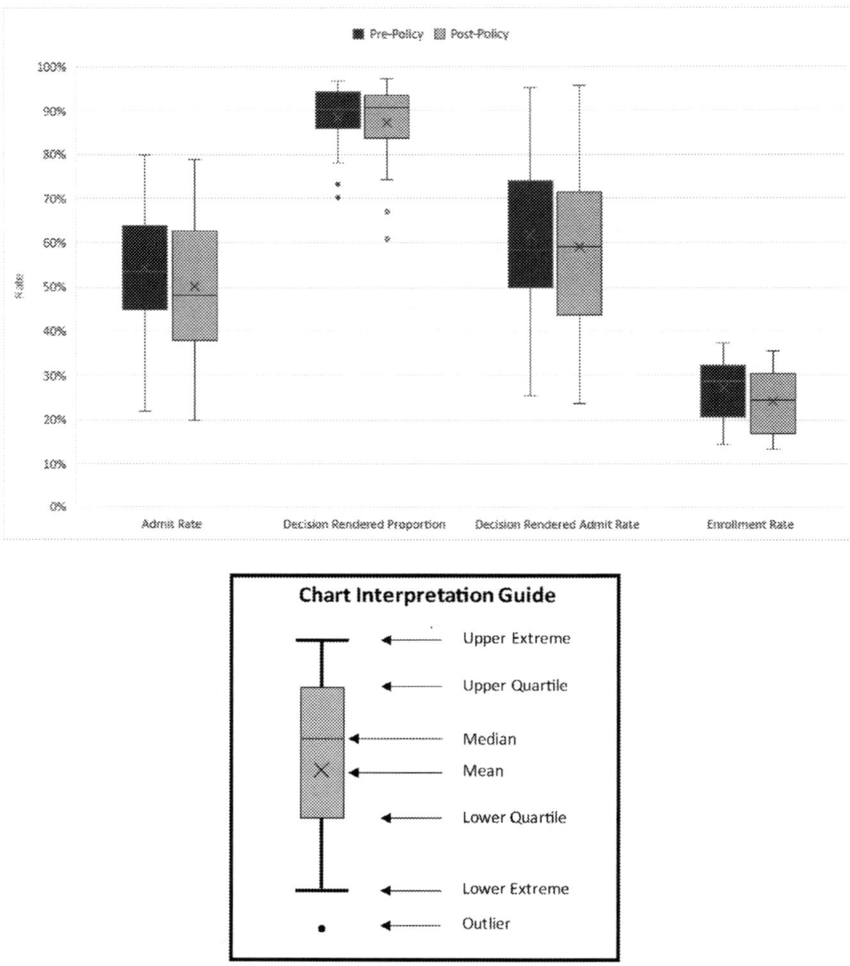

Note. Cohort years 2008–2016. The institutions represented include 13 public and private TOP institutions in the study that provided cohorts immediately preceding and immediately following their adoption of a TOP.

Exclusions: 4 policy early adopters

13 institutions | 656,491 records

Enrollment = 2,000–20,000 (4,000 M) | Endowment per FTE = $4,000–$250,000 ($60,000 M) | Admit rate = 20%–80% (50% M)

Figure 7.6. Pre- and Post-Policy URM Admission Funnel

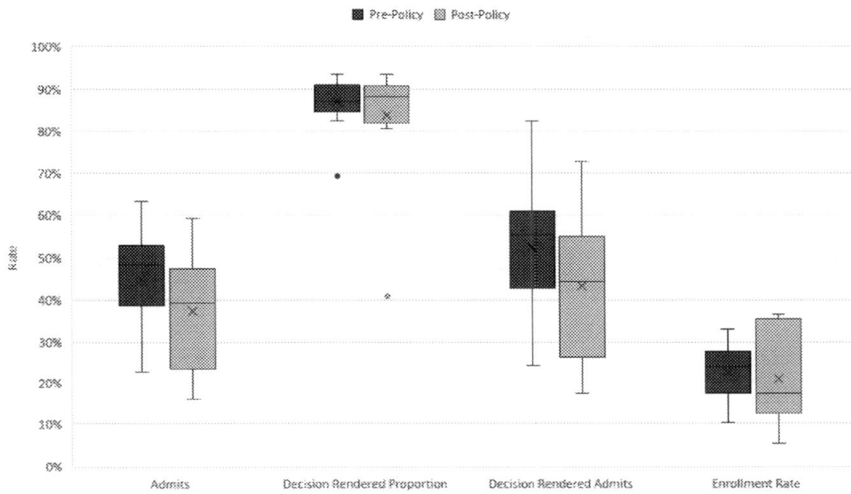

Note. Cohort years 2008–2016. The institutions represented include 13 public and private TOP institutions in the study that provided cohorts immediately preceding and immediately following their adoption of a TOP.

Exclusions: 4 policy early adopters, and 2 that did not have reliable URM data.

13 institutions | 138,482 URM records.

Enrollment = 2,000–20,000 (4,000 M) | Endowment per FTE = $4,000–$250,000 ($60,000 M) | Admit rate = 20%–80% (45% M)

In summary, there is great variation among the experiences of colleges that have adopted test-optional admissions policies. And while it is seductive to believe one can make a single pronouncement about the impact of adopting a TOP, much of that impact varies based upon the specific institution, its competitive position in the world of higher education, and the implementation and promotion of the test-optional policy. Our participating TOP institutions varied in size (~1,500 to ~20,000) and selectivity (with admit rates ranging from ~15% to ~90%). But the experiences of this particular batch of colleges suggests that the adoption of a well-promoted and well-executed test-optional admissions policy can reasonably lead to an increase in overall applications as well as an increase in the URM representation (both numeric and proportionate) within the freshman class. Thus a TOP policy can provide one tool to assist a college in attracting and enrolling a larger contingent of URM students.

Figure 7.7. Overall Admission Funnel Comparing Submitter vs. Non-submitter, with 5-Year Graduation Rates.

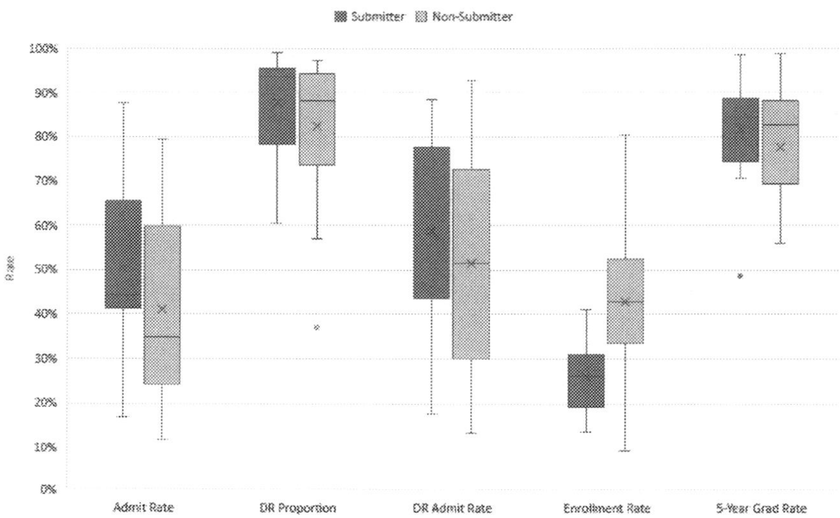

Note. Data represents 14 public and private institutions in the study for which we had 5-year graduation data. Exclusions: 2 institutions with Academic Threshold policies, 1 that did not have non-submitter proportions. 14 institutions | 166,561 records. Enrollment = 1,500–5,000 (2,500 M) | Endowment per FTE = \$5,000–\$800,000 (\$100,000 M) | Admit rate = 15%–80% (45% M)

Non-submitter Profile

Do non-submitters and submitters exhibit different funnel patterns? The answer is yes. Non-submitters are admitted at lower rates, but enroll at significantly higher rates than submitters. Non-submitters go on to graduate at rates equivalent to submitters.

In addition to assessing the broad impact of a test-optional admissions policy on an institution's applicant pool and enrolled classes, this study sought to identify any differences between the funnel patterns of the students who submitted test results (submitters) and those who chose not to submit test results (non-submitters) in the admission process.

There are several notable differences between these two groups at the various stages of the admission funnel (see Figure 7.7).

Perhaps the most significant are that, on average, the 14 institutions in our study that had at least 5-year graduation rates available (i.e., mature TOP institutions) admitted non-submitters at lower rates than submitters, and, on average, those non-submitters enrolled at substantially higher rates and went on to graduate at similar rates. The graduation rates from non-submitters at these mature TOP institutions have a wider range and

Figure 7.8. URM Admission Funnel Comparing Submitter vs. Non-submitter, with 5-Year Graduation Rates

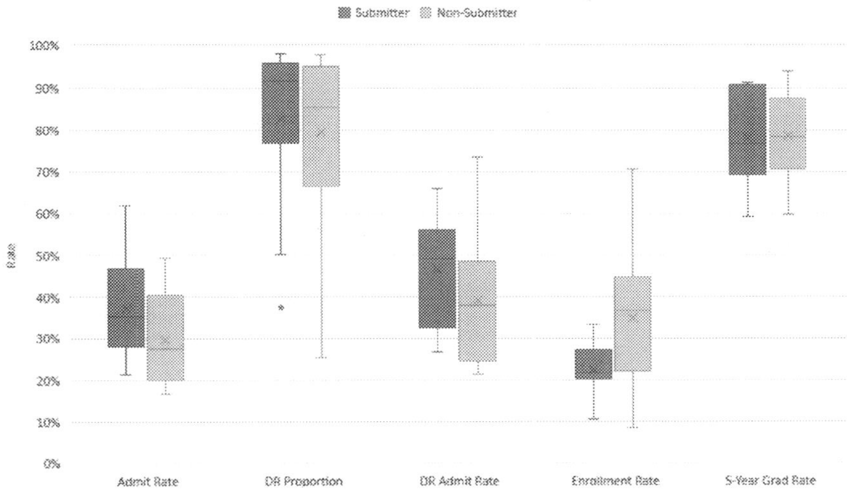

Note. Data represents 12 private TOP institutions with reliable URM data for submitters and non-submitters and 5-year graduation rates. Exclusions: 2 institutions with Academic Threshold policies, 1 that did not have non-submitter proportions, and 2 that did not have reliable URM data. No public institutions had reliable data for this assessment. 12 institutions | 26,245 URM Applicant records Enrollment = 1,500–5,000 (2,500 M) | Endowment per FTE = $44,000–$800,000 ($150,000 M) | Admit rate = 15%–70% (40% M)

lower mean than seen among submitters; however the differences between the two groups' averages and medians are within 3–4 percentage points. It is important to note that this data represents institution averages. As we will illustrate later, pooled student data on average graduation rates shows a comparable, but slightly different, picture.

Using the same lens, the admission funnel for underrepresented minority (URM) students (see Figure 7.8) mimics the patterns seen in the overall admission funnel: Institutions admitted URM non-submitters at lower rates than URM submitters, but the URM non-submitters enrolled at significantly higher rates— an average of 14 percentage points higher than submitters. URM graduation rates are harder to reliably interpret, because graduated non-submitter URM counts are low, but the URM 5-year graduation rates show equivalence between the two groups.

There were eight institutions in our study that adopted TOPs more recently and thus do not yet have graduation rates to report. But the patterns are similar—they admitted non-submitters at markedly lower rates, and non-submitters enrolled at higher rates.

Figure 7.9. Institution Admit and Enrollment Rate Differentials: Non-submitter vs. Submitter.

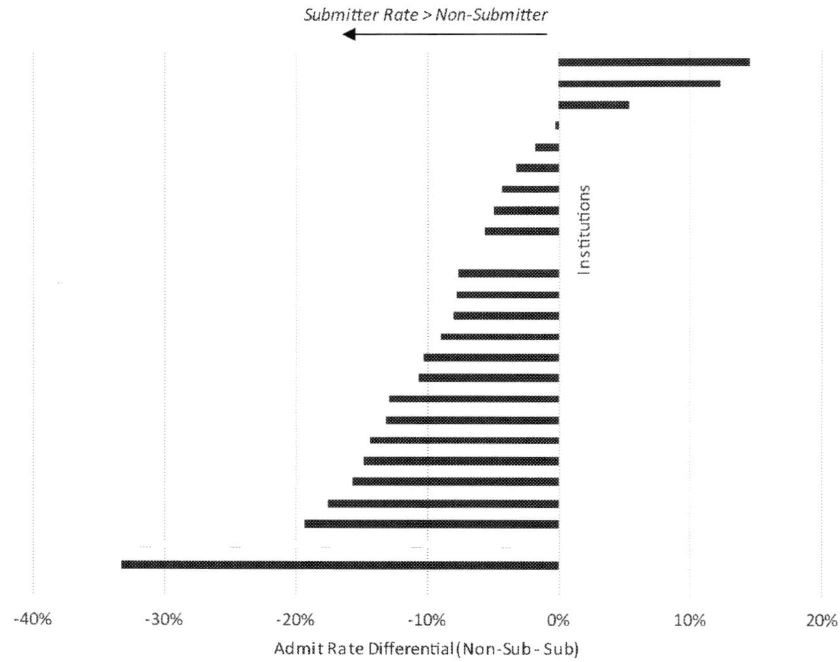

An institution-by-institution comparison of differentials shows that the majority of these institutions (21 out of 25) *admitted non-submitters at lower rates than submitters*. However, all but one of these institutions (24 of 25) saw non-submitters enrolling at higher rates than submitters (see Figure 7.9).

In a few instances, colleges that identified as Optional Plus (with additional requirements on non-submitters, like a required interview or written responses to additional questions), may have increased their gross number of non-submitter applicants, but had a lower average completion rate, thereby depressing the number of their Decision Rendered (DR) non-submitters. In a couple of cases, after adopting a TOP, an increase in URM applications did not carry through to an increase in the number admitted, because there was a large tail-off in the number of URM applicants who received a decision (which we assume was due to lack of completed applications). In fact, a lower proportion of the applicants to Optional Plus institutions than to Optional for All institutions (78% vs. 90%) actually received a decision (see Figure 7.10).

Figure 7.9. Institution Admit and Enrollment Rate Differentials: Non-submitter vs. Submitter, continued.

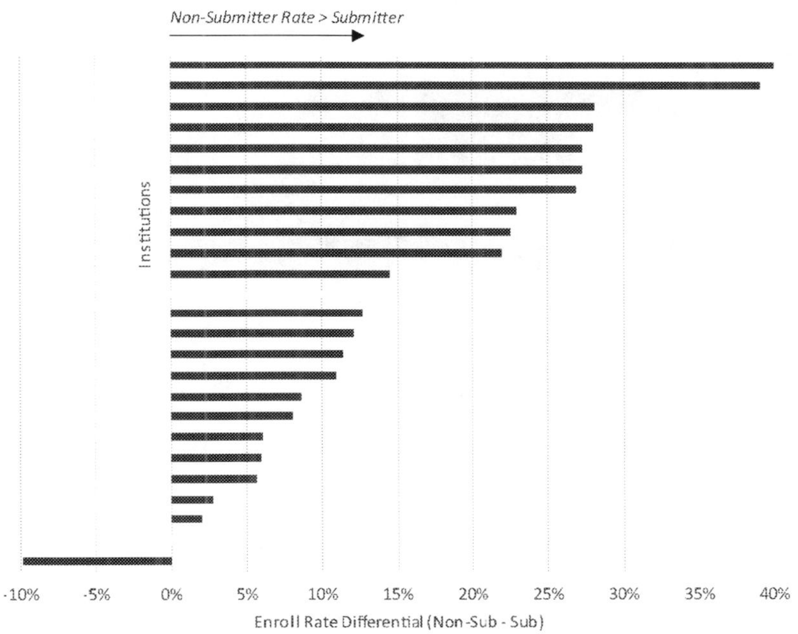

Note. Shaded bars identify the public institutions.

25 public and private institutions with reliable non-submitter data. Exclusions: Two 2 institutions with Academic Threshold policies, one that did not have non-submitter proportions. 25 Institutions | 396,921 Decision Rendered records

Enrollment = 1,500–20,000 (2,500 M) | Endowment per FTE = $5,000–$800,000 ($70,000 M) | Admit rate = 15%–80% (40% M)

Who are the non-submitters of testing? When given the opportunity, who chooses to be a non-submitter? Based on just under 500,000 records of students applying to these 24 colleges under a test-optional policy, we found that some important subgroups of students stood out as using the policy at higher rates than other student subgroups.

As found in our prior study, *Defining Promise* (Hiss & Franks, 2014), the non-submitter student group included larger proportions of URM students, first-generation-to-college students, women, and Pell recipients than seen in the submitter group (see Figure 7.11).

When we considered the distribution of applicants based on racial and ethnic status, Whites have the largest representation among both submitters

Figure 7.10. Admit Rate Comparison: Optional for All versus Optional Plus Policies.

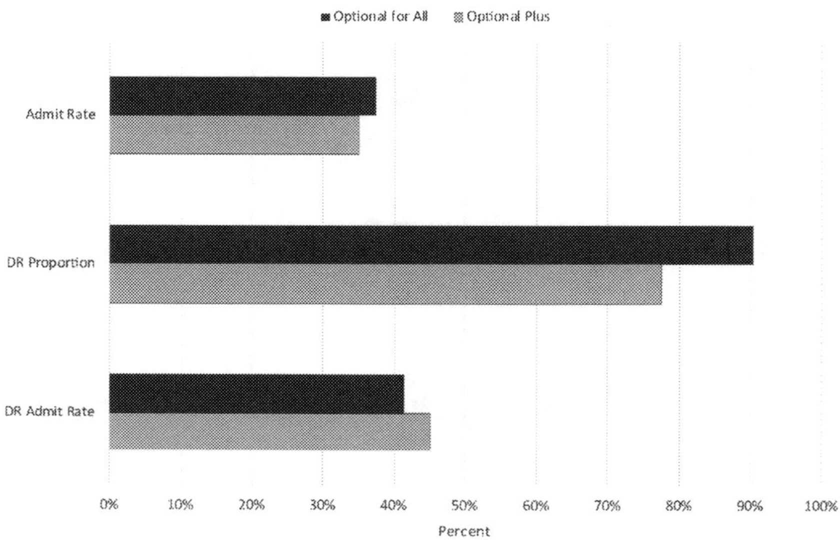

Note. The chart represents data from the 25 public and private TOP institutions with the appropriate policies. Exclusions: 2 institutions with Academic Threshold policies, 1 that did not have non-submitter proportions. Pooled student data.

25 institutions | 479,008 records

Enrollment = 1,500–20,000 (2,500 M) | Endowment per FTE = $5,000–$800,000 ($70,000 M) | Admit rate = 15%–80% (40% M)

and non-submitters. However, Hispanic and Black students both had substantially higher proportionate representation among the non-submitters than among the submitters (see Figure 7.12).

Although the cadre of students choosing to apply as non-submitters has disproportionate representation from the Black and Hispanic groups, it is *not* the case that non-submitters comprise a majority of any racial/ethnic student group.

So, for instance, while a larger proportion of the non-submitters are Black students, among all the Black students, only 35% applied as non-submitters. We were somewhat surprised to find that almost 20% of nonresident aliens listed as non-submitters. In the early years of TOP, almost all nonresident aliens were required to submit testing, on the (perhaps flawed) assumption that institutions needed these tests as evidence of English fluency. It does appear that some international students are now being permitted to apply as non-submitters, perhaps from schools with English as

Figure 7.11. Percentage of Select Student Demographic Segments, Comparing Non-submitters vs. Submitters.

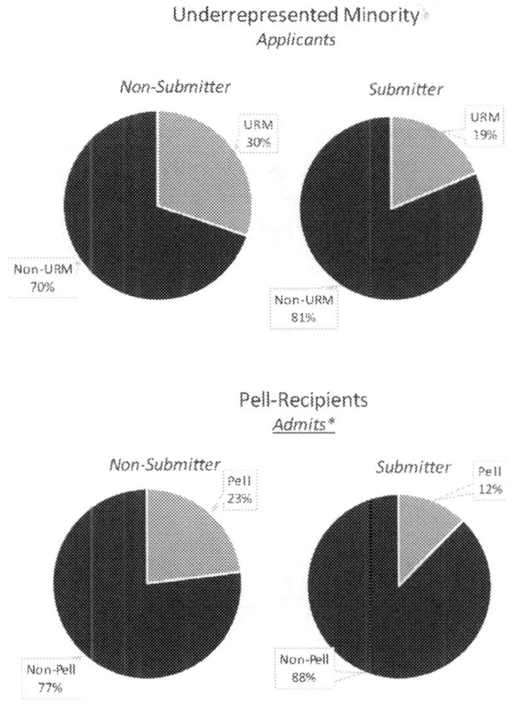

the language of instruction, or because American international admissions officers know schools abroad far better, or perhaps some of these are undocumented students. But we are not completely confident of this non-submitter statistic for internationals. It may be that some students are submitting TOEFLs, IBs, or other tests which are not being recorded with SATs and ACTs in college data files (see Figure 7.13).

Other groups of non-submitters are based on less personal characteristics. For example, higher proportions of students from parochial and independent schools chose to be non-submitters compared to public school students (see Figure 7.14).

But recognizing the average ratios of school counselor to students in these three types of high schools, we might imagine that students in public schools are getting less on-point advice about how to use a TOP to their advantage. The contrasts in school counselor ratios in America are often stark. Nationally, the average ratio of students to school counselors in public schools is approaching 500 to 1. And of course, public school counselors have many other duties besides college counseling. In independent schools,

Figure 7.11. Percentage of Select Student Demographic Segments, Comparing Non-submitters vs. Submitters, Continued

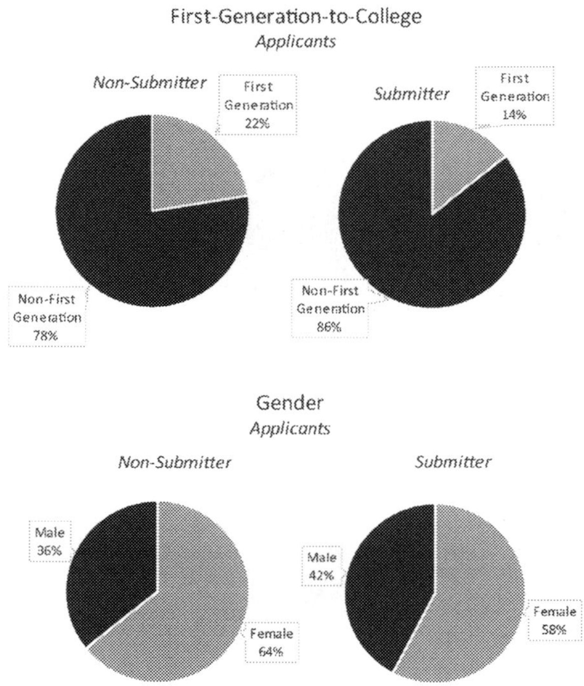

* Pell data is not available at the Applicant stage, so this proportion represents Admits.

Note. Each set of charts represent data from a subset of institutions that provided reliable data. Exclusions: 2 institutions with Academic Threshold policies, one that did not have non-submitter proportions. Pooled student data.

URM: 24 institutions | 470,273 records (of which 99,298 are URM)

First-generation-to-college: 22 institutions | 384,703 records (of which 62,626 are first gen.)

Pell: 16 institutions | 110,901 records (of which 16,016 are Pell Admits)

Gender: 23 institutions | 379,605 records (of which 224,975 are Female). Note that two of our larger institutions did not submit gender data, bringing our count down to 23. An "other" gender category was offered, but there was very limited data to represent, with the exception of one institution where virtually all students were recorded as "other." That institution has also been excluded from this average.

Enrollment = 1,500–20,000 (2,500 M) | Endowment per FTE = $6,500–$800,000 ($100,000 M) | Admit rate = 15%–90% (50% M)

Figure 7.12. Distribution of Non-submitters and Submitters by IPEDS Racial/ Ethnic Student Group.

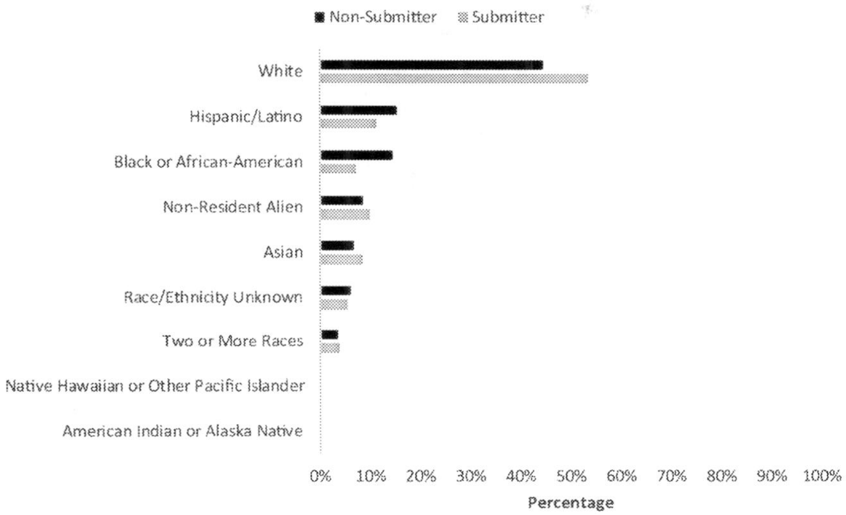

Note. 24 institutions provided reliable submitter and non-submitter URM data. Pooled student data.

Exclusions: 2 institutions with Academic Threshold policies, 1 that did not have non-submitter proportions, and 2 with unreliable URM data.

24 institutions | 470,273 records

Enrollment = 1,500–20,000 (2,500 M) | Endowment per FTE = $6,500–$800,000 ($100,000 M) | Admit rate = 15%–90% (50% M)

the ratio of students to college counselors is often about 50 to 1. Jerome Lucido comments on this issue in his recent essay on optional testing, positing that the gaps in TOP use by high school type may reflect wildly uneven college counseling resources (Lucido, 2018, p. 164–165).

We are not surprised to see TOPs also being steadily used by students with excellent access to college counseling. It is a descriptive rather than judgmental comment that some non-submitters appear to be "accurately playing the corners" in their college applications, helped by advice from college counselors. These students largely do not have high testing in their favor, but they will have an accumulation of other attributes, starting with solid to spectacular transcripts, but often including evaluations for athletics, the arts, leadership, legacy status, geography, language or cultural backgrounds, and service commitments. In this respect, as in so many others, this policy turns out to be a helpful tool for complex and varied pools of students. To be sure, a TOP is a sword that cuts both ways. On the one

Figure 7.13. Percentage of Applicants Who Chose to be Non-submitters by IPEDS Racial/Ethnic Student Groups.

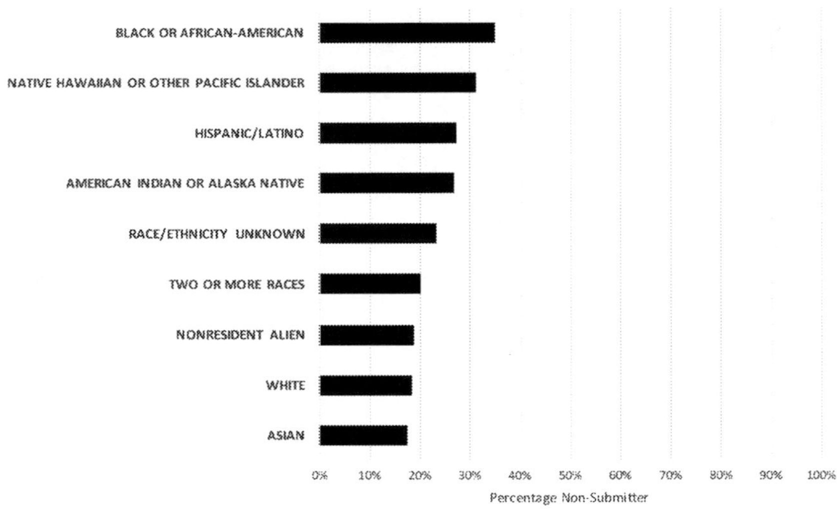

Note. Twenty-four institutions represented with reliable submitter and non-submitter Racial/ Ethnic applicant data.

Exclusions: 2 institutions with Academic Threshold policies, one that did not have non-submitter proportions, and two with unreliable URM data.

24 institutions | 99,370 non-submitter records

Enrollment = 1,500–20,000 (2,500 M) | Endowment per FTE = \$6,500–\$800,000 (\$100,000 M) | Admit rate = 15%–90% (50% M)

hand, it encourages thoughtful, holistic reading, where students can present information that allows admissions officers to understand their multiple gifts. But it also can sometimes advantage students with sophisticated college counseling over those without.

Because standardized tests often present special challenges for students with learning differences (LD), both this study and our 2014 study attempted to ascertain whether LD students gravitated toward being non-submitters. Most of our institutions did not systematically collect this information during the application process, and even after students were enrolled it was not systematically stored as retrievable data. We were, however, able to gather a small pool of information from nine institutions in the study.

We found LD students represented a higher portion of the non-submitters than the submitters (7% vs. 4%). The pool of data is limited, so it can only suggest broader trends. But higher education knows a great deal more

Figure 7.14. Distribution of Non-submitters and Submitters by High School Type.

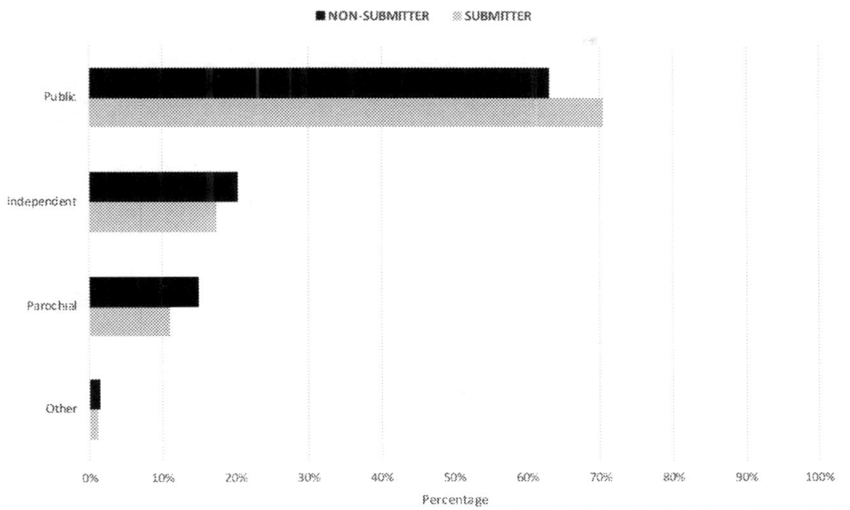

Note. 17 institutions represented with reliable submitter and non-submitter data on high school type. Exclusions: 2 institutions with Academic Threshold policies, 1 that did not have non-submitter proportions. Pooled Student Data

17 institutions | 335,904 records

Enrollment = 1,500–20,000 (2,500 M) | Endowment per FTE = $10,000–$800,000 ($100,000 M) | Admit rate = 15%–80% (43% M)

about learning differences than it did a few decades ago, and most universities and colleges have programs in place to provide accommodations (as required by Federal law) for students with documented LDs. One college that did a careful study found that with basic reasonable accommodations, the CumGPAs of their LD students rose, and their graduation rates almost doubled to reach class averages. With enrollments of LD students increasing to about 8% of their student body and graduating at class averages, the effect was to lift the college's overall graduation rate by several percentage points, not a trivial change. As with other facets of TOP efforts, LD student access is a research project with potentially very high rewards waiting to be done (Hiss & Franks, 2014, p. 31).

In two other groups of students, we found equivalent proportions choosing to be non-submitters and submitters. One group is athletes, which, in the aggregate, we suspect may be a cross-current of opposites. While Division I athletes are required by NCAA regulations to submit testing as part of their applications, a good many of the institutions in the study have teams at the D-III levels and their coaches have demonstrated a proclivity to actively encourage lower-testing athletic recruits to apply as non-submitters.

Similarly, we found equivalent rates of Early Decision or Early Action use among submitters and non-submitters of testing, both at roughly a quarter of the applicants. So these "early" plans seem to have equal appeal to both groups.

Finally, an exploration of the use of TOP based on student home geography revealed a higher share of non-submitters in this study from the Middle Atlantic and New England, but this may be partially explained by the distribution of TOP institutions. While our study includes institutions from 14 states, 20 of our 28 institutions are located in New England or the Mid-Atlantic. And of the 21 that provided data for this geographical comparison, 16 were in those two regions. There are higher concentrations of TOP colleges and universities on the East Coast and non-submitters appear to be somewhat more likely to apply regionally than nationally. According to FairTest's admittedly inclusive listings, there are now TOP institutions in 49 states, the District of Columbia, and most U.S. territories. As TOPs are adopted by more institutions around the country, one would expect the geographic distribution of non-submitters to expand.

How is "expanded diversity" represented among non-submitters? Non-submitters include higher proportions of students representing any combination of first-generation-to-college, Pell recipients, and URM students (i.e., each student counted only once): 42% of the enrolled non-submitters versus 32% of the submitters. These results cast a new light on the attractiveness of a TOP for these underserved students and the opportunity for colleges to use this policy to attract and enroll more of them.

In recent decades, colleges and universities have put a great deal of effort into increasing the diversity of their campus communities. Correctly cited are ethical considerations to have colleges and universities serve social needs and offer access to underserved populations.

There are a multitude of characteristics currently identified in discussions of the "diversity" of a student population, and most center around the educational and developmental values associated with differences in perspective that result from differences in life experience. There is increasing concern and discussion about whether the use of standardized tests (specifically SAT and ACT) unnecessarily limits the admission of otherwise well-qualified students and tends to replicate the status quo in social class and opportunity in our American society.

> . . . test scores appear to calcify differences based on class, race/ethnicity, and parental educational attainment. To come to some resolution, the Commission agrees that without confusing correlation with causation, admission offices must remain aware that test score differences persist among already underserved populations. Part of the public mission of colleges and universities is to ensure that differences that are not attributable to a student's ability to succeed

academically at an institution are mitigated in the admission process. (NACAC, 2008 p. 7)

We highlight three identifiable populations that have traditionally been underrepresented in American higher education: first-generation-to-college, students from lower SES backgrounds (using Pell Grant recipients as an easily identifiable proxy), and students from racial and ethnic groups that have traditionally been underrepresented in college populations (URM). Often these are discussed as three distinct populations, failing to account for the overlap or intersectionality of the three. Thus we offer the construct of "expanded diversity" in which we have included any student identified with any of these three groups.

While we've already shown that each of the three subgroups are more strongly represented among non-submitters, we draw your attention here to a sizable difference in representation of those students who are representatives of a combination of all three of those groups—9% of the enrolled non-submitters versus 3% of the enrolled submitters. This serves to emphasize the attractiveness of a TOP for these underserved students and the opportunity for colleges to use this policy to attract and enroll more of them.

Although only seven institutions provided all of the requisite data at the admit stage, there were 21 institutions in our study that provided reliable data on all three of these groups at the enrolled stage. In this larger pool of enrolled students, 42% of non-submitters identify with one or a combination of these categories, as compared to 32% of submitters (see Figure 7.15).

The differences between non-submitters and submitters are even more pronounced at the individual institutional level, where non-submitters hold higher proportions of total expanded diversity, with the median institution at 43% for non-submitters versus 27% for submitters. Non-submitters also comprise larger proportions of students who identify with more than one underrepresented group:[5] Among these institutions, the median is 19% for non-submitters versus 9% for submitters.

Academic Outcomes

Does adopting a test-optional policy lower the academic quality of the enrolled student body? In a word, no. Applicant average high school grades and SAT scores increased from pre-policy to post-policy at all but one of our institutions.

We sought to answer this question by comparing the average high school GPA and SAT scores from pre- and post-policy years. While we could identify no reasonable way to compare these characteristics for TRP peer institutions, and, in the context of rising grade inflation, we cannot confidently attribute these increases to the adoption of a TOP, we thought it worth sharing the experience of the 13 TOP institutions with cohorts

Figure 7.15. Expanded Diversity Enroll Percentages, Comparing Non-submitters vs. Submitters.

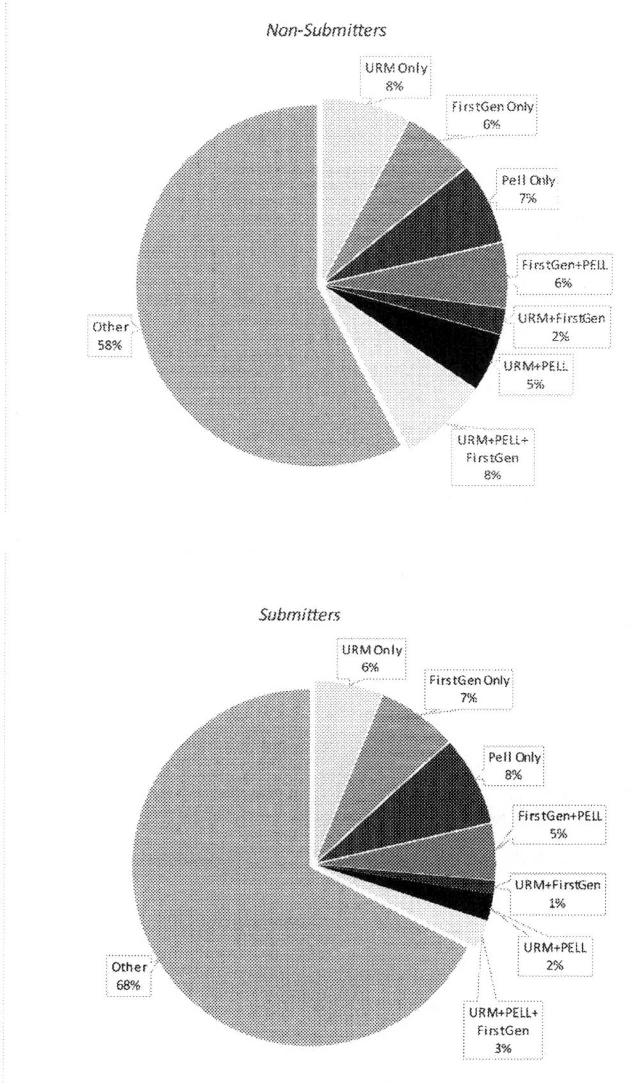

Note. Enrolled students at the 21 public and private institutions that submitted reliable URM, first-generation-to-college, and Pell recipients. Pooled student data. Exclusions: 2 institutions with Academic Threshold policies, 1 that did not have non-submitter proportions.

21 institutions | 36,034 records (of which 12,579 are expanded diversity)

Enrollment = 1,500–20,000 (2,500 M) | Endowment per FTE = $7,000–$800,000 ($100,000 M) | Admit rate = 15%–90% (40% M)

from immediately preceding and following adoption of a TOP. While these institutions experienced only modest gains, all but one of the institutions experienced an increase in the average HSGPA of their applicants, and again all but one saw an increase in their average SAT scores (though this may be the result of some of the applicants with lower SAT scores choosing to apply as non-submitters). This seems to be another broad, if tentative, set of evidence that the adoption of a TOP strengthens, not weakens, the applicant pool at almost all institutions.

How do non-submitters and submitters compare academically at each stage of the admission funnel?

In comparison with submitters, the non-submitters showed slightly lower high school grades (-0.12), academic ratings, and college first year GPAs (-0.17). And the non-submitters for whom we had scores had a significantly lower SAT average score. Once enrolled, non-submitters were less likely to designate a STEM major than submitters.

Based on academic data pooled from virtually all of our participating institutions (see Figure 7.16), the non-submitters had HSGPAs that were marginally lower at all three stages (applicant -0.12, admit -0.09, enroll -0.05). For those with SAT scores (26%, 31%, 35%, respectively, of non-submitters), scores were lower than the submitters by just under 200 points (185, 192, 168 respectively). The only college statistic available at all 25 of these institutions was the FYGPA, and here the non-submitters lagged behind the submitters by 0.17, consistent with the difference in their HSGPAs.

Next, we considered differences between non-submitters and submitters in choice of majors (see Figure 7.17).

Consistent with earlier studies, non-submitters were more likely than submitters to declare majors in humanities and liberal arts, social science, and psychology and social work. In contrast, submitters were more likely than non-submitters to select business, biology and life science, computers and mathematics, and education.

Moreover, non-submitters were less likely to have chosen STEM disciplines than submitters, 18% versus 23%, respectively. So, are non-submitters selecting higher grading disciplines, thereby lifting the overall average GPA for the group? To answer this question, we identified STEM majors and non-STEM majors to assess the impact on the cumulative GPAs of submitters and non-submitters. For this group of 31,000 students there is not a dramatic difference between the GPAs achieved by those majoring in STEM fields versus those in non-STEM fields (Figure 7.18). So, for this sample, the choice of major does not appear to have had a significant influence on the cumulative GPAs of either group.

How do the academic outcomes compare with those of "Defining Promise" (2014)? In short, non-submitters performed quite well in both studies.

Figure 7.16. Academic Profile of Non-submitters vs. Submitters at Each Stage of the Admission Funnel.

	Non-Submitters	Submitters
Applicant numbers	*100,362*	*378,646*
High School GPA	3.40	3.52
Academic Rating	5.61	6.06
SAT	1041	1226
Admit numbers	*36,843*	*192,588*
High School GPA	3.53	3.62
Academic Rating	6.69	6.89
SAT	1095	1253
Enrolled numbers	*10,878*	*38,318*
High School GPA	3.52	3.57
Academic Rating	6.19	6.52
SAT	1082	1226
First-Year GPA	3.07	3.24

Note. Academic rating: 20 of the 25 institutions in this analysis submitted academic ratings. They each submitted their own scales, but for comparison purposes we converted all to a 10-point scale, where 10 is the highest rating. Pooled student data.

Exclusions: 2 with Academic Threshold policies and 1 that did not have non-submitter proportions.

25 institutions | 479,008 records

Enrollment = 1,500–20,000 (2,500 M) | Endowment per FTE = $6,000–$800,000 ($70,000 M) | Admit rate = 15%–90% (40% M)

SAT Score Representation for Non-Submitters: 26% of Applicants, 31% of Admits, and 35% of Enrolls had a score on record.

While their college first-year GPAs and cumulative GPAs were marginally lower than submitters, both this study and the 2014 study confirmed they graduated at rates equivalent to or slightly above submitters (see Figure 7.19).

We examined parallel data points from the 2014 Defining Promise study and the current study: the 4- and 5-year graduation rates of enrolled students. A major finding of the earlier study was that were no significant differences in the first-year GPA, cumulative GPA, or graduation rates between submitters and non-submitters. We analyzed the current data in the same manner and found that the results were strikingly similar.

The HSGPAs were equivalent between submitters and non-submitters, but there was a significant difference in the SAT scores.[6] The non-submitter

Figure 7.17. Academic Outcomes: Major Designation, Comparing Non-submitters vs. Submitters.

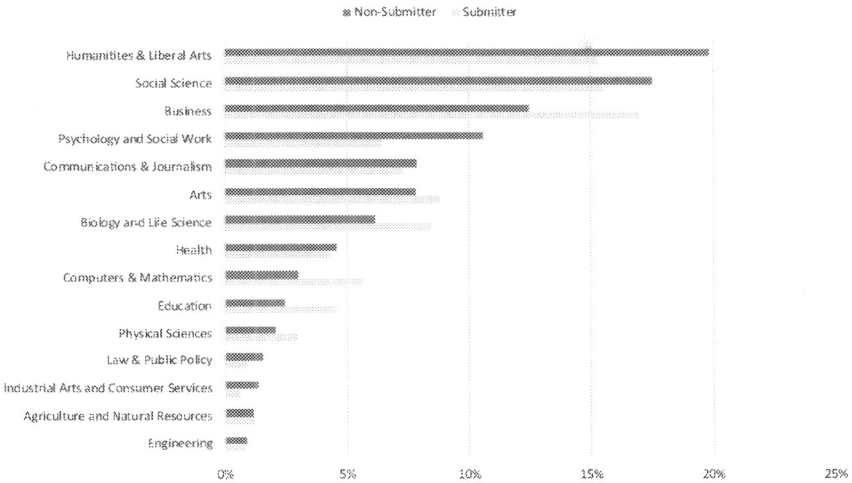

Note. Enrolled students at 20 public and private institutions with at least 2 years of a TOP policy in place in order to have declared majors using Classification of Instructional Programs (CIP) codes, 2010. CIP codes were converted to major categories designated by the Center on Education and the Workforce, Georgetown University. Pooled student data.

Exclusions: 2 with Academic Threshold policies and 1 that did not have non-submitter proportions.

20 institutions | 31,692 records

Enrollment = 1,500–10,000 (2,500 M) | Endowment per FTE = $6,000–$800,000 ($60,000 M) | Admit rate = 15%–90% (43% M)

average was lower by 146 points in the 2014 study and 126 points in the current study.

In college, the non-submitters started their college careers with FYGPAs that were lower than submitters, by 0.10 to 0.18, a GPA pattern that persisted through to graduation. In both studies, both non-submitters and submitters who graduated earned college cumulative GPAs over 3.20, and those who did not graduate (from that institution) posted cumulative GPAs in the 2.7–2.8 range. But in spite of having slightly lower GPAs, both studies found non-submitters graduating at marginally higher rates than submitters.

Because the above data is pooled data from the included colleges, we also examined the comparative submitter and non-submitter graduation rates at the institution level. While the bulk of the colleges reported the same result as the pooled averages above—little difference between submitter and non-submitter graduation rates—there were four private institutions that

Figure 7.18. Average Cumulative GPA of STEM Majors and Non-STEM Majors, Comparing Non-submitters vs. Submitters.

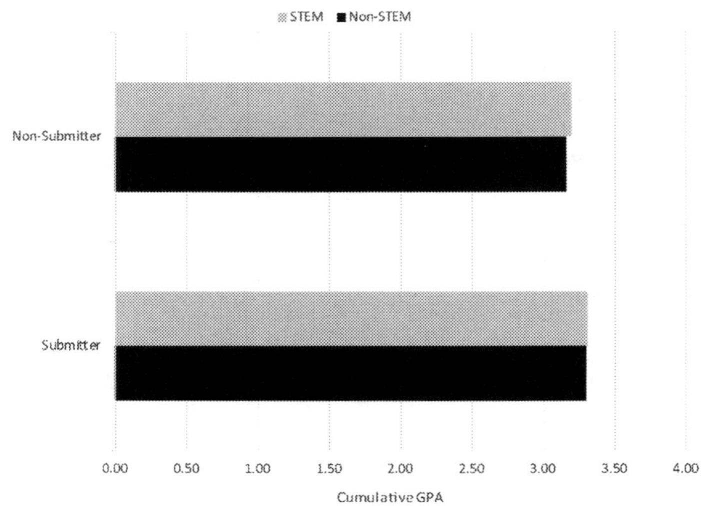

Note. Enrolled students at 20 public and private institutions with at least 2 years of a TOP policy in place in order to have declared majors, using CIP codes, 2010. STEM majors were identified using the Department of Education's Classification of Instructional Programs taxonomy within the two-digit CIP series containing engineering, biological sciences, mathematics, and physical sciences, or a related field. These fields represent research, innovation, or development of new technologies using engineering, mathematics, computer science, or natural sciences (including physical, biological, and agricultural sciences). Pooled student data.

Exclusions: Academic Threshold, institutions with very recent TOP Policies

20 institutions | 31,692 records

Enrollment = 1,500–10,000 (2,500 M) | Endowment per FTE = $6,000–$800,000 ($60,000 M) | Admit rate = 15%–90% (43% M)

experienced significantly lower rates among non-submitters. It is important to note that two of these four were identified earlier in the report as having also experienced lower application growth, lower URM enrollment growth, and lower Pell enrollment growth compared to their matched TRP peers. Looking back into the institutional analyses and interview notes done for each institution in our study, we found some common patterns at these schools:

Figure 7.19. Two-Study Comparison: Academic Profile of Non-submitters vs. Submitters

Defining Promise, 2014 (20 Private Institutions)

	Non-Submitters	Submitters
Enrolled number	*2,427*	*4,064*
High School GPA	3.50	3.52
Academic Rating	6.86	6.78
SAT	1085	1231
First-Year GPA	3.02	3.12
Cumulative GPA (Non-Grad)	2.74	2.83
Cumulative GPA (Grad)	3.24	3.33
Graduation Rate, 4-Year	78.4%	76.8%
Graduation Rate, 5-Year	78.8%	77.1%

Defining Access, 2018 (13 Public and Private Institutions)

	Non-Submitters	Submitters
Applicant number	*37,904*	*110,913*
Applicant High School GPA	3.48	3.60
Applican Academic Rating	5.98	6.90
Applicant SAT	1124	1243
Enrolled number	*4282*	*12,846*
High School GPA	3.63	3.64
Academic Rating	6.05	6.67
SAT	1108	1234
First-Year GPA	3.03	3.21
Cumulative GPA (Non-Grad)	2.70	2.79
Cumulative GPA (Grad)	3.23	3.40
Graduation Rate, 4-Year	79.0%	76.4%
Graduation Rate, 5-Year	82.8%	82.0%

Note. 2014 study: 20 private institutions (no minority-serving or arts institutions represented) that submitted 4- and 5-year graduation rates (students entering cohort 2008 for 4-year; students entering 2007 for 5-year)

Current study: 13 (12 private and 1 public) institutions that submitted 4- and 5-year graduation rates (cohorts entering 2012 for 4-year and 2011 for 5-year). Pooled student data. Exclusions from both studies: Academic Threshold policies. Academic rating: All institutions submitted their respective scales, but for comparison purposes we converted all to a 10-point scale, where 10 is the highest rating. Enrollment = 1,500–5,000 (2,000 M) | Endowment per FTE = $6,000–$800,000 ($100,000 M) | Admit rate = 15%–90% (40% M). Six institutions participated in both studies. However, there is no cohort overlap. Each study represents a different set of students.. Based on the way the data was submitted, the 4-year and the 5-year graduation rates reflect two separate cohorts of students from the same set of institutions.

- Very high levels of self-help in financial aid packages for high-need students.
- Variability in graduation rates from one cohort to the next, with 1 of the 2 cohort years showing disparately poor graduation rates for non-submitters.
- Larger than average gaps in HSGPA (.3) between non-submitters and submitters.

We also isolated the graduation rates of students who were identified as part of the expanded diversity group from "other" students (see Figure 7.20).

Here we note that in the Expanded Diversity group, the non-submitters graduated at a rate 6%–7% higher than submitters, whereas the students represented in the "other" category show more equivalence between submitters and non-submitters.

Under TOP, how well did the high school GPA correlate with college success? High school GPA had a strong positive linear correlation with college cumulative GPA, and it had a stronger relationship with both GPA and graduation rate than the SAT/ACT score. The test scores showed stronger correlation with submitter outcomes than non-submitter outcomes. They also had very strong correlation with expected family contribution (EFC).

Pitting the available admission academic markers—high school GPA and SAT scores—against college success markers—college GPAs and graduation rates—we examined these relationships side by side, using averaged percentiles[7] of student records containing both sets of data points. To be clear, SAT score data include all the students for whom we have a test score. But while these data accurately portray the information for the two groups, the non-submitter group represents only about a third of all the non-submitters. We therefore offer these comparisons not as definitive but simply observational.

Intuition would suggest that those non-submitters with higher scores would be more likely to share them than those with lower scores, but there is no way to validate that hypothesis. At the eight institutions in the study that submitted test scores for more than 50% of non-submitters, however, we found the patterns to be identical.

We found a positive linear relationship between HSGPA and college CumGPA, with a clear pattern of submitters having modestly higher college CumGPAs than their non-submitter classmates who had similar HSGPAs. This difference averages out to approximately the 0.17 of a GPA point that we cited earlier in this study, the difference between 3.23 and 3.40. These two average CumGPAs, while modestly different, are stark evidence that both non-submitters and submitters are achieving academic success.

Figure 7.20. 4- and 5-Year Graduation Rates for Expanded Diversity Students, Comparing Non-submitters vs. Submitters.

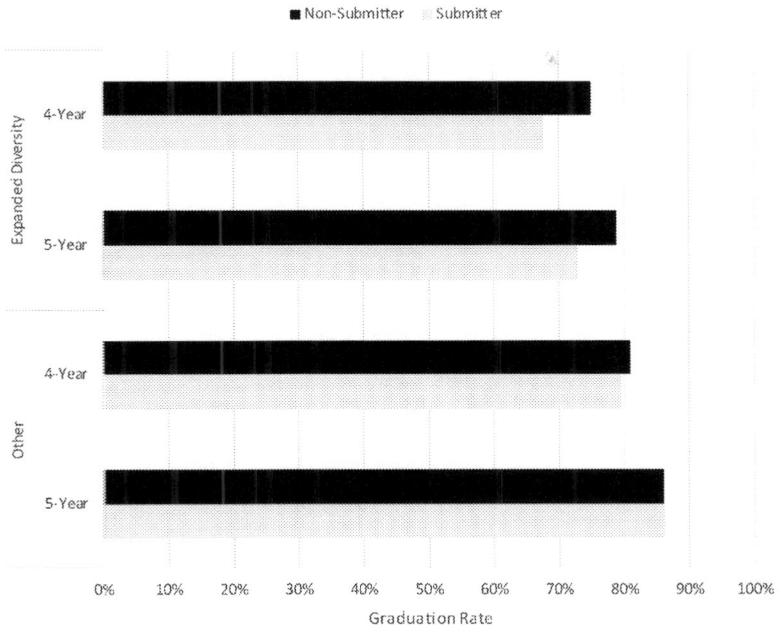

Note. Enrolled students at public and private institutions with mature TOP policies, having 4- or 5-year graduation rates and reliable data on each underrepresented group. Pooled student data.

13 institutions | Expanded diversity: 3814 records | Other: 8696 records

Enrollment = 1,500–7,000 (2,000 M) | Endowment per FTE = $6,000–$800,000 ($125,000 M) | Admit rate = 15%–90% (43% M)

In comparing SAT to CumGPA, the relationship is also positive and linear. However, non-submitter score averages ranged lower than submitters and were more scattered in their college GPAs at any given test score. Interestingly, the non-submitters were more likely to have achieved higher college GPAs than submitters with the same test scores. (The reader must remember that the test scores here represent only 33% of the non-submitters.) (See Figure 7.21).

We also examined HSGPA against same-school graduation rates. While the relationship is not as strong as might be expected, there is a general upward trend correlating higher high school grades with higher college graduation rates. But plotting SAT scores against graduation rates reveals a modestly different pattern. Submitters show a tighter correlation between SAT

Figure 7.21. Relationships Between HSGPA, SAT, and College Cumulative GPA Under TOP Cohort Years, Comparing Submitters vs. Non-submitters.

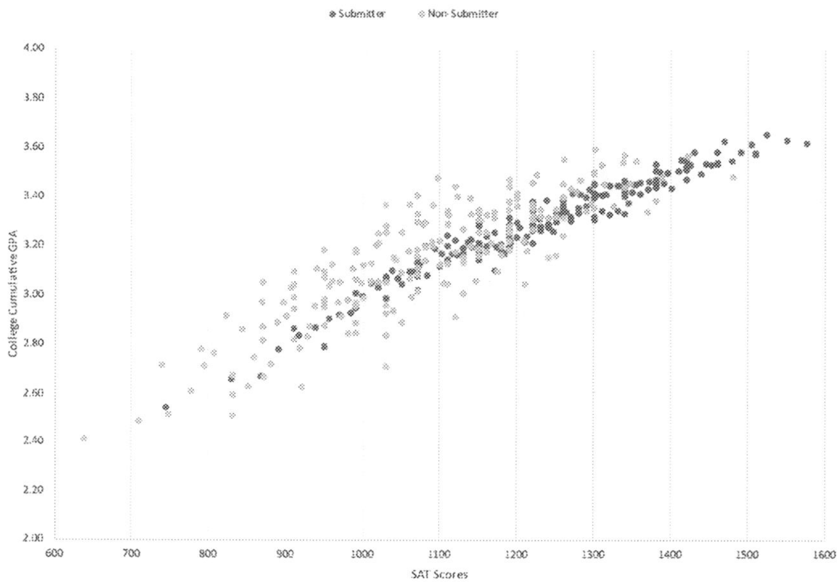

Note. HSGPA vs. CumGPA: Enrolled students at 20 public and private institutions. 41,320 records

Exclusions: Academic Threshold policies and very recent policy adopters.

Enrollment = 1,500–20,000 (2,500 M) | Endowment per FTE = $5,000–$800,000 ($50,000 M) | Admit rate = 15%–80% (43% M)

scores and graduation rates, while a majority of the non-submitters graduated at higher rates than submitters with comparable SAT scores. We also noted that while many of the non-submitters have performed at high levels in college, none of the non-submitters have SAT scores in the highest ranges.

We also found intriguing the patterns of students who applied for financial aid. By definition, we are missing the upper portions of the income ladder, who are not applying for financial aid. We saw a wide lack of relationship between high school grades and expected family contribution (EFC). Non-submitters will tend to be from lower-income families, but many of them have fine high school records. Any clustering has students with both high and low EFCs causing their means to trend toward the middle of the overall range (i.e., for any particular GPA, there are students with a wide range of EFCs).

In contrast, we found a strong correlation between SAT scores and family affluence (in this case using EFC as a proxy for other family financial data). The correlation for submitters is much stronger, with the upper end of the averages of both test scores and income remaining high. The relationship with non-submitter scores is mildly more diffuse, representing a lack of lower EFC students achieving those higher SAT scores. This aligns well with these students' sense that the test scores do not represent them well (see Figure 7.22).[8]

We also again used our construct of "expanded diversity" to explore, for this set of students, the correlations between graduation rates and either HSGPA or SAT scores. In graphing HSGPA against graduation rate, we found more or less equivalent positive relationships for submitters and non-submitters, with a marginally tighter relationship for submitters than for non-submitters, and with non-submitters more often clustered above the submitters in graduation rate for students with a given HSGPA, again out-performing their SATs.

With SATs compared with graduation rate, the differences are more pronounced: a positive relationship for these underrepresented student (expanded diversity) submitters, but a scattershot of graduation rates for non-submitters, mostly on the upper portion of the graph, suggesting that they were more promising students than their SATs would have suggested. (There are only 420 non-submitters, so this is observational, not conclusive.)

So, at least for this sample of non-submitters, high school GPA correlated more strongly than the SAT with success in college, in terms of both college cumulative GPA and graduation rate. The SAT, while showing solid correlations with cumulative GPA for submitters, continues to most strongly correlate with family affluence.

The Financial Side of the Policy

This section includes some of the most complex analyses in the study. In addition to comparing differences between pre- and postadoption cohorts, non-submitter and submitter groups, aspects of diversity, and graduation rates, we have introduced information about the financial need and aid awards of students. Adding another level of interpretative complexity, we were not able to ascertain whether institutions were need-blind or need-aware at any (or all) points in the data of the study. Some (particularly more selective, more affluent) institutions utilize a need-aware admissions policy to carefully regulate their commitment to financial aid. This, obviously, would find expression in the admit rates (particularly of high-need students) as well as in the aid offers made to students. Thus what follows is a representation of the data we had available, without any effort to overlay these factors into our observations.

Figure 7.22. Relationships Between High School GPA, SAT, and Expected Family Contribution Under TOP Cohort Years, Comparing Submitters vs. Non-submitters

1

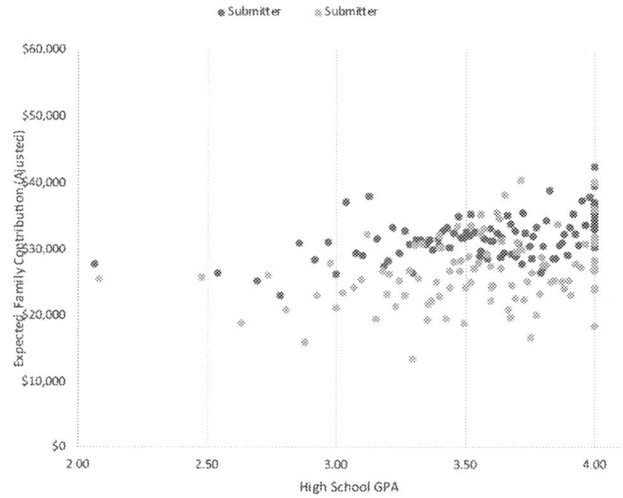

2

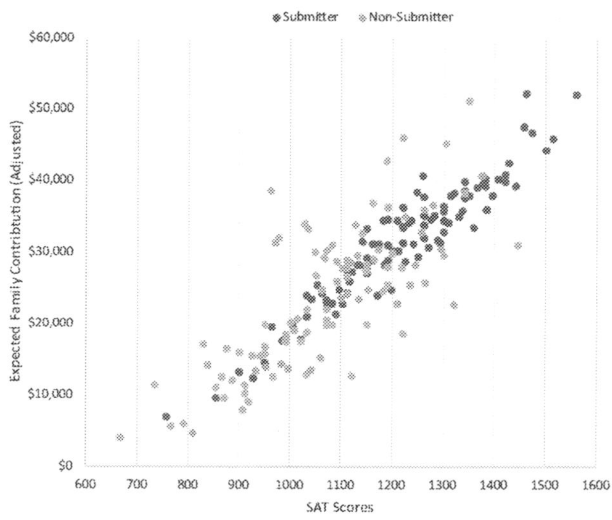

Note. Chart 1. HSGPA vs. EFC: Enrolled students at 20 public and private institutions with reliable HSGPA and EFC data. 25,257 records. Chart 2. SAT vs. EFC: Enrolled students at 20 public and private institutions with reliable SAT and EFC data. 21,333 records. Exclusions: Academic Threshold policies. Enrollment = 1,500–20,000 (2,500 M) | Endowment per FTE = $5,000–$800,000 ($70,000 M) | Admit rate = 15%–90% (43% M)

Additionally, institutions use different protocols in the awarding of aid to international students—some create an EFC, others award aid to international students but record EFCs only for domestic students, and so on—so for the comparisons on aid, we have excluded all students identified as non-resident aliens (international students). By doing so, we hope the observations about need-based aid will be clearer.

Do TOPs place greater financial aid demands on the institution? Our data limits drawing conclusions, but our findings suggest yes. High-need students choose to be non-submitters at higher rates, and gift aid per capita increased pre- to post-policy adoption.

We compared the proportion of students with a qualified need[9] in the pre-policy and post-policy years for the 12 institutions[10] that provided data from the years immediately preceding and immediately following adoption of the policy Among these 12 institutions, the changes in proportion of needy students were roughly evenly split, with five institutions experiencing an increase in the proportion of enrolled needy students, four experiencing a decrease, and three enrolling essentially the same proportion (within +/- 2%). As noted above, some of this may have been the result of need-aware admission policies.

However, while the proportion of enrolled needy students did not necessarily increase with the adoption of a TOP, the average financial need[11] of the needy students did tend to increase at modest levels (corrected for inflation).

Expanding beyond the need of the enrolled students, we attempted to assess the actual financial impact on an institution by generating estimates of gift aid per capita[12] for all enrolled students. Then we compared the cohorts immediately preceding and following the policy adoption and found that per capita costs rose during the TOP cohort years at all but one of these 10 institutions. The smallest increase was $728 per capita, and the largest almost $4,000 per capita (see Figure 7.23).

To what extent is this rise in investment a result of the policy? Although we cannot answer this question directly, we investigated the financial need of the incoming non-submitters for an indication. Our analysis was set up by creating four categories of financial need:

- High demonstrated need: students who need 75%–100% of the cost of attendance.
- Moderate demonstrated need: students who need 25%–75% of the cost of attendance.
- Low demonstrated need: students who need from 2%–24% of the cost of attendance.
- No need: students who did not request financial aid or needed less than 2% of the cost of attendance.

Figure 7.23. Gift Aid per Capita Differential: Pre-Policy vs. Post-Policy

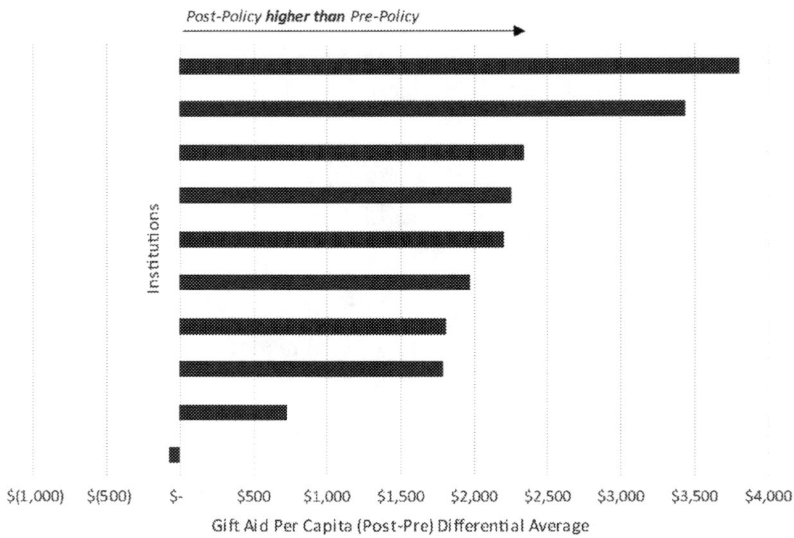

Note. Data from the 10 private and public institutions with gift aid submitted immediately pre- and immediately post-policy adoption.

Exclusions: Early adopters and nonresident aliens

All financial data has been adjusted to 2016-dollar standards.

10 institutions | 56,564 records

Enrollment = 2,000–20,000 (4,000 M) | Endowment per FTE = $4,000–$230,000 ($65,000 M) | Admit rate = 20%–80% (53% M)

Using these segments, we contrasted the pooled data for enrolled non-submitters and submitters at the broader set of 21 institutions with reliable data at the enrolled stage (see Figure 7.24).

As might be expected, due to the attractiveness of the test-optional policy to lower SES students, the non-submitters had a higher proportion of high-need students than submitters (36% vs. 28%). However, on the other end of the financial spectrum, both non-submitters and submitters had substantial proportions (34% and 38%. respectively) of no-need students.

We also made an institution-by-institution comparison of the difference between the demonstrated need of the needy submitters and non-submitters enrolling at the same 21 institutions. At every one of these institutions, the enrolled needy non-submitters had a higher average demonstrated need than the needy submitters, with the median differential being approximately $4,000.

Figure 7.24. Demonstrated Need Segment Proportion Profiles: Comparing Non-submitters vs. Submitters

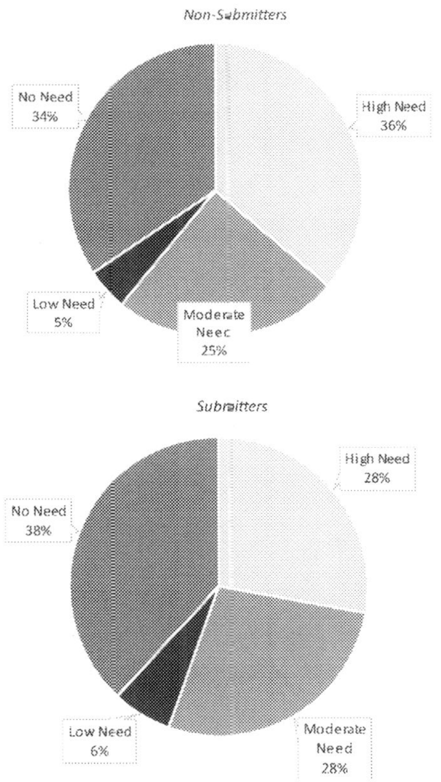

Note. Data from 21 private and public institutions with reliable financial aid data at the enroll stage of the admission funnel. Pooled Student Data. Exclusions: 2 with Academic Threshold policies, 1 that did not have non-submitter proportions, and nonresident aliens. 21 institutions | 34,305 records. Enrollment = 1,500–20,000 (2,400 M) | Endowment per FTE = $6,000–$800,000 ($52,000 M) | Admit rate = 15%–90% (43% M)

Do institutions aid non-submitters differently than submitters? There were substantial differences in awarding strategies between institutions, with the majority having provided less generous (gift) aid packages to both their needy and no-need non-submitters than to their submitters.

We approached this analysis by clustering student financial support in five "need met with gift" segments:

- Need not met with gift: gift aid was less than demonstrated need by at least $1,000.

- Need met with gift: gift aid was approximately equal to the need—with gift within $1,000 above or below need.
- Need exceeded with gift: gift aid exceeds need by at least $1,000.
- No need, and no gift: no demonstrated need, and no gift aid awarded.
- No need, and gift: not applying for aid or no demonstrated need, and gift aid awarded.

Traditionally, an institution meets need with a combination of gift aid (grants and scholarships), student loans, and work-study. However in this study, we evaluated whether demonstrated need had been met solely with gift aid. Thus in these clusters many of the high-need students (and even moderate-need students) will fall into our category of "need not met with gift." In some instances the colleges may have chosen not to meet the full need of the students (commonly called 'gapping'), but the reader should not conclude that students in this category didn't have their need met under the more traditional definition. It should also be noted that some institutions required test scores to be considered for scholarships, which would tend to mildly skew some of these outcomes, particularly in the category of "no need, and gift."

Using the framework of financial aid awards provided above, we used pooled data from 10 institutions that were able to provide the data at both the admit and enrolled stages to represent the "average" experience of a submitter or non-submitter. After comparing the distributions at both stages of the funnel, we found that non-submitters have higher proportions of "need not met with gift" (and "no need and no gift"), and lower proportions of no-need students who received "merit" aid ("no need and gift"). The gap closes slightly between the admit and enrolled stages of the funnel. We also made the same comparison solely at the enrollee stage of 15 institutions and found that the pattern is virtually identical with 5 more institutions.

We then contrasted these same distributions for the enrolled students at a set of highly selective institutions in comparison with some less selective institutions (see Figure 7.25).

At the less selective institutions, we found that there is a larger proportion of non-submitters whose need was not fully met with gift aid, and on the other end of the spectrum, a larger proportion of no-need submitters who received gift aid. We also found that truly "full pay" students ("no need, and no gift") are less than 10% of the enrollees at the less selective institutions, but comprise roughly 30% of the enrollees at the highly selective institutions. We do not know the policies that generate these results, but there are at least two reasonable hypotheses: First, the less selective institutions are not competitive enough to enroll many truly full-pay students, so they utilize "merit" scholarships more extensively (for both submitters and non-submitters) to attract those affluent students. And second,

Figure 7.25. Need-Met-with-Gift-Aid Segment Proportions of Enrolled Students by Submitter Status at Highly Selective vs. Less Selective Institutions

Note. Pooled student data. *Highly Selective*: Institutions with < 40% admit rate and reliable EFC and gift aid data at the enroll level, offering merit aid programs. Exclusions: 2 with Academic Threshold policies, 1 that did not have non-submitter proportions, and nonresident aliens. 5 institutions | 8,313 records. Enrollment = 2,000–5,000 (3,000 M) | Endowment per FTE = $10,000–$230,000 ($180,000 M) | Admit rate = 20%–40% (34% M). *Less Selective*: Institutions with > 60% admit rate and reliable EFC and gift aid data at the enroll level, offering merit aid programs. Exclusions: 2 with Academic Threshold policies, 1 that did not have non-submitter proportions, and nonresident aliens. 5 institutions | 13,445 records. Enrollment = 1,500–10,000 (4,000 M) | Endowment per FTE = $20,000–$60,000 ($38,000 M) | Admit rate = 60%–70% (64% M)

the less selective institutions may have treated submitters more generously than non-submitters in the "no need, and gift," "need exceeded with gift," and "need not met with gift" categories because they were pursuing profile-enhancing test scores in each of those cohorts, which obviously were not available for the non-submitters.

An interesting side note is that very few of our participating institutions currently require test scores of "merit" scholarship candidates, whereas a number of them did in earlier years (perhaps including the cohorts for which there is data in this study). As institutions become more comfortable with their use of TOP, it may be that they feel less compelled to require test scores for merit scholarship consideration.

Are needy non-submitters treated differently than submitters in gift aid allocation? There were substantial differences in awarding strategies between institutions, with the majority having provided less generous (gift) aid packages to their needy non-submitters than to their needy submitters. All the data we used are averages, so they do not account for differences that may have occurred in the awarding of high-need versus low-need students. Nevertheless, comparisons of the financial aid treatment of submitters versus non-submitters suggest that only a couple of institutions appear to have been more generous with non-submitters than with submitters (on average by about $2,000), four treated non-submitters and submitters about equally, while the majority of these institutions appear to have treated submitters more favorably (13 institutions, by an average of $2,600). So while not massive differences, over a 4-year education, non-submitters at these 13 institutions are being asked to carry an average of a little over $10,000 more of expense than are submitters, while often coming from lower-income families.

In addition, the selectivity of the institutions is reflected in the incomes of students who attend. Of the 13 institutions who fund non-submitters less well, 9 are less selective. Perhaps partly with much lower financial resources, but also trying to compete for no-need "full payers," there are at these 13 institutions very large gaps between the "Expected Family Contribution" (EFC) and our calculated "Family Financial Contribution" (FFC). That is, both non-submitters and submitters are being asked to carry much more of the costs than their EFC would suggest they are able to carry, by large amounts: from a low of $2,600 to a high of $18,500, with a majority of these less competitive institutions asking families to shoulder an amount in excess of $10,000 higher than their EFC. In contrast, at all but one of the moderately selective and more selective institutions, the gap between EFC and FFC is much smaller, with most in the $5,000-$8,000 range. So for a non-submitter at a less selective institution, there is often a quite literal "double whammy," with the non-submitters funded less well in comparison to the submitters, and both groups asked to carry large levels of unmet need.

Given these data, we ought not to be surprised when students have difficulty both finishing their degrees without major levels of family and personal debt, and paying off those loans.

Are no-need non-submitters treated differently than submitters in gift aid allocation? In short, yes. Potentially exacerbated by the policy at some institutions to require test scores for scholarship consideration, we found that no-need non-submitters were awarded gift aid at lower rates than no-need submitters. And yet these non-submitters graduated at modestly higher rates than their submitter counterparts.

Considering only the admitted, no-need students, we compared the proportions of the non-submitters and submitters that received gift aid (see Figure 7.26).

As noted elsewhere, a small percentage of these students perhaps may have received non-institutional grants (e.g., Pell) based upon the federal methodology, but have been deemed "no-need" based upon institutional methodology. Our data did not allow us to distinguish these differences. In the pooled data from these 10 institutions, no-need submitters were awarded gift aid at a higher rate (70%) than their non-submitter counterparts (60%). As noted above, for the cohorts included in this study, some of these institutions may have required test scores of anyone seeking consideration for a "merit" scholarship, and if so, it would have contributed to this disparity.

As with many of our comparisons, the pooled data is helpfully augmented by looking at the disaggregated data presented by individual institutions. The same data we discussed above reveals the difference, at the institution level, between the proportions of no-need non-submitters and submitters who received non-need-based grants or scholarships

We found that one institution appears to have treated no-need non-submitters more favorably, but the bulk of the institutions appear to have favored submitters when awarding grants and scholarships to no-need students. Virtually the same pattern is replicated within both admitted and enrolled students.

As noted above, these no-need or "merit" awards may be given for a variety of reasons, from the desire to enhance the institutional profile by enrolling students with high test scores (implicitly excluding non-submitters) to a tacit acknowledgement that the institution cannot enroll the right mix of needy and full-pay students at their published price, and therefore need to discount that price for some students. The situation for the non-submitters is exacerbated at the institutions that specifically require the submission of test scores to receive consideration for their merit scholarship programs. But the effect is the same: The families of higher need students (including a higher proportion of non-submitters), are carrying more "self-help" and smaller grants relative to their need, while no-need students (including a

Figure 7.26. Proportions of "No-Need" Non-Submitters and Submitters Receiving Merit Aid

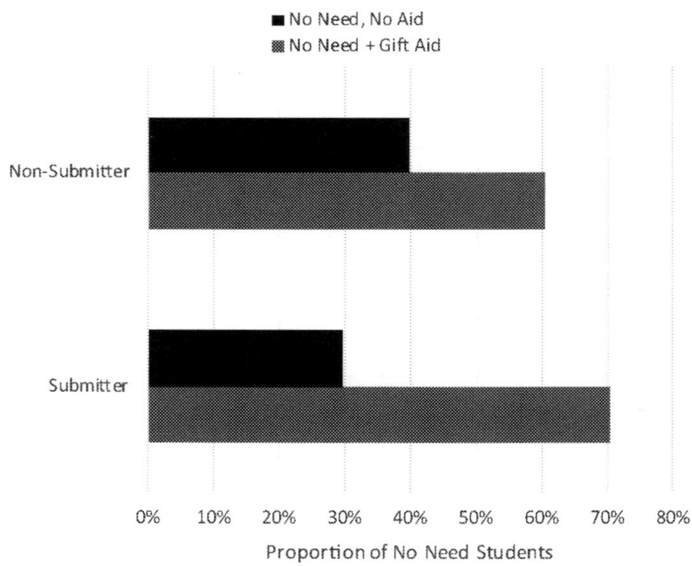

Note. Pooled student data. Institutions with admit level data, merit aid programs, reliable financial data. Exclusions: 2 with Academic Threshold policies, 1 that did not have non-submitter proportions, and nonresident aliens. No public institutions provided data at the admit level. 10 institutions | 33,718 records (students with "no need"). Enrollment = 1,500–7,000 (2,400 M) | Endowment per FTE = $40,000–$500,000 ($63,000 M) | Admit rate = 30%–70% (50% M).

higher proportion of submitters) are given merit awards to reduce the price to the family. At some institutions, the net financial expectations for families with no need and high need were within a few thousand dollars of each other because of the combinations of merit awards and high levels of self-help packaging. But, to summarize, with regard to aid awards at these institutions, on average, non-submitters didn't fare as well as submitters.

How does aid allocation relate to graduation rates? With respect to graduation rates, we found that no-need, non-submitters were less likely to receive gift awards, but they graduated at marginally higher rates than the no-need submitters.

We considered the graduation rates at the 14 institutions that have sufficient aid data and have been TOP long enough to have graduation rates (see Figure 7.27).

Figure 7.27. Need-Met-with-Gift Segment Graduation Rates, Submitters vs. Non-submitters

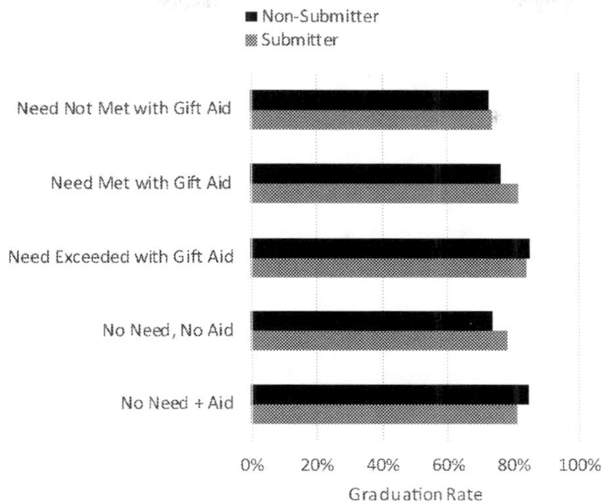

Note. Pooled student data. Public and private institutions selected based on availability of gift aid data at the enroll level, and institutions with 4- to 5-year graduated TOP cohorts. Exclusions: 2 with Academic Threshold policies, 1 that did not have non-submitter proportions, and nonresident aliens. 14 institutions | 17,436 records. Enrollment = 1,500–5,000 (2,400 M) | Endowment per FTE = $6,000–$800,000 ($100,000 M) | Admit rate = 15%–90% (40% M)

At least within this small sample, it appears that the lowest graduation rates were achieved by students whose need was not met fully with gift aid—not surprising, as they were likely the students facing the greatest financial challenges to completing their degrees. Non-submitters whose need was fully met with gift aid and those who were no-need and received no aid graduated at modestly lower rates than their submitter counterparts. However, no-need non-submitters who were awarded gift aid graduated at a modestly higher rate than no-need submitters. And yet the institutions favored the submitters in granting this aid, which may be a counter-productive strategy.

We also looked at the graduates and non-graduates of 17 institutions with 4- or 5-year graduation rates (see Figure 7.28).

The non-graduate submitters and non-submitters appear to be similar in both their high school profiles and in their college academic records—modestly but not dramatically weaker than their graduating peers. On average, it does not appear that they were required to leave for academic reasons. The non-graduates have higher representations of URM, first-generation-to-college, and Pell recipients. But we note a painful reality: comparing the four

Figure 7.28. Academic Outcomes and Financial Contributors: Graduates vs. Non-Graduates

	Graduates		Non-Graduates	
	Non-Submitters	Submitters	Non-Submitters	Submitters
Number	4311	12525	1377	4021
High School GPA	3.62	3.66	3.42	3.48
Academic Rating	6.05	6.69	5.65	6.04
SAT	1115	1249	1057	1177
First-Year GPA	3.11	3.29	2.82	2.90
Cum GPA	3.25	3.40	2.85	2.89
URM	17%	10%	19%	13%
First Generation	15%	11%	20%	14%
Gender (Female)	63%	59%	61%	53%
STEM	23%	32%	12%	16%
Pell	21%	17%	31%	26%
Demonstrated Need	$40,026	$35,576	$41,692	$36,533
Family Financial Contribution	$37,528	$36,450	$39,002	$37,420

In order to view proportions related to gift allocation, the rows below represent a subset of 11 institutions with graduating TOP cohorts and merit aid programs.

Number	2818	8400	992	2666
Exceed Need	10%	11%	6%	7%
No Need + Aid	17%	21%	19%	21%
No Need, No Aid	23%	20%	17%	14%
Need Not Met	46%	45%	55%	55%
Need Met	4%	3%	3%	2%

Note. Enrolled students at 17 institutions with either 4- or 5-year graduation rates. The analysis is valid in comparing the submitters versus the non-submitters for each line item, but each variable represents a different combination of institutions and students. Exclusions: 2 with Academic Threshold policies, 1 that did not have non-submitter proportions, and nonresident aliens (excluded from the bottom section). 17 institutions | 22,234 records. Enrollment = 1,500–5,000 (2,400 M) | Endowment per FTE = $6,000–$800,000 ($100,000 M) | Admit rate = 15%–90% (40% M). SAT Submissions for Graduates: 10,747 Submitters, 1,243 Non-Submitters. SAT Submissions for Non-Graduates: 3,600 Submitters, 340 Non-Submitters. Academic Rating: All institutions submitted their respective scales, but for comparison purposes we converted all to a 10-point scale, where 10 is the highest rating.

categories of graduates and non-grad, non-submitters and submitters, the graduate submitters have both the lowest demonstrated need and the lowest family financial contribution. In contrast, the non-graduate non-submitters have both the highest demonstrated need and the highest family financial contribution. And supporting the observation in the preceding paragraph, the need-not-met students comprise a substantially larger share of the non-graduates than of the graduates. These higher financial expectations suggest that these students may be facing additional challenges to successfully navigating their college careers.

How does aid allocation relate to any gains in diversity? With respect to diversity, we found that institutions will likely need to make additional financial aid commitments to achieve the goal of serving more traditionally underserved populations.

With the adoption of a TOP, the bulk of the schools in this study appear to have increased their enrollment of students from traditionally underrepresented (and generally needier) groups. We have examined the financial impact that may have been required to secure these gains. In this section we align financial aid averages against the proportions and growth of the three identifiable populations we have used earlier: first-generation-to-college, students from lower SES backgrounds (using Pell Grant recipients as an easily identifiable proxy), and students from racial and ethnic groups that have traditionally been underrepresented in college populations (URM). Discussing them as three unique populations fails to account for the overlap or intersectionality of the three. Thus, as we did earlier, we are utilizing the construct of "expanded diversity," in which we have included any student identified with any of these three groups.

For this part of our study we collected only the total gift aid awarded to students and an indication of whether or not they had received a Pell Grant. Because the institutions could not supply the specific breakdown of institutional gift aid, we are unable to draw solid conclusions about the financial impact of the policy on the institution. However, we devised an approximation by summing the total gift aid for all enrolled students (regardless of whether it was need-based or merit) and then dividing that by the total number of enrolled students (whether or not they received aid) to arrive at the "gift aid per capita." Obviously, some of this gift aid was not institutional gift aid (e.g., Pell Grants, state grants, and outside scholarships), but it does allow for a very rough assessment of the relative financial investment made to the pre- and post-policy adoption cohorts.

After reviewing the detailed information about the 12 institutions that were able to submit reliable financial aid data immediately pre- and post-policy adoption (see Figure 7.29), we offer three example case studies of the interplay between financial investment and growth in diversity:

Private Institution 3 —This private institution achieved a 48% growth in the proportion of enrolled URM students (going from 9% to 14%, an increase of 5 percentage points), and also had one of the highest percentage increases in the proportion of needy students (going from 43% to 51%). The average need rose $1,868, and it appears they may have become more generous in their aid award policy, as the gift aid per capita increased by $3,802. They also had substantive increases in Pell recipients and first-generation-to-college students, resulting in one of the largest increases on our expanded diversity measure (an increase of 7 percentage points—which for them represented a 38% increase in the proportion of these populations). So they appear to have made a substantive financial commitment, in addition to adopting a TOP, and have achieved a substantial increase in the diversity of their class.

Private Institution 4—More in the "middle of the pack" is another private institution, with roughly the same proportion of needy students pre- and post adoption. The average need of their enrolled students increased by about $6,100 and their gift aid per capita increased by about $2,300. They also increased the proportion of their URM students by 3 percentage points, their first-generation-to-college students by 8 percentage points and their Pell recipients by 5 percentage points, resulting in a proportional increase to 12% (5 percentage points) in their expanded diversity score. So subsequent to adopting a TOP, they invested more resources in aid and substantially increased the diversity of their student body, particularly in terms of serving first-generation-to-college students.

Private Institution 9—On the other end of the spectrum is a private institution that posted a decline in the proportion of needy students and actually lowered its gift aid per capita a slight amount. But in doing so it suffered substantive declines in the proportions of both URM and Pell recipients.

So, while it is not possible to arrive at definitive conclusions from the small sample we had available, it is reasonable to state that if an institution is interested in increasing its diversity, a test-optional admissions policy can provide a valuable tool; but, unsurprisingly, to achieve the goal of serving more traditionally underserved populations, the institution will likely need to make additional financial aid commitments.

SUMMARY AND IMPLICATIONS

Conclusions About Test-Optional Policies. No research can provide definitive answers to the questions we have explored about the use of a test-optional

Figure 7.29. Table of Financial Aid Variables Pre- and Post-Policy for Enrolled Students

			Private 1	Private 2	Private 3	Private 4	Private 5	Private 6	Private 7	Public 1	Public 2	Private 8	Private 9	Private 10
FINANCIAL AID DATA	Qualified Need Proportions Enrolled	PRE	44%	34%	41%	74%	44%	52%	69%	81%	75%	77%	64%	76%
		POST	56%	37%	51%	74%	48%	56%	67%	81%	75%	67%	61%	68%
		DIFF	12%	3%	9%	0%	5%	4%	-2%	0%	-1%	-10%	-4%	-8%
	Average Demonstrated Need --Needy Students-- Enrolled	PRE	$ 29,071	$ 34,177	$ 37,106	$ 39,464	$ 45,431	$ 41,853	$ 35,598	$ 24,180	$ 21,389	$ 35,372	$ 28,716	$ 42,942
		POST	$ 34,812	$ 38,786	$ 39,503	$ 45,602	$ 48,784	$ 41,582	$ 37,974	$ 25,582	$ 22,731	$ 34,836	$ 30,414	$ 40,308
		DIFF	$ 5,740	$ 4,609	$ 2,397	$ 6,138	$ 3,352	$ (272)	$ 2,376	$ 1,401	$ 1,343	$ (536)	$ 1,698	$ (2,634)
	Gift Aid Per Capita --All Students-- Enrolled	PRE	*No Data Submitted to Study*	$ 11,306	$ 14,082	$ 25,127	$ 17,367	*No Data Submitted to Study*	$ 19,102	$ 10,704	$ 5,106	$ 20,850	$ 10,477	$ 15,436
		POST		$ 13,505	$ 17,884	$ 27,461	$ 19,620		$ 22,539	$ 11,432	$ 6,894	$ 22,819	$ 10,407	$ 17,238
		DIFF		$ 2,199	$ 3,802	$ 2,334	$ 2,253		$ 3,437	$ 728	$ 1,788	$ 1,969	$ (71)	$ 1,803
	Average Gift Aid -- Needy Students -- Enrolled	PRE	*No Data Submitted to Study*	$ 27,526	$ 33,451	$ 28,171	$ 41,654	*No Data Submitted to Study*	$ 24,601	$ 12,544	$ 6,953	$ 25,197	$ 13,308	$ 26,753
		POST		$ 32,316	$ 36,297	$ 30,734	$ 44,486		$ 28,027	$ 13,901	$ 7,769	$ 29,288	$ 13,599	$ 24,752
		DIFF		$ 4,790	$ 2,846	$ 2,563	$ 2,832		$ 3,426	$ 1,357	$ 815	$ 4,091	$ 291	$ (2,001)
DIVERSITY OUTCOMES	URM Enrolled Proportions	PRE	10%	11%	9%	13%	16%	10%	12%	16%	6%	10%	8%	13%
		POST	19%	13%	14%	16%	18%	11%	15%	19%	4%	13%	6%	9%
		DIFF	*9%*	*2%*	*5%*	*3%*	*2%*	*1%*	*3%*	*3%*	*-1%*	*3%*	*-3%*	*-4%*
		% Change	*85%*	*17%*	*48%*	*23%*	*12%*	*13%*	*29%*	*19%*	*-22%*	*36%*	*-34%*	*-29%*
	Pell Enrolled Proportions	PRE	11%	7%	9%	27%	16%	15%	21%	28%	30%	24%	18%	14%
		POST	19%	10%	15%	32%	18%	17%	20%	28%	31%	22%	13%	13%
		DIFF	*7%*	*3%*	*5%*	*5%*	*2%*	*1%*	*-1%*	*0%*	*1%*	*-2%*	*-4%*	*0%*
		% Change	*65%*	*42%*	*56%*	*18%*	*11%*	*9%*	*-3%*	*0%*	*2%*	*-8%*	*-25%*	*-1%*
	First-Generation-to-College Enrolled Proportions	PRE	5%	5%	12%	24%	14%	13%	12%	34%	22%	23%	*No Data Submitted to Study*	21%
		POST	10%	7%	14%	31%	16%	15%	11%	36%	21%	21%		17%
		DIFF	*6%*	*2%*	*2%*	*8%*	*2%*	*2%*	*-1%*	*2%*	*-1%*	*-1%*		*-3%*
		% Change	*117%*	*31%*	*21%*	*33%*	*11%*	*16%*	*-8%*	*5%*	*-3%*	*-6%*		*-17%*
	Expanded Diversity Enrolled URM, Pell and or FG--each student counted once	PRE	21%	19%	18%	43%	29%	29%	31%	51%	43%	39%	22%	32%
		POST	35%	22%	25%	48%	31%	30%	32%	52%	44%	38%	15%	29%
		DIFF	*14%*	*3%*	*7%*	*5%*	*2%*	*1%*	*0%*	*1%*	*0%*	*-1%*	*-7%*	*-2%*
		% Change	*67%*	*19%*	*38%*	*12%*	*6%*	*4%*	*1%*	*2%*	*1%*	*-1%*	*-30%*	*-7%*

Note. Data from 12 private and public institutions with reliable financial aid data at the enroll level, submitted immediately pre- and immediately post-policy adoption. Exclusions: Early adopters and nonresident aliens. 12 institutions | 38,047 records. Enrollment = 2,000–20,000 (4,000 M) | Endowment per FTE = $4,000–$230,000 ($65,000 M) | Admit rate = 20%–80% (53% M)

admission policy, and we do not claim to have done so. Every institution has a slightly different experience. We are not presumptuous enough to believe we can identify any single outcome (nor even strong tendency) that should be expected by every institution adopting a TOP. There is simply too much variation between institutions in their commitment to mission, location in the educational marketplace, student population being served, affluence, and institutional goals. Instead, we have provided many perspectives on the possibilities that a TOP may help an individual institution to achieve.

Thus qualified, our findings suggest that a TOP works well at a variety of institutions. Almost all institutions in our study increased enrollment of underserved populations, with many showing proportionate increases exceeding those found at test-requiring peer institutions. And the policy transition occurred without any signs of academic slide: GPAs and graduation rates didn't suffer, and, according to reports from the deans, many faculty were very pleased with the quality and character of the incoming classes.

This success, however, appears to come with some degree of additional financial investment. The proportion of needy students rose at roughly half of our TOP institutions. Almost all the institutions saw an increase in the average demonstrated need from the pre-policy to the post-policy cohort years and increased the gift aid per capita. Most of our participating institutions appear to have provided less generous gift aid packages to non-submitters (both needy and no-need) than to submitters.

The institutions in our study appeared to treat non-submitters differently than submitters, admitting them at a lower rate and, on average, treating them a little less generously in the financial aid process, particularly with merit scholarships. The admitted non-submitters, however, enrolled at higher rates at virtually all of our institutions.

These non-submitters comprised significantly larger proportions of underrepresented minorities, first-generation-to-college, Pell recipients, and women than did submitters. As a group, non-submitters showed slightly lower academic performance both in high school and college, but graduated from college at equivalent, or in some cases, higher rates than submitters. The largest distinguishing academic difference we found was the lower test scores for the non-submitters (though we had test scores for only about a third of them).

Furthermore, this study helps to punctuate the question of what is meant when we refer to "success in college," a phrase frequently used to argue for the predictive value of the SAT and ACT. There is general agreement that those tests, when used in conjunction with high school grades, do a marginally better job than high school grades alone of predicting the first year college GPA of students. However, whether they predict evenly across populations of students has been widely debated. And an increasing number of voices are challenging the notion that predicting whether a student is likely to achieve, say, a 3.3 GPA versus a 3.2 at the end of their first year in college is synonymous with predicting "success in college," and are rejecting that phrase as an obfuscation of the actually limited value of the tests. Quoting again from the NACAC Commission on the Use of Standardized Tests in College Admission:

> Commission members unanimously agreed that college success is a term of sufficient breadth that it includes degree attainment, a wide range of GPAs, and the acquisition of experiences and skills that will propel a student into the workforce, graduate education, or responsible citizenship. (NACAC, 2008, p. 11)

We also found that this group of non-submitters represented approximately a quarter of the applicant pool, a finding that highlights an interesting intersection between findings published by the testing agencies. Their meta-analysis of studies also found a quarter to a third of all students with "discrepant performance," either students with high HSGPAs and low testing, or the reverse, modest HSGPAs but high testing (Sanchez & Mattern, 2018). Within this group, approximately half of them have high school grades that are higher than what the tests would predict. And it is worth noting the parallels between the proportions noted in the above studies and the median percentage (23%) of students choosing to be non-submitters at the institutions in this study.

We also agree with characterizations of the most likely students to have strong HSGPAs and low testing: women, first-generation-to-college, low-income students, and students who speak a second language at home (Hiss & Doria, 2011.).[13] Furthermore, those most likely to be discordant with weaker HSGPAs and stronger testing are males, Whites, and those of higher income (Sanchez & Edmunds, 2015).

We would suggest another, largely parallel language for thinking of these students. Many researchers, especially in medical fields, will speak of "false negatives" and "false positives." A false negative occurs when the test suggests that something will not happen, but it does. A false positive suggests that something will happen, but it doesn't. We assert that most TOP non-submitters are "false negatives": the SAT and ACT tests suggest that they will not perform well in college, but these students perform fine, and graduate at equal or higher rates than the submitters.

Finally, this study also confirmed that the SAT and ACT do have a positive correlation with college cumulative GPA for some students, more commonly submitters—the students who made an informed decision that their testing represented their ability. We do not argue that institutions should entirely eliminate consideration of the ACT and SAT for all their students. We do not promote the simplistic notion that these tests are either "all bad" or "all good."

The argument from the testing agencies that colleges should want every piece of significant information to make their decisions misses a key point. A student's decision to apply to TOP colleges, and not to have test scores considered in the admissions decisions, *is* significant information, often profoundly important for both student and institution. The students have made a key decision, saying to the admissions offices, "I am a better student and potential citizen than these tests would suggest." The research findings from this study and others cited suggest that the students are right.

Deans Reflect on Test-Optional Policy At the start of the study, we interviewed the participating deans of admission about their experience with TOP. Then we reviewed their comments in light of the data submission, which was subject to a thorough analysis. Pulling apart some of these unique findings from each institution enabled us to see patterns in similar experiences.

- The motivations cited for adopting a test-optional policy were fairly consistent across the institutions in the study, relating primarily to improving the access of underserved students: "TOP arose from the decision to pursue access to higher education among underrepresented groups." "It was important to our commitment to access, in particular to First-Generation students and students from under-resourced schools. Also felt it might help us reach students who might previously not have considered."
- The adoption of the policy was also described as way to simply formalize what they had been doing in practice all along: "We never weighted testing heavily—always weighted classroom performance more heavily"*;* "We always pitched that the scores were not given much weight."
- While the policies varied in terms of specifics, most employed an Optional for All policy with a few exceptions, for example, requiring test scores from international students, homeschooled students, or students applying to specialty programs. Some had started with an Academic Threshold or Optional Plus policy, and then migrated to the more open variation of the policy, Optional for All, indicating an increased comfort level with making sound admission decisions without testing.
- The group that employed some form of an Optional Plus policy had mixed reviews. A few seemed pleased with their interviews, essay questions, or other formats designed to solicit information from students on noncognitive skills. However, others felt that it was too time-consuming and did not yield the results they wanted: "The [additional requirement] added very little to our reading or prediction, and took up big shares of time." These institutions are actively considering eliminating the additional admission materials and migrating to an Optional for All policy.
- Most of the institutions had not employed a marketing campaign to

promote their new policy. Many claimed to simply "put out a press release and some FAQs on website" or "launched it by notifying on the Common App and on the website, and included it in a counselor update newsletter."

- A few institutions launched TOP as part of a larger initiative: "TOP was a component of a substantive shift of the institution as more hands-on skill building, and felt standardized tests did not fit well with this shift."
- Most described the policy buy-in process as taking some time and effort, particularly with faculty members. Yet many claimed that after TOP adoption, constituents reported being satisfied with it. As one dean claimed, "We are very happy with the policy and there is no discussion of rolling it back. We also listen heavily to the comments of faculty about their students and hear no concerns."
- Many described the process of transitioning to TOP as largely painless, just requiring an additional step in the direction of focusing greater attention on the rigor of the coursework in the context of the quality of the high school. One noted, "a little more training with our readers, and it has increased our focus on the rigor of the high school curriculum."
- Some institutions mentioned adding interviewers or temporary readers to handle the application increase. One of the institutions, as highlighted in the introductory case study, hired additional temporary readers because of the increased volume of applications, and the additional time required for non-submitter applications. "When you have a test score that is consistent with the academic record and other documents, it gives you confidence to spend less time on the application. When there's no test score as 'confirming' evidence, you'll typically look more closely at the high school record, the rigor of the curriculum, and the school profile for context."
- Most of the deans described their policy experience in glowing terms as a success in achieving admission goals:
    - » "We are attracting more Students-of-Color due to the policy."
    - » "We are seeing lots of kids who have done everything right except have high tests."
    - » "It has absolutely worked. First year academic performance and freshman–sophomore retention have improved. We've seen a steady increase in ethnic diversity."
- A few had more limited success and had to make some adjustments to the policy over time:
    - » "Only issue that did not play out as well as we had hoped with students of color, First Gen, and working-class kids. But we have fixed the financial aid budget now."

» "It has worked, though it is not nearly as popular (widely used) as we thought it would be . . . maybe most of the students who would traditionally have been attracted to TOP were already applying without being overly concerned if their test scores didn't represent them well."

Ideas for Future Research This study has provided many insights into the use of a test-optional policy. However, while our study is both broad and detailed, we identified numerous related topics that reasonably could be addressed in future research, including in no particular order of priority or importance:

- Our study focused on analyzing data from student records provided by institutions and did not delve into the nature and behavior of non-submitters. Qualitative research techniques, such as interviews and focus groups with prospective students and enrolled non-submitters, would be an insightful follow-up to this study.
- While graduation rates were a pivotal feature of this study, the specifics of student retention were not investigated. Much could also be learned about the success of the policy in light of the on-campus learning and social environment that receives non-submitters.
- We received test scores for a limited proportion of non-submitters. A more comprehensive collection of test scores from non-submitters would allow a more definitive assessment on the alignment of HSGPA and test scores with college outcomes.
- LD student access to higher education is a future research project with potentially very high rewards, given the growing understanding and identification of this population of students.
- While we elicited complex findings on financial aid, there is much room for additional investigation, including the review of the policy in light of institutional aid numbers.
- Academic Threshold policies offer a degree of lessened reliance on testing, but are a very different breed of policy when compared against the Optional for All model, whereby students have the free will to choose their admission credentials. There is much room to learn more about the ins and outs of this type of policy.
- The concept we introduced of "expanded diversity," whereby each student is considered in terms of all the rich diversity he or she brings to campus life and learning, could be used to underpin a substantial rethinking about how we as researchers understand diversity in higher education. This concept has potential to encompass an even broader range of students than we did in this study, for instance, those with learning differences, nontraditional students, international students, and nonnative speakers.

NOTES

1. The FairTest list includes many colleges that are "for profit," and others that are "Test Flexible"—allowing applicants to choose which form of testing to submit. The 28 institutions in this study, all not-for-profit and none using a Test Flexible policy, are drawn from two groups on the FairTest lists: the 129 National Liberal Arts Colleges and National Universities, and the 174 Regional Colleges and Universities.

2. Only one institution submitted a few ACT test scores from students after 2016. For this institution, the more recently adopted concordance table was used (though its validity has been disputed by ACT).

3. Data was pulled from IPEDS Data Center. The following criteria were used to select (from the list of peer-competitors identified by the dean) the best possible test-required peer: (1) Control type—public or private; (2) similar URM proportion during the TOP pre-policy cohort years; (3) similar Pell proportion, or if unavailable, similar federal aid award proportion, during the TOP pre-policy cohort year; (4) similar application pool size; (5) same general geography; (6) Carnegie Classification: size and setting.

4. IPEDS enrollment data on undergraduates entering fall 2016.

5. Combined total proportion of students who identify as URM + FirstGen, URM + Pell, FirstGen + Pell and URM + FirstGen + Pell.

6. The scores for enrolled non-submitters represent only 41% and 30% of the non-submitters, respectively, though it can be argued that it is unlikely that non-submitters with higher scores would disproportionately choose not to share them. As more institutions have become comfortable with TOP, fewer of them seem to feel compelled to collect test scores from matriculating students to allow them to conduct research—hence the lower proportion of test scores available for non-submitters in the current study.

7. The points in the scatterplots were calculated using Analytics software, by Rapid Insights. The points represent records that contained both academic measures. The data was calculated into percentiles, then averaged for each cluster. For example, in the case of HSGPA vs. CumGPA, each submitter point is represented by 300 data points or 3% of the data.

8. Remember that the SAT and EFC charts represent test scores from approximately a third of the non-submitters, and also do not include the upper part of the income ladder, since it only captures students who filed a financial aid application.

9. The proportion of students who demonstrated a need for financial aid (demonstrated need > 0).

10. Three of our institutions provided data for only postadoption cohorts; there were several years of separation between the pre- and postadoption cohorts for others of our other institutions; and still others were unable to provide reliable financial aid data for all their cohorts.

11. Demonstrated need was calculated as: total cost of attendance, adjusted – EFC, adjusted.

12. Gift aid per capita was calculated as: sum of total gift aid-adjusted/total enrollment.

13. A 25-year study of optional testing at Bates found a thick band of non-submitters whose homes ran across the top of ME, NH and VT. Often American

citizens for several generations, they were of French Canadian backgrounds. Being close to the border, they had kept up cultural and linguistic ties, with students speaking French at home and learning English at school.

REFERENCES

Belasco, A. S., Rosinger, K. O., & Hearn. J. C. (2015). The test-optional movement at America's selective liberal arts colleges: A boon for equity or something else? *Educational Evaluation and Policy Analysis, 37*(2), 206–223.

Bowen, W. G., Chingos, M. M., & McPherson, M. S. (2009). *Crossing the finish line: Completing college at America's public universities*. Princeton, NJ: Princeton University Press.

Buckley, J., Letukas, L., & Wildavsky, B. (Eds.). (2018). *Measuring success: Testing, grades, and the future of college admissions*. Baltimore, MD: Johns Hopkins University Press.

College Board. (2009). *ACT and SAT concordance tables*. Retrieved from research.collegeboard.org/sites/default/files/publications/2012/7/researchnote-2009-40-act-sat-concordance-tables.pdf

College Board. (2016). *Instructions for concording new SAT scores to old SAT scores*. Retrieved from collegereadiness.collegeboard.org/pdf/higher-ed-brief-sat-concordance.pdf

Davis, M. A. (Director/Producer). (2018). *The test and the art of thinking* [Motion picture]. Belvedere Tiburon, CA: Canobie Films. Retrieved from thetestdoc.org/

FairTest, National Center for Fair & Open Testing. (2019). More than 1000 accredited colleges and universities that do not use ACT/SAT scores to admit substantial numbers of students into bachelor-degree programs. Retrieved from www.fairtest.org/university/optional

Hiss, W. C., & Doria, K. (2011, June 3). *Defining promise: Twenty-five years of optional testing at Bates College, 1984–2009*. Paper presented at conference titled *Diamonds in the rough: Why every institution of higher learning wants to attract and admit dyslexic students,* Stanford University School of Business, Stanford, CA.. Retrieved from www.bates.edu/admission/optional-testing/

Hiss, W. C., & Franks, V. W. (2014). *Defining promise: Optional standardized testing policies in American college and university admissions*. Retrieved from www.nacacnet.org/globalassets/documents/defining-promise-poster--optional-standardized-testing-policies.pdf

Hiss, W. C., & Franks, V. W. (2015). Brave new world: How test-optional policies could (and should) change college admission. *The Journal of College Admission, 228,* 32–34.

Kobrin, J. L., Camera, W. J., & Milewski, G. B, (2002, January). *Students with discrepant high school GPA and SAT I scores* (Research Notes, RN-15). New York, NY: The College Board.

Lucido, J. A. (2018). Understanding the test-optional movement. In J. Buckley, L. Letukas, & B. Wildavsky (Eds.), *Measuring success: Testing, grades, and the future of college admissions* (pp. 164–165). Baltimore, MD: Johns Hopkins University Press.

Mattern, K. D., & Patterson, B. F. (2014). *Synthesis of recent SAT validity findings: Trend data over time and cohorts* (Research in Review No. 2014-1). New York, NY: The College Board. Retrieved from files.eric.ed.gov/fulltext/ED556462.pdf

Mattern, K. D, Shaw, E. J., & Kobrin, J. L. (2010, May). *A case for not going test-optional: Students with discrepant SAT and HSGPA performance.* Paper presented at the annual meeting of the American Educational Research Association, Denver, CO. Retrieved from files.eric.ed.gov/fulltext/ED563419.pdf

McNeish, D. M., Radunzel, J., & Sanchez, E. (2015). *A multidimensional perspective of college readiness: Relating student and school characteristics to performance on the ACT* (ACT Research Report Series 2015-6). Iowa City, IA: ACT Inc. Retrieved from eric.ed.gov/?id=ED563774

Mulugetta, Y. M. (2015). *Understanding the impacts of the test optional admission policy.* Retrieved from www.ithaca.edu/ir/docs/testoptionalpaper2.pdf

National Association for College Admission Counseling (NACAC). (2008). *Report of the Commission on the use of standardized tests in undergraduate admission.* Arlington, VA: NACAC.

National Association for College Admission Counseling (NACAC). (2016). *Use of predictive validity studies to inform admission practices.* Retrieved from www.nacacnet.org/globalassets/documents/publications/research/testvalidity.pdf

Sanchez, E., & Edmunds, A. (2015, May). *How discrepant high school GPAs, test scores, and engagement impact persistence.* Paper presented at the annual convention of the Association for Institutional Research (AIR), Denver, CO.

Sanchez, E., & Mattern, K. (2018) When high school grade point average and test scores disagree: Implications for test-optional policies. In J. Buckley, L. Letukas, & B. Wildavsky (Eds.). *Measuring success: Testing, grades, and the future of college admissions* (pp. 118–141). Baltimore, MD: Johns Hopkins University Press.

Soares, J. A. (Ed.). (2012). *SAT wars: The case for test-optional college admissions.* New York, NY: Teachers College Press.

U.S. Department of Education, National Center for Education Statistics, Integrated Postsecondary Education Data System (IPEDS). (2017).

Compare the institutions. Retrieved from nces.ed.gov/ipeds/use-the-data.

U.S. News and World Report (2018) U.S. News Best Colleges, National and Regional. Retrieved from www.usnews.com/rankings

Weissbourd, R., & Thacker, L. (2016). *Turning the tide: Inspiring concern for others and the common good through college admission.* Cambridge, MA: Harvard Graduate School of Education. Retrieved from mcc.gse.harvard.edu/files/gse-mcc/files/20160120_mcc_ttt_execsummary_interactive.pdf

The FBI Sting and Moments That Define a Profession

Jon Boeckenstedt

Our collective ability to recall where we were and what we were doing at certain defining points in history serves as a powerful anchor to us, drawing a line between what once was and what now is. Certain events, ranging from the mundane to the profound, stay with us forever, and days that started like any other end up permanently affixed in our memories.

No Boston Red Sox fan will ever forget the moment the ball rolled between Bill Buckner's legs in the 10th inning of the sixth game of the 1986 World Series. Others remember with clarity the first time they saw the theater go dark and the words "A long time ago, in a galaxy far, far away . . . " scroll across the screen. But for people who aren't baseball fans or sci-fi buffs, these moments probably lost most semblance of meaning shortly after they happened.

The morning of March 12, 2019, seemed normal enough, a day as unlikely as any other to live in the collective minds of America or even in the minds of any specific groups of Americans. But by midmorning, the story of the "College Admissions Scandal," as the press quickly dubbed it, had broken.

Within minutes of the first tweets being sent, admissions professionals were being bombarded with emails and social media posts from high school counselors, colleagues inside the university, and the media. At first, it wasn't clear what exactly was transpiring, or why it was so newsworthy: It is hardly a secret in the admissions profession that wealthy, famous, and otherwise privileged people can use their influence to get much of what they want, including admission for their children to the nation's most prestigious and selective colleges and universities. Was this simply the media overreacting to realities most of us had already reluctantly acknowledged? Did it warrant the special code name—Operation Varsity Blues—that the FBI had created for it? Was it that big?

It was. As the day unfolded, and details became more apparent, the plot thickened. Moment by moment, as dozens of well-known and high-income celebrities and otherwise-famous people were placed under arrest and taken into custody by law enforcement officials who charged them with a host of federal crimes, even the most seasoned and cynical people in the profession were rendered incredulous. Why—and more interestingly how—would parents seek to bribe people both inside and outside universities to guarantee admission for their children, in some cases paying almost half a million dollars to do so? Nothing like this had happened in recent memory, and only a 2002 scandal of much smaller proportion at Oxford University in England (www.telegraph.co.uk/news/uknews/1388770/Two-quit-in-Oxford-cash-for-places-scandal.html) even seemed to come close.

Once revealed, the allegations were shocking and fell into three broad categories of criminal behavior: Bribing coaches to advocate for "student athletes," many of whom qualified only marginally as the former and not at all as the latter; manipulating physicians to get a diagnosis of a learning disability, taking advantage of legitimate accommodations for students with learning differences that allow extended time and special, individual proctoring, and then having imposters take the SAT or ACT for them; and overly zealous parents having their child's test results doctored by proctors who changed the test answers after the student had turned in the test booklet. To top it all off, some parents apparently had the audacity to take tax deductions for the payments they made for donating to the "Foundation" of the mastermind of the scheme, who then used the cash to pay off the coaches, proctors, and test takers who were part of the process (www.latimes.com/local/lanow/la-me-ln-cheating-scandal-donations-20190312-story.html).

While every fan of Division I college sports certainly must know that athletes gain special favor in the admissions process, and while most Americans have had a sense that a parent's ability to build a new library or science center can give applicants a considerable boost in the admissions process, and while many people have heard or already knew that the ACT and SAT can be manipulated to help students obtain a better score, this was a macabre and grotesque twisting of those realities into something almost everyone found repugnant.

The harm inflicted upon legitimate candidates who applied for admission in the same cycle ranges from nebulous to specific. While admission officers can always find room to sneak a few "advancement cases" into the group of admitted students without affecting those who were admitted via traditional means, spots on athletics teams are finite and often quite valuable. If a coach had six slots on a rowing team, for example, it is almost certain that the student who was legitimately ranked number six on the list would have been denied admission so that the faux athlete could be granted one of the scarce opportunities.

As this book went to press, many of the parents in the Varsity Blues scandal have been sentenced. Some have been sent to jail, some have been hit with substantial fines approaching $100,000; others have been sentenced to jail time; and still others have received probation (www.vice.com/en_ca/article/ne89vz/all-the-parents-going-to-jail-in-the-college-admissions-cheating-scandal).

What details have surfaced so far suggest that the shock those admissions people felt that morning was justified (www.foxnews.com/world/college-admissions-scandal-greg-abbott-marcia-abbott). Collectively, the profession appears to be finding solace in the fact that no admissions officers have been implicated in any crimes, yet there is some guilt and confusion about the effects of being too trusting of colleagues in the university, and being too naive about how simple it might be to corrupt the weakest links in the admission chain.

The events that unfolded on March 12 will live in the minds of admissions professionals as the day their profession changed. It seems clear that this scandal will affect the way they do business for a long time, but whether this scandal will similarly be embedded in the collective consciousness of *all* Americans is still yet to be determined. If so, it will likely be due to the significant increase in the attention the media, the public, and even lawmakers pay to the admissions process and the admissions profession going forward.

As admissions professionals watched this unfold, and prepared for increased scrutiny, another curious collective response seems to be gaining traction: That perhaps the SAT and ACT shouldn't be considered as much—if at all—in the admissions process. For those who have long seen and understood the limited value of standardized testing in predicting academic success, and who have witnessed the blind acceptance of the SAT and ACT by otherwise well-meaning professionals, this victory is perhaps a hollow one.

Years of research and proof that admissions without standardized tests not only works but succeeds have made only the slightest dent in the minds of the public, while a single scandal, involving perhaps fifty celebrities and their children, has the potential to bring the whole system down, or at least alter the course of college admissions for decades to come. It's unlikely anyone could have predicted this; still, many people, whether explicitly anti-standardized–testing, or simply proponents of test-optional admissions, will likely take the win.

It's fair to assume the tests will live on, for the time being. While the Varsity Blues scandal illuminated the role testing plays in college admissions and embedded a moment in the collective psyche of admissions officers, it also brought to mind for many of us defining memories in our own college search. These moments are not singular, focused national events, of course, but rather deeply personal and memorable for other reasons, much like other rites of passage that occur to most people at different times of our individual lives: Jumping off the high dive, a first kiss, or getting a driver's license, all come to mind as important milestones in the lives of young people. Many people would add to this list the memory of taking their college admissions examinations.

It's simultaneously ironic, comic, and tragic that this ritual stays with us, given what we now know about the limited value of standardized tests and what they tell us about a student applicant. Perhaps it is because their meaninglessness is juxtaposed with the importance that they press upon our consciousness. Or perhaps it is because our attitude toward standardized testing is so American.

The tests are uniquely American in several ways: Apropos of the great current political divide many of us see today, proponents talk about them as being conceived as "engines of educational opportunity," while critics describe their genesis as one of creating "tools of exclusion." Absent a national American high school college-prep curriculum, the tests cannot measure with precision what has been taught in the classroom, so they were created to test "aptitude" or "native intelligence," or to screen out "undesirable" candidates for admission to universities that were originally all male, almost all White, and almost exclusively for the wealthy.

Unlike other countries where college admissions exams make up the bulk—if not all—of the basis for admission, the American tests are designed to be a companion to the high school record, which is most often used to determine whether a particular student is the type of student a particular college is seeking. They are designed to add something to the high school record, but no one is quite sure what that something is, or how much weight it should be given. Most important, in perhaps the most American way possible, the tests reward the obsessive behavior of the wealthy people and the well-resourced school districts that rely on them to maintain their positions in the social strata.

Additionally, while many countries with admissions examinations develop the tests in conjunction with some official ministry or bureau of education, in America the tests are created by independent, nominally not-for-profit agencies whose sole original purpose was to create a single test that could be used by hundreds or thousands of colleges to measure "potential." (Both testing agencies have branched out considerably, and now consider standardized admissions tests as just one—albeit the most well-known—component of their portfolio of assessments and other products.)

In other words, as is befitting a capitalist society, two private agencies responsible to no one but themselves have an oversized role in determining who goes to college, or perhaps more accurately, who goes to *which* college. Suppose, for example, that you go to a meeting at the College Board in New York City and then come out of the building and grab lunch at one of the many hotdog stands one finds in Manhattan. In the span of 10 minutes, you've interacted with two companies. Yet the hotdog cart, with no brand name, no national presence, having no effect on 99.999% of all Americans, is bound by more government regulations and accountable to more state and federal agencies than the College Board is. The hotdog vendor must prove the "all-beef franks" are really all beef by using USDA-approved products, it must prove that it keeps food at a proper temperature to ward off the potential for food poisoning, and it must demonstrate that the people who handle the food use proper hygiene.

The College Board and ACT don't have to provide any proof to back up any of their claims to anyone, despite their enormous presence and intrusion into the educational system of almost three million high school graduates every year. What testing is done is distributed to the ultimate client, the colleges, to make their own decisions based on in-house evaluations. The students—who may be either the beneficiary or the victim of the tests and their biases—get little satisfaction, and few answers. Even simple demands for accountability, like requiring the agencies to release previously administered tests, meets with resistance.

It is no wonder that the morning of the SAT or ACT is impressed so clearly on the minds of so many people, and why—decades later—so many people who scored well on the exams are eager to tell everyone how well they did on them. These scores have insidiously become a part of an individual's identity; it has been suggested that the score one obtains on the tests is tantamount to a forehead tattoo for which students believe they will be praised or shamed the rest of their lives.

The unflinching acceptance and ubiquity of the tests might be explained by their high-stakes nature, coupled with the undeniable reality that universities are populated with professors and administrators who owe much of their educational pedigree to scoring well on tests, leading to what economists would call "rent-seeking" behavior.

In the past decade, colleges and universities have begun to question and, in some cases, abandon standardized tests as a requirement for admission. FairTest lists over a thousand test-optional colleges and universities on their website. Many of these institutions most likely never required tests for admission in the first place, such as DeVry University, Divine Word College and Seminary, and Dharma Realm Buddhist University (to name just a few from the D category on the alphabetical list). Of course, if you go back far enough in American history, no college required standardized tests for admission. Long before colleges sought to make it easy to apply for admission (increasing application numbers and decreasing selectivity), many universities required their own examination, usually created by the faculty and often testing things we would find superfluous or irrelevant today.

The tests, as we know, have spawned an entire industry of test preparation services that have dissected and analyzed the test design and structure and offered students clues and strategies into deciphering the code to choose the "most correct" answer from those given, notwithstanding the fact that this very specific skill is of limited value in most college classes and even less value in life after college. The testing agencies, fighting back for years against the test prep companies, argue that claims of score increases brought about by test preparation were greatly exaggerated (and they may have been) and insist that "tricks" and "hacks" could never replace a mastery of the content in order to achieve a high score.

Of course, both testing agencies have recently released their own versions of online test preparation in a classic case of vertical industry integration, attempting to own a larger piece of the process from start to finish. Similarly, the sudden rise and rapid adaptation of test-optional policies have generated an interesting subindustry of its own within the testing agencies. Books have been written, blog posts have appeared, and events have been sponsored, all with the apparent purpose of criticizing colleges who have made testing an optional component of the admissions process, but all with a clear warning: Tests are important, and you abandon them at your peril. The arguments are familiar ones, focusing on grade inflation, context awareness, and—the most specious of all—the desire for "more information" in the admissions file. "Why," they ask, "would you want to throw away additional information?" These claims are all based on research, yet the majority of the research cited is conducted by, sponsored by, or tangentially connected to one of the testing agencies themselves.

Why are testing companies so inflamed about whether or not a college is test-optional? Why should they care what a college does? If Goucher College wants to admit students based on a video, or the University of Chicago wants to admit a stellar student who chooses too many "nearly correct" rather than "mostly correct" answers on a standardized test, or if Hampshire College wants to ignore tests altogether, why do those decisions—decisions that are effectively meaningful to only the student and the college itself—matter to the testing agencies?

The answer is not hard to find, and it has to do with simple economics. Per-unit costs of test development go down when more students take them, and the view of a future in which some students could go to college without ever taking—let alone submitting—tests is likely of great concern to the revenue of these agencies. They respond as one would expect from someone so threatened: by defending their tests and asking true believers to help sway public opinion and by diversifying portfolios that allow them to influence and direct the nature of content and instruction in both high schools and even elementary schools. State-mandated administration of college admissions tests—even for students who are not candidates for college admission—is the new battlefield, and in this instance, it's the testing agencies fighting each other for the contracts, instead of fighting students and colleges over the need and importance of tests.

With very few exceptions, test-optional colleges have found that they continue to make good decisions on student applications when they don't have standardized tests to rely on, and it appears that it will be impossible to stop the snowball that is now rolling downhill, as dozens more announce every year. A few court decisions, another highly selective institution adopting test-optional, or a state system of higher education finally seeing the light may bring about the avalanche the testing companies must fear.

About the Contributors

Jon Boeckenstedt is vice provost of Enrollment Management for Oregon State University, formerly the associate vice president for Enrollment Management at De Paul University.

Michael DeWitt is a data scientist in Wake Forest University's Office of Institutional Research.

Paul Fain is news editor at *Inside Higher Ed*. An award-winning journalist, he has written for *The Chronicle of Higher Education*, *The New York Times*, and *Mother Jones*.

Valerie W. Franks is a former assistant dean of admissions at Bates College. The lead researcher and coauthor with William C. Hiss of the first national study on test-optional policy, *Defining Promise* (2014), she is now serving the same role in the follow-up "Defining Access" study.

Saul Geiser is a research associate at the Center for Studies in Higher Education, University of California–Berkeley, and the former director of admissions research for the University of California system. He is coauthor with Richard C. Atkinson of "Reflections on a Century of College Admissions Tests" (*Educational Researcher*, 2009).

Philip Handwerk is director of Wake Forest University's Office of Institutional Research.

William C. Hiss served Bates College for 35 years as Dean of Admissions and Financial Aid. In 2014 he coauthored with Valerie Franks *Defining Promise*, the first national, peer-reviewed study of optional testing at 33 private and public institutions.

William C. Kidder was law clerk to the Honorable Edward M. Chen, Northern District of California. He was a researcher for *Testing for the Public*, Berkeley, California; consultant for the student intervenors defending affirmative action in *Grutter v. Bollinger*; and researcher on affirmative action for the Society of American Law Teachers (SALT).

Jay Rosner is the former executive director of the Princeton Review Foundation. He was an expert witness before the U.S. Supreme Court in the landmark *Grutter v. Bollinger* case, which upheld the affirmative action admissions policy of the University of Michigan Law School.

Robert A. Schaeffer is public education director at the National Center for Fair and Open Testing (FairTest), Cambridge, MA. He is the author of "Standardized Tests and Teacher Competence" (*School Voices*, Fall, 1996), coauthor of *Standing Up to the SAT* (1989), and a contributor to *SAT Wars: The Case for Test-Optional College Admissions* (2012).

Joseph A. Soares is a professor of sociology at Wake Forest University. His book *The Power of Privilege: Yale and America's Elite Colleges* (2007) was instrumental in Wake Forest's decision to go test-optional. An earlier book on universities in the UK, *The Decline of Privilege: The Modernization of Oxford University* (1999), won a national award from the American Sociological Association. He edited *SAT Wars: The Case for Test-Optional College Admissions* (2012), a New York Times recommended book, cited by the U.S. Supreme Court in *Fisher v. UT Austin.*

Steve Syverson is assistant vice chancellor for Enrollment Management at the University of Washington–Bothell, formerly a director of admissions at Pomona College and a dean of admissions and financial aid at Lawrence University. He served on the National Association for College Admissions Counseling's (NACAC) Board of Directors (2011–2014), as NACAC Vice President for Admission Practices (1988–1991), and on the NACAC Commission on the Use of Standardized Testing in Undergraduate Admissions in 2008.

Index